VICTORIAN PERSPECTIVES

Victorian Perspectives

SIX ESSAYS

Edited by

JOHN CLUBBE
Professor of English
University of Kentucky

and

JEROME MECKIER
Professor of English
University of Kentucky

MACMILLAN
PRESS

First published 1989

Published by
THE MACMILLAN PRESS LTD
Houndmills, Basingstoke, Hampshire RG21 2XS
and London
Companies and representatives
throughout the world

Typeset by Wessex Typesetters
(Division of The Eastern Press Ltd)
Frome, Somerset

Printed in Hong Kong

British Library Cataloguing in Publication Data
Victorian perspectives
1. English fiction—19th century—
History and criticism
I. Clubbe, John   II. Meckier, Jerome
823'.8'09   PR871
ISBN 0–333–44334–9

Contents

Notes on the Contributors

Richard D. Altick, Regents Professor Emeritus of English at Ohio State University, is the author or editor of numerous works covering the range of Victorian literature and society. His most recent books are *The Shows of London* (1978) and *Paintings from Books: Art and Literature in Great Britain, 1760–1900* (1985).

Jerome Hamilton Buckley is Gurney Professor of English at Harvard University. His many books include *The Victorian Temper* (1951), *Tennyson: The Growth of a Poet* (1960), *The Triumph of Time* (1966), *Season of Youth: The Bildungsroman from Dickens to Golding* (1974) and *The Turning Point: Autobiography and the Subjective Impulse since 1800* (1984).

David J. DeLaura, Avalon Foundation Professor of the Humanities at the University of Pennsylvania, is the author of a number of major articles on the Victorians and of *Hebrew and Hellene in Victorian England: Newman, Arnold, and Pater* (1969). He has edited, among other volumes, the Norton Critical Edition of Newman's *Apologia Pro Vita Sua*.

George P. Landow, Professor of English at Brown University, has written *The Aesthetic and Critical Theories of John Ruskin* (1971), *William Holman Hunt and Typological Symbolism* (1979) and *Victorian Shadows: Biblical Typology in Victorian Literature, Art, and Thought* (1980). He has also edited *Approaches to Victorian Autobiography* (1979).

J. Hillis Miller, Professor of English at the University of California, Irvine, published his pathbreaking *Charles Dickens: The World of His Novels* in 1958. Among his subsequent books on the Victorians are *The Disappearance of God: Five Nineteenth-Century Writers* (1963), *Thomas Hardy: Distance and Desire* (1971) and *Fiction and Repetition: Seven English Novels* (1982).

Donald D. Stone, Professor of English at Queen's College, CUNY, is the author of *Novelists in a Changing World: Meredith, James, and the Transformation of English Fiction in the 1880s* (1972) and *The Romantic Impulse in Victorian Fiction* (1980).

The editors, John Clubbe and Jerome Meckier, are Professors of English at the University of Kentucky. Both have made significant contributions to scholarship on nineteenth- and twentieth-century English literature. Clubbe has published books on Hood and Carlyle, has written extensively on Byron, and co-authored *English Romanticism: The Grounds of Belief* (London: Macmillan, 1983). Meckier inaugurated the modern study of Huxley with his *Aldous Huxley: Satire and Structure* (1969), has written widely on Victorian and modern authors – Dickens, Huxley and Waugh, most particularly – and recently published *Hidden Rivalries in Victorian Fiction*, a study of the literary interactions among the major Victorian novelists.

Introduction

Over the past decade, more than a dozen eminent Victorians have delivered lectures or enlivened graduate seminars at the University of Kentucky.* The idea for this volume originated during a semester-long symposium on 'Victorian Literature and Society' held in the spring of 1982. The six essays that make up *Victorian Perspectives* are not in all cases the papers their authors presented in Lexington, then or at other times, but they commemorate those fine occasions and exemplify the new avenues of thought that the visiting scholars opened up. The essays in this volume not only testify to a resurgence of interest in Victorian studies at one American university; they also make major contributions to the ongoing revaluation of the Victorians that has been one of the most interesting phenomena of recent literary scholarship.

J. Hillis Miller's ' "Hieroglyphical Truth" in *Sartor Resartus*: Carlyle and the Language of Parable' examines 'a fundamental paradox' underlying Carlyle's art: why does someone who believes a writer should 'keep silent or say the truth that is in him directly and plainly' write *Sartor Resartus*, a fiction that rivals in complexity of diction and presentation works such as Faulkner's *Absalom! Absalom!* or Conrad's *Nostromo*? Or as Miller puts the matter subsequently: 'The question is why being sincere, speaking and writing sincerely, in Carlyle's case, requires such indirection, such recourse to figures, to ironies and to rhetorical extravagancies of all kinds.' To present his argument Miller juxtaposes *obiter dicta* on Carlyle by Emerson and Nietzsche. Emerson reports Carlyle's repudiation of 'high art' and his belief that 'a sincere man will see something and say nothing'; Nietzsche 'sees Carlyle's propriety as the impropriety of a constant passionate dishonesty against himself'. Which is the real Carlyle? How to resolve the paradox? Miller's lucidly argued study has Carlyle 'both, or neither'. His focus on *Sartor Resartus* leads him to a wide-ranging reconsideration of the nature of Carlyle's art and of contemporary narrative theory.

---

* A partial listing includes, aside from the contributors to this volume, William F. Axton, Duane DeVries, Robert Giddings, James Gindin, Karl Kroeber, Jerome J. McGann, David Paroissien, David Perkins, Andrew Sanders, Mark Spilka and, on two separate occasions, Michael Slater.

George P. Landow's 'Elegant Jeremiahs: The Genre of the Victorian Sage' contends that the great Victorian prose writers borrowed extensively from classical and biblical traditions to create a genre of sagistic writing. Defining the sage as the Victorians conceived him, Landow takes up Carlyle, Arnold, Ruskin (and Thoreau) as writers who owe their tone and a willingness to castigate their contemporaries to Old Testament prophecy. Such prophecy, Landow explains, was just as interested in diagnosing the age's spiritual condition as in predicting the future. The former activity is, in fact, the basis for the latter. Landow examines the way sagistic writings draw on related genres, such as the novel, neoclassical satire and Victorian sermons. He identifies traits and techniques that make interpreting the discursive prose of the Victorian sages a valuable literary exercise as well as a study in the history of ideas.

Donald D. Stone singles Trollope out as the only great Victorian novelist to treat the father–son theme with the fulness and fairness it deserves. In 'Prodigals and Prodigies: Trollope's Notes as a Son and Father', Stone measures Trollope's handling of the father–son relationship against less successful examinations in, among others, Dickens, Butler and Joyce. According to Stone, Trollope's advantage lay not merely in knowing both sides of the struggle between the generations but in being able to sympathise with the demands of each station, which explains the unprecedented number of fully realised fathers and sons his fictional world contains. Beginning with Trollope's remarks about his own father, Stone progresses to partial portraits of that father in Trollope's novels, then explores the novelist's feelings for his own sons. In the process, Stone accounts for the legion of prodigals, both *père et fils*, that Trollope created. For moderns such as Waugh and Huxley, splits between fathers and sons signify the gulf separating the post-war world from the value systems of its Edwardian predecessor. Stone's valuable addition to the study of a pervasive concern in nineteenth- and twentieth-century fiction shows that Trollope was able to view the father–son theme in a kindlier light: it was his means of studying society's transition from one generation to the next. A son's love of his father, he argues, stands for acceptance of the past, while a father's decision to yield to his son's wishes connotes acceptance of the future.

Throughout his career David J. DeLaura has honed our awareness of the Victorian cultural context: religious, political, social, artistic no less than literary. His 'Ruskin, Arnold and Browning's Grammarian: "Crowded with Culture" ' supplies 'a more complex matrix' for 'A Grammarian's Funeral'. The context out of which the poem emerged includes Browning's other poems of the early 1850s, particularly 'Cleon' and 'Fra Lippo Lippi'; his reading of Carlyle, Arnold and Ruskin (particularly of *The Stones of Venice* II and III); and his personal interactions with these writers. The ramifications that DeLaura analyses are of considerable complexity, yet he threads his way through them with surety of touch. Even short excursuses into Browning's language – for example, his use of the words 'world' and 'culture' – have relevance to the larger picture. DeLaura's essay illuminates not only 'A Grammarian's Funeral' but other works before and after. In the process he increases our knowledge of the mid-Victorian cultural scene. Three appendices – on 'Browning and Arnold's "Empedocles on Etna" ', on 'Browning and Culture' and on 'Cleon versus Empedocles' – complement and complete his argument.

Matthew Arnold is not the first author who will come to mind when broaching the subject of Victorian comedy. Like Hillis Miller on *Sartor Resartus*, Richard D. Altick in 'The Comedy of *Culture and Anarchy*' reconsiders a seminal work: like Miller and occasionally DeLaura, he focuses on his author's handling of language. Where Miller questions Carlyle's purpose in his chosen artistic method, Altick examines Arnold's language for its comic and ironic effect. In so doing he gives the language of *Culture and Anarchy* the most thorough analysis it has yet received. The resultant perspective on Arnold's literary art – and on Arnold himself – offers a few surprises. By making a number of subtle rhetorical discriminations, Altick specifies the humour that contemporaries would have caught but that eludes most modern readers. He forces us to confront Arnold as a writer whose comedy is but moderately successful and whose tone can be uncertain. 'It is probably just as well that the comic touches are brief', Altick concludes. No one who ponders this essay will read *Culture and Anarchy* – or other prose works by Arnold – in quite the same way again.

In 'The View from John Street: Richard Whiteing's Social Realism', Jerome Hamilton Buckley resurrects a late-Victorian political satirist remarkable for 'intelligence, originality, and wit'. *No. 5 John Street* impresses Buckley as a good example of the nature of realism in the 1890s. Indeed, writes Buckley, Whiteing compares well with the best London realists of that decade. Like Maugham in

Liza of Lambeth, he could find plenitudes of drama in a single London slum-street. Buckley also rehabilitates Whiteing's Swiftian satire *The Island*, because *No. 5 John Street* works best as a sequel to it. In the 1888 novel, the stranded narrator finds 'edenic' conditions on Pitcairn Island preferable to Victoria's England. The 1889 sequel is a report to the islanders on the situation in London at the time of the Queen's Diamond Jubilee. *No. 5 John Street* supplies the key for a radical vision of late-Victorian England as an island composed of islands, its slums ironically juxtaposed with pockets of wealth. As a reviewer of *The Victorian Temper* noted, Buckley has always been willing to go 'into the highways and byways of Victorianism' after a more accurate perspective. He travels in this essay to an unfrequented address in an unfashionable street to discover characters and situations prototypical for Shaw and Conrad. He concludes that *No. 5 John Street* furnishes a missing link in the tradition of a specifically British realism that runs from Dickens to Trollope, through Whiteing, to the Edwardian accomplishments of Bennett and Wells.

To a surprising degree for papers composed independently, the essays in *Victorian Perspectives* complement each other. They focus on major figures, major works or major themes and movements. The function of language engages Miller, DeLaura and Altick. Altick's view of Arnold as a sage with an irresistible urge towards comedy bears closely upon Landow's definition of the high seriousness that sagistic prose requires, and vice versa. Creating a new genre for such prose is akin to shedding light on a neglected phase of literary realism, particularly since Richard Whiteing, the realist in question, patterned his anger on Carlyle's and learned his zeal for political justice from Ruskin. All the essays attempt to fill in gaps while participating in the volume's recurring concern with contexts and stratagems of presentation. Most of all, these essays share a preoccupation with newness. They strive for fresh perspectives, whether it be a fuller grounding for Browning's poetry, a reconciliation of the contrary views that Emerson and Nietzsche held on Carlyle's narrative techniques, a clearer awareness of the role of comedy in Arnold's prose (not omitting his deficiencies as a comedian), a new chapter in English literary realism, or a look at Trollope as a crucial addition to his era's exhaustive studies of changing and highly symbolic parent–child relationships.

The essays in *Victorian Perspectives* have been published in the

belief that each is of consequence to the Victorian specialist, yet
readily accessible to scholars with related interests and to readers of
English literature generally.

J. C.
J. M.

1

'Hieroglyphical Truth' in *Sartor Resartus*: Carlyle and the Language of Parable

J. HILLIS MILLER

In gesture, rather than in speech

Ralph Waldo Emerson made his second visit to England in 1847–8. One of the high points of his year there was his excursion with Thomas Carlyle in July of 1848 to see Stonehenge, Wilton, Salisbury and Winchester. In *English Traits* Emerson recounts the episode and tells the reader a bit of their conversation on the way to Amesbury by train and carriage. Carlyle attacked art generally and ornament in particular:

> Art and 'high art' is a favorite target for his wit. 'Yes, *Kunst* is a great delusion, and Goethe and Schiller wasted a great deal of good time on it:' – and he thinks he discovers that old Goethe found this out, and, in his later writings, changed his tone. As soon as men begin to talk of art, architecture and antiquities, nothing good comes of it. He wishes to go through the British Museum in silence, and thinks a sincere man will see something and say nothing. In these days, he thought, it would become an architect to consult only the grim necessity, and say, 'I can build you a coffin for such dead persons as you are, and for such dead purposes as you have, but you shall have no ornament.'[1]

I take this as a parable of a fundamental paradox about Carlyle. The man who rejects ornament, who praises sincere seeing and knowing above all, and who associates sincere knowing and seeing with silence, is at the same time far from silent, even in his praise of silence to Emerson. He publishes works that add up to thirty closely

1

printed volumes in the collected edition, and, far from composing in a style like a plain coffin, enwreathes everything he writes with fantastic and ostentatious ornament.

In the case of *Sartor Resartus*, which I take here as my main focus and as the *locus classicus* in Carlyle's writing of 'ornament', the ornament takes two forms. One is the local form of the openly elaborated style, 'Carlylese'. Carlylese is mostly metaphor or other figure which displays itself, which calls attention to itself as figure, by its hyperbolic elaboration. Examples are legion, but would include these several not wholly compatible metaphors for the book as a whole: the image of a chaos of documents fitfully illuminated by intermittent flashes of light; or the image of Palingenesis, the image both of society and of Teufelsdröckh as a phoenix about to arise again from the flames of its own self-consuming; or the image of Teufelsdröckh's life as like a stream plunging over a waterfall and dispersing in vapour, to reform itself here and there in visible splashes and puddles; or the image of nature and the human heart as hieroglyphic writing to be deciphered; or, finally, the image, drawn ironically from Milton, of the Editor's reconstruction of Teufelsdröckh's life and opinions as the making of a bridge over chaos:

> Daily and nightly does the Editor sit (with green spectacles) deciphering these unimaginable Documents from their perplexed *cursiv-schrift*; collating them with the almost equally unimaginable Volume, which stands in legible print. Over such a universal medley of high and low, of hot, cold, moist and dry, is he here struggling (by union of like with like, which is Method) to build a firm Bridge for British travellers. Never perhaps since our first Bridge-builders, Sin and Death, built that stupendous Arch from Hell-gate to the Earth, did any Pontifex, or Pontiff, undertake such a task as the present Editor. For in this Arch too, leading, as we humbly presume, far otherwards than that grand primeval one, the materials are to be fished-up from the weltering deep, and down from the simmering air, here one mass, there another, and cunningly cemented, while the elements boil beneath: nor is there any supernatural force to do it with; but simply the Diligence and feeble thinking Faculty of an English Editor, endeavouring to evolve printed Creation out of a German printed and written Chaos, wherein, as he shoots to and fro in it, gathering, clutching, piecing the Why to the far-distant

Wherefore, his whole Faculty and Self are like to be swallowed up.[2]

The other mode of ornament in *Sartor Resartus* is the more comprehensive, large-scale, all-encompassing form of the complex narrative machinery which makes *Sartor Resartus* of great interest, among Victorian works, for contemporary narrative theory. *Sartor Resartus* is as complex and involuted a form of storytelling as, say, William Faulkner's *Absalom, Absalom!* or Conrad's *Nostromo, Lord Jim* or *Under Western Eyes*. In Carlyle's *Sartor*, as in novels by Conrad or Faulkner, the act of narration, in which someone retrospectively reconstructs the past from ambiguous evidence and ambiguous documents, is foregrounded as a problematic and uncertain enterprise. In all these cases the book becomes in part about the act of narration, about the act of achieving knowledge by a process of reminiscent retelling, retailoring the tailor, repatching the patcher, sartor resartus. Both in local style and in overall narrative conception Carlyle, in *Sartor Resartus*, does the thing that takes the most doing. The book, *Sartor Resartus,* about the book, Diogenes Teufelsdröckh's *Die Kleider, ihr Werden und Wirkung*, which purports to have been published by Stillschweigen and Co^{gnie} [Keep Still and Company], is one of the noisiest books among the classics of English literature. I shall concentrate here on an attempt to answer the question: Why is this? What is the function of all that 'ornament' and indirection in Carlyle? Why does this sincere man not keep silent or say the truth that is in him directly and plainly, like a coffin made of six flat slabs of wood, fit for his dead English readers, and have done with it? It will not do to say he could not help writing the way he wrote. The question is why he could not help it, given the circumambient condition he was in and the purposes he had in writing.

A clue to an answer or at least to a clearer definition of the question may be given by a passage from Chapter Ten of Book Second of *Sartor Resartus* entitled 'Pause'. It is the chapter which follows the grand climax of *Sartor Resartus*, 'The Everlasting Yea':

Here, indeed, at length, must the Editor give utterance to a painful suspicion, which, through late Chapters, has begun to haunt him; paralysing any little enthusiasm that might still have rendered his thorny Biographical task a labor of love. It is a suspicion grounded perhaps on trifles, yet confirmed almost into certainty by the more and more discernible humoristico-satirical tendency of Teufelsdröckh, in whom under-ground humours and intricate sardonic rogueries, wheel within wheel, defy all reckoning: a suspicion, in one word, that these Autobiographical Documents are partly a mystification! What if many a so-called Fact were little better than a Fiction; if here we had no direct Camera-obscura Picture of the Professor's History; but only some more or less fantastic Adumbration, symbolically, perhaps significantly enough, shadowing-forth the same! Our theory begins to be that, in receiving as literally authentic what was but hieroglyphically so, Hofrath Heuschrecke, whom in that case we scruple not to name Hofrath Nose-of-Wax [it means literally, of course, 'grasshopper'] was made a fool of, and set adrift to make fools of others. (p. 202)

This passage functions simultaneously as a real statement demystifying another set of statements as fictional and at the same time as a fictional statement working obliquely and ironically to give the reader directions for how to read the whole of *Sartor Resartus*, including the passage itself we are reading. The reader is invited to read the whole as hieroglyphical rather than as literal truth, as a 'more or less fantastic Adumbration' or indirect 'shadowing-forth' of the truth. It is the effect of the application to the passage itself which is hardest to see. It is able to be glimpsed only in the blink of an eye or out of the corner of the eye. This glimpse most concerns me here. In the following paragraph another purported deciphering, quotation and translation from a small slip of paper in one of those notorious paper-bags pins down in a few phrases as good a guide as the reader is ever given to the right way to try and read *Sartor Resartus*: 'What are your historical Facts; still more your biographical? Wilt thou know a Man, above all a Mankind, by stringing-together beadrolls of what thou namest Facts? The Man is the spirit he worked in; not what he did, but what he became. Facts are engraved Hierograms, for which the fewest have the key' (p. 203).

The problem, the reader will see immediately, in a blink of the eye, is that though *Sartor Resartus* may indeed be engraved Hierograms shadowing-forth a transcendent meaning, those Hierograms, in this case, are not facts at all but outrageous and hyperbolic fictions. *Sartor Resartus* differs in this radically in its mode of language from most of Carlyle's other works, *The French*

Revolution, *The Life of John Sterling, The Letters and Speeches of Oliver Cromwell, On Heroes and Hero-Worship* and the *History of Frederick the Great*. The latter have a solid historical or biographical base, however much they make that base the hieroglyphic vehicle of an otherwise invisible spiritual truth. That base is missing in *Sartor*, except by way of the exceedingly oblique and indirect presence of the facts of Carlyle's own life story behind the life of Teufelsdröckh. No one who did not already know those facts, however, for example the story of Carlyle's conversion experience in Leith Walk, could possibly extract them as such from *Sartor*. My questions here are the following: What, exactly, is the mode of language of *Sartor Resartus*? Why did Carlyle find it necessary to use such a fantastic mode of indirection to say the truth that was in him? What does it say about the nature of that truth that it needed to be said in such a roundabout and parabolic fashion?

That Carlyle's goal was to say that truth and convey it to his readers there can be no doubt. In his letter to *Fraser*'s offering them the manuscript of *Sartor* he roundly affirms that, 'The Creed promulgated on all these things [Art, Politics, Religion, and the rest], as you may judge, is *mine*, and firmly *believed*.'[3] In his letter of 12 August 1834 to Emerson about *Sartor* he says, apologising for the extravagancies of style, 'My Transoceanic brothers, read this earnestly, for it *was* earnestly meant and written, and contains no *voluntary* falsehood of mine', and then adds, 'Since I saw you, I have been trying, am still trying, other methods, and shall surely get nearer the truth, as I honestly strive for it. Meanwhile, I know no method of much consequence, except that of *believing*, of being *sincere*: from Homer and the Bible down to the poorest Burns's *Song* I find no other *Art* that promises to be perennial.'[4] The question is why being sincere, speaking and writing sincerely, in Carlyle's case, requires such indirection, such recourse to fictions, to figures, to ironies and to rhetorical extravagancies of all kinds.

It is this element of sincerity, as of a man speaking directly to other men and women the truth that is substantially in him and makes up his substance as a person, since it is based on his God-given intrinsic nature, which Emerson emphasises in his memorial address or brief character sketch of Carlyle presented in Boston in Emerson's old age, in February 1881. This was written just after Carlyle's death, but was primarily based on a letter written in 1848, after Emerson's second visit to Carlyle. 'Great is his reverence for realities,' says Emerson of Carlyle, for all such traits as spring from the intrinsic nature of the actor. . . . He preaches, as by cannonade, the doctrine that every noble nature was made by God, and contains, if savage passions, also fit checks and grand impulses, and, however extravagant, will keep its orbit and return from far. . . . His guiding genius is his moral sense, his perception of the sole importance of truth and justice; but that is a truth of character, not of catechisms.[5]

Friedrich Nietzsche's view of Carlyle was very different, so different as to raise the question of whether they could have been speaking of the same person. Nietzsche, as is well known, greatly admired Emerson's work, carried a copy of Emerson's *Essays* in his knapsack, and when he lost it, went to some trouble to acquire another. In *Twilight of the Idols* (*Die Götterdämmerung*), Nietzsche praises Emerson for having that spiritual agility and gaiety, in the sense of *Die fröliche Wissenschaft*, gay science or joyful wisdom, a power of constant self-renewal or self-transcendence, which Nietzsche most prized in himself and in others. Emerson, says Nietzsche, is

one who instinctively nourishes himself only on ambrosia, leaving behind what is indigestible in things. . . . Emerson has that gracious and clever cheerfulness which discourages all seriousness; he simply does not know how old he is already and how young he is still going to be; he could say of himself, quoting Lope de Vega: '*Yo me sucedo a mi mismo* [I am my own heir]'.[6]

Nietzsche's judgement of Carlyle, which just precedes his comments on Emerson in *Twilight of the Idols*, is strikingly different. It too uses the figure of eating and of digestion, certainly a maliciously appropriate figure for Carlyle:

I have been reading the life of *Thomas Carlyle* [presumably he means Froude's *Life*],[7] this unconscious and involuntary farce, this heroic–moralistic interpretation of dyspeptic states. Carlyle: a man of strong words and attitudes, a rhetor from *need*, constantly lured by the craving for a strong faith and the feeling of his incapacity for it (in this respect, a typical romantic!). The craving for a strong faith is no proof of a strong faith, but quite the contrary. If one has such a faith, then one can afford the beautiful luxury of scepticism: one is sure enough, firm enough, has ties enough for that. Carlyle drugs something in himself with the fortissimo of his veneration of men of strong faith and with his rage against the less simple-minded: he *requires* noise. A constant passionate dishonesty against himself – that is his *proprium* [i.e. his propriety, what is proper to him]; in this respect he is and remains interesting. . . . At bottom, Carlyle is an English atheist who makes it a point of honor not to be one.   (*Ibid.*, p. 521)

Which judgement is the correct one: Emerson's, which sees Carlyle as the type of the honest or sincere man, speaking from the heart, or Nietzsche's, which sees Carlyle's propriety as the impropriety of a constant passionate dishonesty against himself? My argument will be that Carlyle is both, or neither, that it is in principle impossible to tell which he is, for reasons which are essential to his situation as a human being, to his strategy as a writer, and to the meaning of the doctrine he preached. The reasons are the same as those which make it necessary for this admirer of sincerity and silence to write works which are so indirect in rhetorical strategy and so stylistically noisy.

In a letter to John Sterling Carlyle defends himself from the *'awful* charge' that he does not believe in a *'Personal'* God by imagining Teufelsdröckh replying to such a charge by laying his hand on his heart and making a gesture of 'solemnest *denial*'. 'In gesture, rather than in speech; for "the Highest *cannot* be spoken of in words". . . . *Wer darf ihn NENNEN?* I dare not, and do not.'[8] If, for Carlyle, the highest cannot be spoken of in words, and if the aim of *Sartor Resartus*, which is precisely words, words on the page to be read, and by no means simply gestures, is to speak of the highest, which clearly *is* its aim, then that speaking must necessarily be of the most oblique and roundabout sort. It must be a speaking which, in one way or another, discounts itself in its act of being proffered.

Symbols, for Carlyle, are words or other signs, hieroglyphical emblems, which are used to name the highest, the unnamable. *Wer darf ihn nennen?* This infinite reality lies hidden behind the garment of nature, of words or other signs, and of human consciousness, all three. It might be said that for Carlyle the almost wholly metaphorical character of ordinary language loosens that language up. Ostentatious metaphor prevents language from being caught in a short-circuit of empirical naming of physical objects. The metaphorical nature of language makes it apt as an ingredient of symbol, but a symbol is not an ordinary metaphor. It is an oblique name for the unnamable. The traditional rhetorical name for such a use of language is 'catachresis', the forced and abusive transfer of a name from its ordinary or at least seemingly literal use to a new realm. There it functions to name something which can be named in no other way, which has no literal name. Who dares name the highest? Such a word is neither literal nor figurative: not literal because it is carried over into a realm where it is improper, and not figurative because the definition, since Aristotle, of figure is that it substitutes for the proper name. In this case there is no proper name, no other name at all but the symbolic one. It can be said that all *Sartor Resartus*, all its exuberant ornament of local style and narrative involution, is both an example of symbol in this sense and written for the sake of making clear what symbols are. If Christ's parables are parables about parable, *Sartor Resartus* is an hieroglyphical work about hieroglyphs. It cannot be otherwise, for it is impossible to speak other than hieroglyphically in this region.

Carlyle makes a crucial distinction between two forms of symbol, the extrinsic and the intrinsic. His distinction is parallel but not quite identical to the one he makes elsewhere in *Sartor* between metaphor and those few primitive elements of natural sound. Carlyle's distinction corresponds closely to the distinction made by Hegel in paragraph twenty of the *Encyclopedia* and in the *Lectures on Aesthetics* between sign and symbol. This is not to argue that Carlyle was here influenced by Hegel but to indicate that the distinction was one he shared with his German Romantic contemporaries. For Hegel a sign is arbitrary and unmotivated. A sign is not similar to what it stands for. It is a proposition put forth by the human mind in its act of understanding. A sign is evidence of the power of the mind over what it thinks, in its endless process of appropriation and self-appropriation in the gradual fulfilment of spirit. A symbol, on the other hand, is similar to what it stands for. It participates in its meaning. It is, so to speak, the natural embodiment of its meaning. A symbol is found there already rather than proposed or arbitrarily set forth. In the *Encyclopedia* Hegel validates sign over symbol. In the *Aesthetics* he appears to validate symbol over sign in the section on symbolic art, but then, rather surprisingly, in the section on the sublime, which he makes parallel in functioning, again surprisingly, to allegory, fable, parable and other such indirect forms of language, Hegel gives the sublime a high place in aesthetic modes. The sublime is defined as a mode of sign rather than of symbol, since it is characterised by the distance and non-correspondence between the embodiment and what it stands for or expresses.

In a somewhat similar way, Teufelsdröckh, Carlyle's spokesman in *Sartor*, distinguishes between two forms of symbol, those with an extrinsic and those with an intrinsic value, 'oftenest the former only'. Extrinsic symbols may be the glimmering expression of some divine idea of duty or daring, but there is no necessary correspondence between the symbol and what it symbolises. Carlyle gives as examples the clouted shoe the peasants rallied round in the *Bauernkrieg* or the Wallet-and-staff which was the ensign of the Netherland *Gueux*, coats of arms and military banners generally, 'national or other sectarian Costumes and Customs': 'Intrinsic significance these had none; only extrinsic' (p. 223). Even the Cross itself, the highest symbol of Christianity, is, amazingly enough, said by Carlyle to have 'had no meaning save an accidental extrinsic one' (p. 223). Examples of intrinsic symbols are 'all true works of Art', 'the Lives of heroic God-inspired Men', the body of a loved-one in death, and, highest of all, 'those [Symbols] wherein the Artist or Poet has risen into Prophet, and all men can recognise a present God, and worship the same: I mean religious Symbols', of which 'our divinest Symbol' is

> Jesus of Nazareth, and his Life, and his Biography, and what followed therefrom. Higher has the human Thought not yet reached: this is Christianity and Christendom; a Symbol of quite perennial, infinite character; whose significance will ever demand to be anew inquired into, and anew made manifest. (pp. 223–4)

Intrinsic symbols embody the infinite in the finite. The impetus for the conjunction comes from above not from below, and so the similarity between the above and the below, their intrinsic participation in one another, is guaranteed from above.

This seems clear enough and unequivocal enough, but is it? For one thing, it appears that in his highest example, Carlyle is talking not about Jesus himself, but about his biography, that is, I take it, the Gospels and the other books of the New Testament, and he is speaking of these books as human accomplishments: 'Higher has the human Thought not yet reached'. The Gospels are simply the highest form of the work of art generally, in which 'Eternity look[s] through Time' and the 'God*like*' (Carlyle's word, my emphasis) is 'rendered visible' (p. 223). Moreover, it will be noted that Carlyle does not speak of the intrinsic symbolic validity of anything Jesus said, for example in those parables which were a main mode of his teaching. It is Jesus himself, the man and his life, what he did, his wordless gestures, so to speak, which make him 'our divinest Symbol'. What aspect of that life, the reader might ask parenthetically, is intrinsically symbolic, if even the Cross itself, as he had said a moment before, is an extrinsic symbol? This displacement of symbolism from what a man said to what he did is reinforced by the inclusion of 'the Lives of heroic God-inspired Men' in the hierarchy of intrinsic symbols, 'for what other Work of Art', asks Teufelsdröckh, 'is so divine?' (p. 224). Most of Carlyle's writing in his long career after *Sartor* was, as any reader of his knows, devoted to exploring various examples of 'heroic God-inspired Men'. Carlyle is primarily a biographical writer, even in *The French Revolution*.

Finally, though Carlyle (through Teufelsdröckh), speaks of Jesus as a symbol of quite perennial, infinite character, nevertheless the significance of the life of Jesus will ever demand to be anew inquired into and anew made manifest. I take it this means that, perennial and infinite though it is, Jesus as symbol will fade and become inefficacious if it is left solely as embodied in the lives of Jesus written by Matthew, Mark and Luke. New Gospel-makers are constantly required to make even this symbol manifest for a new time. The new Gospel will, of course, to some degree at least be a new garment for the infinite. It will therefore be a transformation of the symbol depending absolutely for its efficacy upon the existence of what Teufelsdröckh calls a new 'Poet and inspired Maker; who, Prometheus-like, can shape new Symbols, and bring new Fire from Heaven to fix it there' (p. 225). It is difficult to discern the difference between an old symbol made new (old wine in new bottles) and an altogether new symbol (new wine in new bottles), since in both cases a new insight through the finite into the infinite is required.

This becomes especially evident when the reader confronts Teufelsdröckh's affirmation of a subdivision with the category of intrinsic symbols which complicates the apparently firm opposition between intrinsic and extrinsic symbols. There are perennial intrinsic symbols and others only 'with a transient intrinsic worth' (p. 224) even in that highest category of religious symbols. Moreover, the two categories of symbol will not stay neatly divided. The extrinsic is constantly superimposing itself on the intrinsic and contaminating it. Many even of religious symbols have 'only an extrinsic' worth, for example the Cross, while to many works of art which have a genuine intrinsic value extrinsic meanings come in time to be added, man-made interpolations which cover over the original shining-through of infinity in time: 'Here too,' says Teufelsdröckh, 'may an extrinsic value gradually superadd itself: thus certain *Iliads*, and the like, have, in three-thousand years, obtained quite new significance' (pp. 223–4).

The reader will see the problem here. Carlyle, or his spokesman Teufelsdröckh, is not confused. The difficulties are intrinsic, if I may use that word, to what he is trying to say. They arise from what is distinctive about Carlyle's theory of symbol. This distinctiveness is shared, of course, with others in the period called Romanticism. It even appears perennially in one way or another throughout the centuries in our tradition. One such distinctive feature is the introduction of the dimension of fleeting time or transiency. The other is the presentation of symbol as a form of catachresis, that is, as neither figurative nor literal, since, as I have said, it is the only possible expression of what it says and therefore may not be compared to any alternative form of expression, either figurative or literal. The difficulties might be defined by saying that on the one hand the distinction between arbitrary and motivated symbols, between extrinsic and intrinsic, is altogether clear and evidently necessary, while on the other hand the more carefully the distinction is analysed the more difficult, even impossible, it becomes to make it. It becomes harder and harder to discern clearly between one kind of symbol and another. They merge into one another, or each turns out to be a version of the other, not its opposite. As soon as Carlyle allows for the notion of a symbol, with 'a transient intrinsic worth', and it is the essence of his doctrine to do so, then he is granting a particular place in time, a particular man, writer, hero or prophet, an essential role in determining the efficacy of the symbol. It is impossible, in principle, to distinguish this from the notion that the symbols are created or projected, by a kind of performative fiat, through the man himself who proffers the new symbol. This is especially true because there is, as I have said, nothing outside the symbols against which to test their authenticity. They must speak for themselves and carry on their own faces the testimonies or witnesses of their validity. For Carlyle no symbol retains its efficacy beyond its own time. It must be replaced by new ones or by a revalidation, a reinterpretation of the old which makes the old effectively new. Carlyle's vision of human history is of the constant appearance through the medium of particular men of transient new symbols, symbols which stand for a moment or a day. They then fade and vanish, to be replaced with new ones. These are brought into the world by new 'Hierarchs', 'Pontiffs', new 'Poets and inspired Makers'. Teufelsdröckh's image of the Phoenix, constantly reborn from its own immolation, expresses well enough this vision of human history as a perpetually renewed process of death and rebirth, as does the projected title of the second volume of his clothes philosophy: *On the Palingenesia, or Newbirth of Society*. Essential to this picture of human history is what Teufelsdröckh calls, in a phrase the Editor hesitantly quotes from one of the Professor's 'nebulous disquisitions on religion', the 'perennial continuance of Inspiration' (p. 193).

It is all very well for Teufelsdröckh to distinguish between intrinsic and extrinsic symbols, but if no symbol can be counted on to remain permanently valid, then no symbol has the kind of permanent and logical relation to the kingdom of heaven ascribed to them, for example, in medieval Christian allegorical interpretations of the Bible. This both defines the Infinite as something incompatible with fixed symbols and breaks down the division between intrinsic and extrinsic symbols by indicating an arbitrary, impermanent and not wholly adequate quality even to an intrinsic symbol. If it were wholly adequate, would it not go on being adequate? How could one tell, for sure, in a given case, whether a given symbol is intrinsic or extrinsic, since there is no conceivable yardstick or criterion outside their own force to distinguish them by and since the permanence of the intrinsic symbol has been abandoned as its distinguishing feature? Might makes right here,[9] as in Carlyle's later theory of the political leader, and the new right displaces the old right. The Professor may preserve the nominally Christian character of his speculations by distinguishing between transient intrinsic symbols and those of quite perennial, infinite character, of which the only example he gives is the life of Christ as recorded by the Gospel-makers. Nevertheless, if even Christ has to be 'anew inquired into, and anew made manifest', presumably by new Gospels, then it is hard to see how Christ as symbol is not liable to transience like the rest. Without the new Gospel, product of the perennial continuance of inspiration, he would fade like the rest.

The centre of Carlyle's chapter on symbols is an eloquent paragraph on the fundamentally temporal and temporary character of symbols. The paragraph rises to a hyperbolic climax in which *all* things, even the manifestations of the infinite and the finite, are said to be conditioned by time, valid only for a time. It is difficult to see how Christ as symbol would be exempt, any more than 'many an African Mumbo-Jumbo and Indian Pawaw' from the sweeping inclusiveness from this 'all':

> But, on the whole [writes Teufelsdröckh], as Time adds much to the sacredness of Symbols, so likewise in his progress he at length defaces, or even desecrates them; and Symbols, like all terrestrial Garments, wax old. Homer's Epos has not ceased to be true; yet it is no longer *our* Epos, but shines in the distance, if cleaner and clearer, yet also smaller and smaller, like a receding Star. It needs a scientific telescope, it needs to be reinterpreted and artificially brought near us, before we can so much as known that it *was* a Sun. So likewise a day comes when the Runic Thor, with his Eddas, must withdraw into dimness; and many an African Mumbo-Jumo and Indian Pawaw be utterly abolished. For all things, even Celestial Luminaries, much more atmospheric meteors, have their rise, their culmination, their decline.
>
> (pp. 224–5)

One final, or at least penultimate, question remains to be briefly asked and briefly answered. What of *Sartor Resartus* itself, which is one of those works that is obliquely about its own nature and efficacy? Is *Sartor* an example of extrinsic or of intrinsic symbol, transient or intransient? Or, if those distinctions indeed do not hold, what, exactly, is the result of this fact for our reading of *Sartor*? Any interpretation of *Sartor Resartus* must centre or culminate in a reading of the 'Everlasting Yea', and to an explication of that chapter I turn before concluding.

It would seem that the answer to my question would be easy to give decisively. The conversion experience in the rue de l'Enfer, echo of Thomas Carlyle's own experience in Leith Walk and echo in turn of all those conversion experiences going back through Augustine to Saul of Tarsus, is followed by the 'Centre of Indifference' and then by the ringing affirmations of the 'Everlasting Yea'. In that 'Yea'-saying Teufelsdröckh asserts his divine vocation as a writer. He testifies that he is one of those God-inspired men through whom Eternity enters into Time. He is another 'Poet and inspired Maker, who, Prometheus-like, can shape new Symbols, and bring new Fire from Heaven to fix it there [in the world]'. 'Feel it in thy heart and then say whether it is of God!' cries Teufelsdröckh. 'This is Belief; all else is Opinion' (p. 194).

The examples that Teufelsdröckh gives of God-inspired men are all of real historical personages, Jesus for example. What difference does it make that Teufelsdröckh is a fictive character in a work of fiction, someone who never existed as such on land or sea, but in *Weissnichtwo*? Does that not make him rather a model or simulacrum of such men, proffered for the reader's better understanding of what they might be like when encountered in real life, though not really one himself, only the cunning image of one? Does that not discount, ironise or hollow out Teufelsdröckh's claim to present genuine Promethean Hieroglyphs or to be such a one in himself? He is not a real God-inspired man but a diabolical image of one, or worse, the mere detritus of such an image, its remnant written down on the pages of a work of fiction, in short, Teufelsdröckh, 'devil's dung'. On the other hand, Teufelsdröckh (and presumably Carlyle behind him) names the true work of Art, the *Iliad*, for example, as an example of intrinsic symbol, and I have suggested that in speaking of Jesus as an intrinsic symbol, it is impossible to know whether Carlyle means that life as such, in itself, or that life as written down by Matthew, Mark or Luke, with whatever fictive additions and ornamentations. Might not *Sartor Resartus* obliquely claim to be another such divinely inspired work of art, even though from the point of view of historical reality it is fictive through and through? On the other hand again, insofar as *Sartor Resartus* is, in one way or another, Thoms Carlyle's own disguised or indirect autobiography, the story of his conversion and his saying yes to his vocation as a writer transmuted, redressed, as hieroglyphic myth, can the reader not see it as, in fact, historically based and having as much ground in reality as even the Gospels? Back and forth among these various possibilities the reader alternates, without being able by the utmost interpretative efforts to find evidence allowing a decisive choice among them. It is of the nature of ironic fictions like *Sartor* to be in this particular way undecidable.

Even if this oscillation is momentarily suspended and the 'Everlasting Yea' taken 'straight', a further undecidability emerges in the nature of that 'Everlasting Yea' itself. Here the interpreter is aided by a now familiar modern distinction which is showing itself to be of great, but perhaps of dangerous or enigmatic, power for the interpretation of literature. I mean the distinction between performative and constative utterances. The distinction was introduced by Austin, developed by Searle, and has been criticised and appropriated for literary studies by, among others, Derrida, de Man and Fish.[10] The distinction between performative and constative language in turn echoes Nietzsche's distinction between *ersetzen* and *erkennen*, to posit and to know. A constative utterance expresses, accurately or inaccurately, a prior state of affairs, a state of affairs which exists independently of the language which names it. Such a statement records an act of knowledge and is to be judged by its truth of correspondence. A performative utterance makes something happen. It is a way of doing things with words. A performative utterance brings something new into the world, something which did not exist a moment before, as when the minister says, 'I pronounce you man and wife', or when the proper person in the proper circumstances says, 'I christen thee the Queen Mary'. A performative utterance does not correspond to anything already there. It is not the result of an act of knowledge, but is a groundless positing, an *Ersetzung*, thrown out by the words themselves to change the world. A performative creates rather than discovers. Or rather, it should be said that whether or not performatives are groundless is just the point of most controversy about them. Into the intricacies of this controversy there is not enough space to enter here, but for me a grounded performative is an oxymoron, not in fact a true performative positing, but a species of constative utterance, based on a prior act of knowing, as in the case of God the Father's *fiat lux*. God already knows before he names.

In any case, which form of utterance is Teufelsdröckh's 'yea'? My argument is that it appears to be a constative statement but is in fact performative, or, to be more precise, that on the basis of Carlyle's own language about it, ascribed of course to Teufelsdröckh, it is impossible to tell for sure which it is, in a systematic ambiguity which is, once more, not Carlyle's fault, but an essential feature of what he is trying to say.

At first Teufelsdröckh's 'Yea' seems unequivocally constative, another version of Isaiah's answer to God's 'Whom shall I send?': 'Here am I, Lord. Send me.' Has not Teufelsdröckh heard God's call in his own heart, and is not his 'Yea' in answer to that a knowledge of his vocation which justifies what he is, what he does and what he says? His speech is in answer to speech of the Eternal, and it is this which justifies his claim to express unconditioned truth hieroglyphically or environed with earthly conditions, to name the unnamable in symbols which are intrinsically valid rather than extrinsic or arbitrary. Teufelsdröckh's answer of 'Yea' to the divine call makes him one of those working 'to embody the divine Spirit of [the antiquated Christian Religion] in a new Mythus, in a new vehicle and vesture, that our Souls, otherwise too like perishing, may live' (p. 194).

On the other hand, Teufelsdröckh makes it clear that his 'Yea' is not to be a knowledge but an action, a gesture, if you will, a form of conduct not the result of speculation, in short, a performative. 'But indeed Conviction,' affirms Teufelsdröckh,

> were it never so excellent, is worthless till it convert itself into Conduct. Nay properly conviction is not possible till then; inasmuch as all Speculation is by nature endless, formless, a vortex amid vortices: only by a felt indubitable certainty of Experience does it find any centre to revolve round, and so fashions itself into a System. Most true it is, as a wise man teaches us, that 'Doubt of any sort cannot be removed except by Action'. (pp. 195–6)

Action or conduct precedes conviction and the knowledge (or conviction of knowledge) conviction brings, not the other way around. One must do before one can know. Performance precedes knowledge. What sort of conduct, action or performance does Teufelsdröckh (or Carlyle) have in mind?

The famous paragraph immediately following about doing the duty that lies nearest you in the actual is given the widest applicability to constructive action of any kind:

> Yes here, in this poor, miserable, hampered, despicable Actual, wherein thou even now standest, here or nowhere is thy Ideal: work it out therefrom; and working, believe, live, be free.
> (p. 196)

The terms Teufelsdröckh uses, however, his basic hieroglyphical figure here for conduct or action, as well as his account in the next chapter of his acceptance of 'Authorship as his divine calling' (p. 198), indicate that what is especially in question here is the proffering of language as gesture, action or conduct, in fact a form of action like Carlyle's in writing *Sartor Resartus*. Carlyle's basic figure for this, or the figure he attributes to Teufelsdröckh, is the analogy between a man's act of taking up the pen and writing a work like Teufelsdröckh's clothes philosophy or like *Sartor Resartus*, and God's act of creating the world through the divine fiat, 'Let there be light'. 'Hast thou not a Brain', asks Teufelsdröckh in the chapter following 'The Everlasting Yea',

> furnished, furnishable with some glimmerings of Light; and three fingers to hold a Pen withal? Never since Aaron's rod went out of practice, or even before it, was there such a wonder-working Tool: greater than all recorded miracles have been performed by Pens. . . . The WORD is said to be omnipotent in this world; man, thereby divine, can create as by a *Fiat*. Awake, arise! Speak forth what is in thee; what God has given thee, what the Devil shall not take away.   (p. 199)

Teufelsdröckh's use of this same figure in the next to last paragraph of 'The Everlasting Yea' shows what is problematic about it. In spite of the phrase 'what God has given thee', it is impossible to tell whether the fiat of the man who holds the pen and wields it as a magic wand is a response to God's call or whether it is an autonomous act, a performance which on its own turns chaos into an organised world spinning round a centre and making a coherent system. The ambiguity, or, more properly, undecidability, turns on the uncertain reference of the 'it' in Carlyle's formulation 'it is spoken'. Is the 'it' speech of God or is it speech of man the performative penwielder? If 'it' is the first, then conduct for Carlyle is based on a prior knowledge, and it is God who brings light, intellectual illumination and order. If 'it' is the second then man's own autonomous act as a producing writer creates the order, posits it as a manbegotten fiction, along with the conviction that the conviction is Godbegotten. It is, I argue, altogether impossible to tell which it is. This impossibility is the essential meaning of the 'Everlasting Yea', therefore of Carlyle's book or indeed of his work as a whole. 'Divine moment', writes Teufelsdröckh,

> when over the tempest-tossed Soul, as once over the wild-weltering Chaos, *it is spoken* [my emphasis]: Let there be Light! Ever to the greatest that has felt such a moment, is it not miraculous and God-announcing; even as, under simpler figures, to the simplest and least. The mad primeval Discord is hushed; the rudely-jumbled conflicting elements bind themselves into

separate Firmaments: deep silent rock-foundations are built beneath; and the skyey vault with its everlasting Luminaries above: instead of a dark wasteful Chaos, we have a blooming, fertile, heaven-encompassed World   (p. 197)

The figure here is a good example of Teufelsdröckh's 'Hierograms'. The august figure of God's creation of the world out of chaos is applied to the ordering of man's inner world when he abandons speculation and acts, doing the duty that is nearest him, to make something, for example a book. This is then followed by the famous affirmation or self-exhortation of the last paragraph of the chapter. This, in the light of what has preceded it, would seem to tip the balance in the direction of saying it is man's unaided power of production, plunging blindly ahead to create something, which makes a world out of chaos, were it not for the phrase at the end, 'in God's name'. This could be no more than a strong expletive, or it could mean man's production of order out of chaos is valid only if it is sanctioned and justified by God's election of the writer. This returns the reader once more to that impossibility of deciding which I am trying to identify. 'I too could now say to myself: Be no longer a Chaos, but a World, or even Worldkin. Produce! Produce! Were it but the pitifullest infinitesimal fraction of a Product, produce it, in God's name!' (p. 197).

It will be seen now what I meant by saying that it is impossible to tell whether Emerson or Nietzsche is right about Carlyle. Both and neither are right. Surely no one has ever spoken more sincerely or more from the heart than Carlyle here in the guise of Teufelsdröckh, nor has anyone more persuasively praised the productive chaos-taming power of sincere speaking and writing. On the other hand, Nietzsche, with his astute and disquieting psychological insight, is right too. What Nietzsche names as Carlyle's passionate dishonesty against himself, his need to be a rhetor and speak in ostentatious ironic figures, we can see as an inescapable necessity of the position that Carlyle was affirming through Teufelsdröckh. Once any symbol of the infinite is seen as transient and as having that sort of inadequacy which is intrinsic to any catachresis, or name for the unnamable, then there is no way in which Carlyle can affirm one version of his doctrine of hieroglyphic truth without at the same time affirming the counter version. What Nietzsche calls Carlyle's passionate dishonesty against himself, I am calling the intrinsic, undecidability of his doctrine.

If this is the case, it will allow me to come, finally, full circle and to indicate the answer to the question with which I began. The justification for all Carlyle's 'ornament', the stylistic ornament of 'Carlylese' and the narrative elaboration of fictive narrator within fictive writer, ironies within ironies, wheels within wheels, is that only in this way can Carlyle be true to the double orientation of his doctrine of writing as production. Only a form of writing which constantly destroys itself and renews itself, as figure follows figure, like phoenix after phoenix in a constant process of palingenesis, will be true to Carlyle's fundamental insight, which is 'that all Forms are but Clothes, and temporary' (p. 267). And only the self-subverting irony of a fictive dramatisation of this truth will be able simultaneously to be one of those works of art which may function as an intrinsic symbol, the Infinite embodied in the circumstantial dress of the Finite, and at the same time openly a fictive product, the positing of an imaginary world or worldkin, complete with a hero, places for him to live, and a life-story, with no grounds for their existence but the fiat of Carlyle's magic power of the pen. The Editor too is a narrative necessity. What does his activity do but mime the pontifical process of making order out of chaos, as the Editor more than once says? The chaos in this case is that monster book by Teufelsdröckh and the disordered contents of those six famous paper-bags, but these are in turn a 'Hierogram' for Carlyle's own internal chaos, brought into order and made a worldkin by the production of *Sartor Resartus*.

Notes

1. Ralph Waldo Emerson, *English Traits, Works*, Concord Edition, v (Boston, Mass., and New York: Houghton Mifflin, n.d.) p. 274.
2. Thomas Carlyle, *Sartor Resartus: The Life and Opinions of Herr Teufelsdröckh*, ed. Charles Frederick Harrold (New York: Odyssey Press, 1937) pp. 79–80. Further citations from *Sartor* will be identified by page numbers from this edition.
3. *The Collected Letters of Thomas and Jane Welsh Carlyle*, ed. Charles Richard Sanders, Kenneth J. Fielding, Ian Campbell, John Clubbe and others (Durham, N.C.: Duke University Press, 1970–) vi, 396. (Hereafter cited as *CL*.)
4. *CL*, vii, 266.
5. Emerson, *Works*, x, 494, 495.
6. Friedrich Nietzsche, *Twilight of the Idols, The Portable Nietzsche*, trs. Walter Kaufmann (New York: Viking, 1959) p. 522.

7. *Twilight of the Idols* was written in 1888. Froude's *Life* was published in two sections of two volumes each in 1882 and 1884, but probably Nietzsche was reading a German translation, *Das Leben Thomas Carlyles* . . . Übersetzt, bearbeitet und mit Anmerkungen versehen von T. A. Fischer, 3 vols (Gotha, 1887).
8. *CL*, VIII, 136.
9. But see Carlyle's clarifying comment in *Two Reminiscences of Thomas Carlyle*, ed. John Clubbe (Durham, N.C.: Duke University Press, 1974) pp. 98–9.
10. For a penetrating discussion of what is problematic about applying the notion of performative utterance to literature, see Rodolphe Gasché, ' "Setzung" and "Übersetzung": Notes on Paul de Man', *Diacritics*, XI (Winter 1981) 36–57.

2

Elegant Jeremiahs: The Genre of the Victorian Sage

GEORGE P. LANDOW

In the introduction to *Culture and Anarchy*, Matthew Arnold wryly complained that a newspaper had labelled him 'an elegant Jeremiah'.[1] Although Arnold may not have been pleased by the *Daily Telegraph*'s placement of him in the company of the Old Testament prophet, its remark does indicate that Arnold's Victorian readers perceived his obvious relation to an ancient literary tradition – one, to be sure, whose zeal and self-proclamation made the urbane, gentlemanly Arnold feel more than a little ill at ease however much he drew upon it. Readers of Carlyle and Ruskin similarly perceived their obvious indebtedness to Jeremiah, Isaiah, Daniel and other Old Testament prophets. Walt Whitman, we remember, commented that 'Carlyle was indeed, as Froude terms him, one of those far-off Hebraic utterers, a new Micah or Habbukak. His words bubble forth with abysmic inspiration', and he approvingly quotes Froude's description of him as 'a prophet, in the Jewish sense of the word', one of those, like Isaiah and Jeremiah, who have 'interpreted correctly the signs of their own times'.[2] All three Victorians in fact owed more than just their tone and their willingness to castigate their contemporaries to Old Testament prophecy, a scriptural genre that devotes itself as much to diagnosing the spiritual condition of an age as to predicting the future.

Recognising the specific elements of Old Testament prophecy that the Victorian sages drew upon not only reveals the nineteenth-century intonation of this ancient tradition but also helps define the genre they created. Indeed, one of the most useful approaches to the Victorian sage begins in the recognition that his writings form a clearly identifiable genre, the definition of which offers readers crucial assistance since genre determines the rules by which one reads, interprets and experiences individual works of literature. As

Alastair Fowler has pointed out, 'Traditional genres and modes, far from being mere classificatory devices, serve primarily to enable the reader to share types of meaning', and in fact the reader's understanding is 'genre-bound: he can only think of *Oedipus Tyrannus* as a tragedy, related to other tragedies. If he ignores or despises genre, or gets it wrong, misreading results.'[3] A good many of the problems which twentieth-century readers have had with the writings of the Victorian sages derive, I suspect, from precisely such ignorance of genre and a consequent failure to recognise those signals it directs at them. Therefore, if we can determine the particular techniques that define what we may call the genre of sagistic writing, then we can also better determine how to read the works of Carlyle, Arnold, Ruskin and their heirs.

Such generic description of the works of the sage offers several attractive possibilities, the first and most important of which is that it promises to provide a method of studying non-fiction as literature and not just as data for the study of history-of-ideas and the cultural background for other literary forms.[4] Second, by placing this prose tradition within the context of biblical, oratorical and satirical ones, it provides a means of relating this Post-Romantic form of non-fiction to earlier genres and modes, just as it also suggests an obvious way of relating its major nineteenth-century practitioners in England and America to one another and to their twentieth-century heirs. Third, it offers the possibility of finding a means, which does not depend solely upon ideology, of evaluating discursive prose.

One begins the definition by recognising that this genre supplements the techniques of the Old Testament prophet with others drawn from the Victorian sermon and neoclassical satire, and it does so in order to create credibility for the interpretations made by the sage, a figure who, like Jeremiah, Isaiah and Daniel, stands in conscious opposition to his society and who presents it with interpretations of contemporary phenomena necessary for its survival. Like the Old Testament prophet, the sage is therefore an interpreter, an exegete, one who can read the signs of the times. The sage, in other words, writes as a semiotician, as one who assumes that reality exists encoded with messages. In fact, the kind of enterprise that semioticians like Roland Barthes and anthropologists like Claude Lévi-Strauss undertake has a long history in the Anglo-American tradition, for like these fashionable French thinkers, their nineteenth-century predecessors proceed on the assumption that things make sense – that, in other words, the phenomena they interpret exist in a complex signifying relationship to other phenomena and that, moreover, anyone who knows the key or who perceives the underlying logic of these relationships can read (or decode) such phenomena.

The sage, however, writes as more than a mere interpreter, since, like the Old Testament prophet, he not only interprets contemporary phenomena but also advances interpretations of them that clash with received opinion and then urges that these attacks are essential to his audience's well-being. As Thomas Scott pointed out in a Bible commentary that remained popular throughout much of the nineteenth century, the Old Testament prophets 'were, in general, extraordinary instructors, sometimes in aid of the priests and Levites; but more commonly to supply their defects, when they neglected their duty'.[5] Furthermore, according to Scott, these Old Testament prophets

> were also bold reformers, and reprovers of idolatry, iniquity, and hypocrisy; they called the attention of the people to the law of Moses, especially the moral law, the standard of true holiness; they shewed the inefficacy of ceremonial observances, without the obedience of faith and love.

In other words, the prophet offered no essentially new message: 'The prophets did not teach any new doctrines, commands, or ordinances, but appealed to the authenticated records.' Scott's description of the Old Testament prophet, who unexpectedly comes forth to instruct his fellows on their spiritual and moral failings in order to help his nation survive, applies to the Victorian sage in every respect but one – Scott's evangelical emphasis that these figures from the Old Testament also 'kept up and encouraged the expectation of the promised Messiah'.

The Victorian sage, furthermore, adopts not only the general message of the Old Testament prophet but also the quadrapartite pattern with which he usually presents it. According to Scott, who presents the orthodox view of his subject, the prophets of the Old Testament first called attention to their audience's present grievous condition and often listed individual instances of suffering; second, they pointed out that such suffering resulted directly from their listeners' neglecting – falling away from – God's law; third, they promised further, indeed deepened, miseries if their listeners failed to return to the fold; and fourth, they completed the prophetic pattern by offering visions of bliss that would be realised if their listeners returned to the ways of God. Many of these visions took the form of predictions of divine vengeance upon the irreligious heathen, who, having served as God's agent for punishing the wayward Israelites, would in future serve as an informing example of punishing wrath. For example, the Book of Isaiah

> opens with sharp rebukes of the people for this idolatry and iniquity, and denunciations of divine vengeance upon them; but intermixed with encouraging intimations of mercy, and predictions of Christ. Afterwards follow various prophecies of judgments about to be executed on several nations, as well as on Judah; through all of which the reader is led to expect future deliverances and glorious times to the Church of God.[6]

This prophetic pattern of interpretation, attack upon the audience (or those in authority), warning and visionary promise provides the single most important influence of the Bible upon the writings of the Victorian sage, for it produces many of, though not all, the devices that make up this characteristically Victorian genre.[7] These devices of the sage include a characteristic alternation of satire and positive, even visionary statement, which is frequently accompanied by a parallel alternation of attacks upon the audience and attempts to reassure or inspire it; a frequent concentration upon apparently trivial phenomena as the subject of interpretation; an episodic or discontinuous literary structure that depends upon analogical relations for unity and coherence;[8] a reliance upon grotesque contemporary phenomena, such as the murder of children, or grotesque metaphor, parable and analogy; satiric and idiosyncratic definitions of key terms; and an essential reliance upon *ethos*, or the appeal to credibility. All but the last two of these sagistic techniques obviously derive from the prophetic pattern, and they both function to accommodate it to the situation in which the Victorian sage finds himself – to the situation, that is, in which he no longer speaks literally as the prophet of God. After briefly examining the sage's use of *ethos* and definition in the following pages, I shall devote the remainder of my brief description of this genre to looking at a few instances of its use of the grotesque.

Rhetoricians have traditionally held that one can argue by means of *logos*, the appeal to logic or reason; *pathos*, the appeal to emotion;

or *ethos*, the appeal to credibility. Of course, all argumentation tries to convince the listener or reader that the speaker deserves credence, and every convincing instance of logic, authority or testimony demonstrates that he has earned it. But the writings of the sage are unique in that their central or basic rhetorical effect is the implicit statement to the audience: 'I deserve your attention and credence, for I can be trusted, and no matter how bizarre my ideas or my interpretations may at first seem, they deserve your respect, your attention and ultimately your allegiance because they are correct and they are necessary to your well-being.'

Many of the sage's techniques contribute to the creation of such *ethos*. The use of tone and technique drawn from contemporary sermons, like the frequent citation of Scripture and commonplace scriptural exegetics, struck just the right note with many portions of the Victorian audience. Carlylean zeal, like that of Ruskin and Thoreau, proved similarly effective, as on occasion did Arnoldian urbanity. Paradoxically, both assertions of strength and admissions of weakness can contribute to the sage's credibility. Although Carlyle generally writes with the extreme confidence of the biblical prophet, Ruskin and Thoreau generally admit weakness or error as a way of winning the audience's allegiance. Thus Thoreau's insistence that he was forced to defend John Brown, like Ruskin's claim that he delivered 'Traffic' to the citizens of Bradford against his will, create credibility, and similarly, Ruskin's extensive commentary on his former views and mistakes in the footnotes to later editions of *Modern Painters* convinces the reader of his openness and willingness to admit error – and hence guarantees the authenticity of his present views. Such self-deprecation often appears near the beginning of a work in this form. Ruskin's admission in 'Traffic' that most members of his audience consider him little more than a man-milliner and Arnold's in *Culture and Anarchy* that he is a product of the aggressively uncultured middle classes cultivate their audiences' sympathy. Finally, the sage's primary claim, that he is an unusually perceptive and reliable interpreter, obviously lends itself to creating such *ethos* since every time the sage convinces the audience that under his gaze some phenomenon reveals unexpected meaning, he proves himself more worthy of belief than do exponents of those opposing views initially accepted by his audience.

As this last example makes clear, sagistic techniques, like those of Old Testament prophecy, tend to blend together, and I have only separated them somewhat arbitrarily for the sake of clarity. In practice, as we shall observe in the works of Carlyle, Ruskin and Arnold, a particular interpretation of contemporary history or customs can take the form of a grotesque analogy (or begin in one) and yet also often attack the audience's basic beliefs satirically and play a role as part of some crucial definition as well.

I have elsewhere discussed the genre of the sage in relation to a single brief work, Ruskin's 'Traffic'.[9] In the following pages I should like in contrast to range more widely and demonstrate the presence of several of the main components of sagistic prose in works by four authors of the Victorian age, three British and one American. Since Thomas Carlyle in essence invents this form of non-fiction, I shall draw upon several of his works more frequently than I shall those by the other authors.

Like the Old Testament prophet, the Victorian sage begins his statements by announcing the crucial need to understand some unhappy fact or event in contemporary life. In *Chartism*, the particular puzzling phenomenon Carlyle uses as his point of departure is the discontent of the working classes:

> What means this bitter discontent of the Working Classes? . . . How inexpressibly useful were true insight into it; a genuine understanding by the upper classes of society what it is that the under classes intrinsically *mean*; a clear *interpretation* of the thought which at heart torments these wild inarticulate souls, struggling there, with inarticulate uproar, like dumb creatures in pain, unable to speak what is in them! Something they do *mean*; some true thing withal, in the centre of their confused hearts.[10]

The sage, we are to understand, must interpret the meaning of contemporary events and political movements; and in so doing, he becomes the eloquent voice of inanimate phenomena and the inarticulate masses.

Carlyle's own metaphors for the sage's interpretive enterprise, which he draws from classical mythology and the Old Testament, first emphasise the essential importance to the community of his acts of interpretation. *Chartism*, for instance, presents the longed-for interpreter of contemporary political phenomena as Oedipus confronting the Sphinx: 'What are the rights, what are the mights of the discontented Working Classes in England at this epoch? He were an Oedipus, and deliverer from sad social pestilence, who could resolve us fully!' (xxix.123). In yet another Carlylean metaphor events appear as fire-letters or writing on the wall: 'France is a pregnant example in all ways. Aristocracies that do not govern, Priesthoods that do not teach; the misery of that, and the misery of altering that, – are written in Belshazzar fire-letters on the history of France' (xxix.161–2). Carlyle alludes, of course, to the Book of Daniel, in which the prophet comes forth to read the undecipherable letters of warning that have appeared on the wall of Belshazzar's palace.[11]

This situation in which the prophet, an outsider, comes forth to testify of God's imminent punishment to those in power becomes paradigmatic for Carlyle, who alludes to it frequently. In *Past and Present*, for example, the Peterloo Massacre appears as such a crucial event that prompts the prophet to come forward:

> Some thirteen unarmed men and women cut down, – the number of the slain and maimed is very countable: but the treasury of rage, burning hidden or visible in all hearts ever since, more or less perverting the effort and aim of all hearts ever since, is of unknown extent. . . . In all hearts that witnessed Peterloo, stands written, as in fire-characters, or smoke-characters prompt to become fire again, a legible balance-account of grim vengeance; very unjustly balanced, much exaggerated, as is the way with such account: but payable readily at sight, in full with compound interest! . . . And this is what these poor Manchester operatives, with all the darkness that was in them and round them, did manage to perform. They put their huge inarticulate question, 'What do you mean to do with us?' in a manner audible to every reflective soul in this kingdom. (x.16–17)

All England heard the question, though few understood it; all England saw the fire-letters, the writing on the wall, though few grasped their meaning. 'All England heard the question', says Carlyle. 'England will answer it; or, on the whole, England will perish' (x.17). This is the basic message of the sage: reform or perish. It is the message, for example, of Ruskin's *Stones of Venice* and all of Thoreau's anti-slavery speeches and essays. Their interpretations, like those of Carlyle, reveal that their contemporaries have abandoned or fallen away from the divine laws that inform the universe and that without such guides they are wandering towards a dreadful destruction.

According to Carlyle, it is with entire societies as with individual human beings: when one is miserable, complaining does no good at all.

> Had he faithfully followed Nature and her Laws, Nature, ever true to her Laws, would have yielded fruit and increase and felicity to him: but he has followed other than Nature's Laws; and now Nature, her patience with him being ended, leaves him desolate; answers with very emphatic significance to him: No.   (x.27)

And the situation is the same, urges Carlyle, with nations. The ancient guides – 'Prophets, Priests, or whatever their name' (x.28) – would point out that his fellows had taken the wrong path, but the 'modern guides of nations, Journalists, Political Economists, Politicians, Pamphleteers, have entirely forgotten this, and are ready to deny this' (x.28). One cannot deny truth, however, and survive for long.

> When a Nation is unhappy, the old Prophet was right and not wrong in saying to it: Ye have forgotten God, ye have quitted the ways of God, or ye would not have been unhappy. It is not according to the laws of Fact that ye have lived and guided yourselves, but according to the laws of Delusion, Imposture, and wilful and unwilful *Mistake* of Fact.   (x.28)

Carlyle finds the task of the sage difficult because in the nineteenth century, as in ancient times, the prophet's listeners do not wish to understand:

> A God's-message never came to thicker-skinned people; never had a God's-message to pierce through thicker integuments, into heavier ears. It is Fact, speaking once more, in miraculous thunder-voice, from out of the centre of the world; – how unknown its language to the deaf and foolish many; how distinct, undeniable, terrible and yet beneficent, to the hearing few: Behold, ye shall grow wiser, or ye shall die! . . . Such is the God's-message to us, once more, in these modern days.
>
> (x.29–30)

Having claimed the minatory function of the prophet, Carlyle employs his voice and stance. Thus, having examined the present condition of his country and compared it to a past instance of proper government and earthly order, Carlyle begins with the emphasis made by the voice from the whirlwind in Job:

> I say, you did *not* make the Land of England; and, by the possession of it, you *are* bound to furnish guidance and governance to England! That is the law of your position on this God's-Earth; an everlasting act of Heaven's Parliament, not repealable in St. Stephen's or elsewhere! True government and guidance; not no-government and Laissez-faire; how much less, *mis*-government and Corn Law! There is not an imprisoned Worker looking out from these Bastilles but appeals, very audibly in Heaven's High Courts, against you, and me, and every one who is not imprisoned, 'Why am I here?' His appeal is audible in Heaven; and will become audible enough on Earth too, if it remain unheeded here.   (x.176)

The sage's task when he confronts his audience is to make the appeals of such facts audible – to speak or write as a ventriloquist for dumb fact – and he employs a wide range of literary devices to attract his audience's attention and win its allegiance.

One of his most important techniques in this endeavour is definition, a device found in all kinds of discourse. In sagistic writing, definition takes three basic forms – simple, corrective and satiric. The first two have ancient roots in the homiletic tradition, for the preacher's means of bringing truth to his congregation has often relied upon first instructing its members in the proper meaning of key terms, such as 'Christian', 'faith', 'Gospel scheme', 'type' and 'salvation'. Such acts of definition, which limit and shape key ideas, seize control of the discourse, for the audience, whether listener or reader, depends entirely upon the person who knows the true meanings of things. Like the preacher, the sage uses acts of definition to demonstrate that without him the members of his audience cannot even communicate effectively with one another. The essence of such a far-reaching claim is that the sage knows, as others do not, the true relation of language to reality. Just as his moral claim rests on the fact that he recognises the good whereas his audience does not, so too his intellectual claim here rests on his demonstration that he alone can use language correctly. In fact, the sage implicitly – and sometimes explicitly – claims that he, and he alone, can restore language to its authenticity and effectiveness.

Matthew Arnold's famous definition of culture well exemplifies what I have termed corrective definition. At the opening of *Culture and Anarchy*, Arnold directly confronts opposing points of view, claiming that those who hold them simply do not understand the words they use. According to him, 'the disparagers of culture make its motive curiosity; sometimes, indeed, they make its motive mere exclusiveness and vanity' (p. 90). These latter opponents of culture claim that 'it is valued out of sheer vanity and ignorance or else as an engine of social and class distinction, separating its beholder, like a badge or title, from other people who have not got it'. Like Ruskin, Arnold well knew the standard code words that had such appeal to many Evangelicals in his intended audience, and he uses one of them – *serious* – to advance his cause. Many raised as Evangelicals both within and without the Church of England remained puritanically suspicious of secular culture because they believed that the truly serious person, the person concerned with the things of Christ, did not have much time, energy or attention for such essentially trivial activities. Confronting this source of opposition head on, Arnold, who uses a device especially popular with the Evangelical sermon, claims that those who thus interpret the meaning of the word *culture* both do not know the meaning of the word and also, by their misuse of it, demonstrate that they themselves are not *serious* people: 'No serious man would call this *culture*, or attach any value to it, as culture, at all' (p. 90). As Arnold, who would have made a fine advertising copywriter, well knew, his charge that his opponents were not 'serious' implied that such intellectual lightness and frivolity derive from an unenviable moral and spiritual state. Then, having turned the tables upon his self-righteous opponents by appropriating one of their favourite cant terms, Arnold again turns the tables on them when he argues that he and all other lovers of culture are the truly 'serious' men, for according to him, culture implies both the 'desire to see things as they are' and a corollary 'balance and regulation of mind'. Culture, he adds, is 'properly described' as deriving from 'the love of perfection; it is a *study of perfection*. It moves by the force, not merely or primarily of the scientific passion for pure knowledge, but also of the moral and social passion for doing good' (v.91). Culture, in other words, hardly implies, as its opponents had charged, either idle curiosity or exclusiveness and vanity. Rather culture turns out to be an essentially moral and religious matter – a matter, in fact, of particularly high seriousness, a matter to engage the minds and souls of all truly earnest Victorians.

The sermons of Charles Kingsley reveal how directly this device, which Arnold employs as part of a prophetic pattern, derives from the sermon tradition. For example, arguing that the Bible instructs us 'not to be religious, but to be godly', he points his audience's attention straight at this crucial matter of language, words and definition; and immediately after so doing he makes the preacher's usual claim to understand the correct meaning of essential words – and his further claim to restore true meaning to such words and thereby place his audience once again in a proper, healthy, vital relationship to reality. He begins by telling his listeners that he realises that they may think there is no important difference between being godly and being religious:

You may think there is no difference, or that it is but a difference of words. I can tell you that a difference in words is a very awful, important difference. A difference in words is a difference in things. Words are very awful and wonderful things, for they come from the most awful and wonderful of all beings, Jesus Christ, the Word. He puts words into men's minds. He made all things, and He makes all words to express those things with. And woe to those who use the wrong words about things! For if a man calls anything by its wrong name, it is a sure sign that he understands that thing wrongly, or feels about it wrongly; and therefore a man's words are often honester than he thinks; for as a man's words are, so is a man's heart . . . and, therefore, by right words, by the right names which we call things, we shall be condemned.[12]

Furthermore, Kingsley also sounds a familiar theme of the sages when he emphasises in 'The Spirit and the Flesh' that 'according to a nation's godliness, and wisdom, and purity of heart, will be its power of using words discreetly and reverently' (p. 43). Placing such importance upon the ability to use langauge correctly, Kingsley as preacher expectedly opens many sermons with such questions of definition.[13]

Looking across the Atlantic, we see Thoreau employing acts of definition within the context of a satiric attack upon the spiritual bankruptcy of the age. In 'Slavery in Massachusetts' (1854) Thoreau uses the definition to argue that the seizure of a single person of another race not only is relevant to the lives of every member of his audience but is centrally important to them, since this act directly limits – and threatens – their own freedom, their own lives. Thoreau, a fine satirist, proceeds by using the sagistic and satiric technique of definition to demonstrate that, since the Governor, the chief executive officer of Massachusetts, did not guard the rights of one who lived in his domain, he has therefore proved himself not to be a governor at all.

Thoreau begins his definition by taking the satirist's pose of the ingenuous novice – the honorable, childlike idealist who believes all he is told:

> I had thought that the Governor was, in some sense, the executive officer of the State; that it was his business, as Governor, to see that the laws of the State were executed; while, as a man, he took care that he did not, by so doing, break the laws of humanity. . . . Perhaps I do not know what are the duties of a Governor; but if to be a Governor requires to subject oneself to such much ignominy without remedy, if it is to put a restraint upon my manhood, I shall take care never to be Governor of Massachusetts.[14]

Much in the manner of Evangelical ministers and writers of tracts, he thus proceeds by claiming that the Governor is a false governor, not a true one – a governor only in name not in act. Thoreau relates that when he searches for a governor, he only finds an empty simulacrum, a shell, a pageant-Governor:

> I listen to hear the voice of a Governor, Commander-in-Chief of the forces of Massachusetts. I hear only the creaking of crickets and the hum of insects which now fill the summer air. The Governor's exploit is to review the troops on muster days. I have seen him on horseback, with his hat off, listening to a chaplain's prayer. It chances that that is all I have ever seen of a Governor. I think that I could manage to get along without one. If he is not of the least use to prevent my being kidnapped, pray of what important use is he likely to be to me. When freedom is most endangered, he dwells in the deepest obscurity.

Even before pointing out that the governor who does not defend one's freedom does nothing, Thoreau implicitly defined him as one who does nothing: 'A distinguished clergyman told me that he chose the profession of a clergyman because it afforded the most leisure for literary pursuits. I would recommend to him the profession of a Governor' (p. 132). As these examples reveal, Thoreau combines straightforward acts of definition with those of a more purely satirical nature. Having first stated the true meaning of a central term, he then mocks those who have not lived up to the meaning of it.[15] The implication of such a manner of proceeding, of course, is that the speaker, the definer of important terms, resides at the centre of meaning. He alone knows what things mean. He also sees clearly enough to warn others that they have fallen away from the ways of God and Nature. The best way to find that way, claims Thoreau the sage, is first by understanding the true meaning of words, and therefore he begins with the meaning of the word 'governor' and follows this definition with others, such as 'slavery', which are even more central to his argument.

By the time that Thoreau has finished attacking the Governor of Massachusetts with this satirically employed definition, he has transformed him, his office and the element of sham they share into a grotesque metonymy of his age and nation. This transformation of contemporary phenomena into what Ruskin termed a 'Symbolical Grotesque' exemplifies another major technique of the sage.[16]

Like Thoreau, Ruskin and Arnold, Carlyle liberally salts his works with such instances of contemporary phenomena that, according to his prophet's eye, embody the spiritual condition of his age. Many of these grotesque signs of the times turn out to be obviously significant things or events, such as his well-known citation of the death of a malnourished Irish widow in *Past and Present*. Drawing upon William P. Alison's *Observations on the Management of the Poor in Scotland* (1840), Carlyle cites the case of the poor woman who could only prove to the citizens of a modern city her common humanity by infecting them fatally with disease:

A poor Irish Widow, her husband having died in one of the Lanes of Edinburgh, went forth with her three children, bare of all resource, to solicit help from the Charitable Establishments of that City. At this Charitable Establishment and then at that she was refused; referred from one to the other, helped by none; – till she had exhausted them all; till her strength and heart failed her: she sank down in typhus-fever; died, and infected her Lane with fever, so that 'seventeen other persons' died of fever there in

> consequence. The humane Physician asks thereupon, as with a
> heart too full for speaking, Would it not have been *economy* to help
> this poor Widow? She took typhus-fever, and killed seventeen of
> you! – Very curious.   (x.149)

Then, continuing to provide a voice for unarticulate fact, Carlyle
speaks the meaning contained in the widow's act – indeed, in her
very existence. She demands of her fellow creatures that they give
her their help and asserts that she deserves it because 'I am your
sister, bone of your bone; one God made us: ye must help me!' The
inhabitants of Edinburgh responded by denying her appeal – 'No;
impossible; thou are no sister of ours', but, as Carlyle emphasises,
she 'proves' her sisterhood when her typhus kills them: 'They
actually were her brothers, though denying it! Had human creature
ever to go lower for a proof?' (x.149). In thus demonstrating the
relevance of such contemporary phenomena, in thus thrusting
upon the audience its need to see deeper into such apparently trivial
events, Carlyle as prophet employs a form of the Symbolical
Grotesque in which the significance of evil and suffering plays a
major part. Such citation of grotesque evil plays an important part in
this genre from Carlyle to the present day, for it forces upon the
reader the immediate need to understand what is essentially not
finally understandable – the presence of pain and suffering in
human existence. Their very horribleness makes them of interest.

Past and Present, which in so many ways can stand as the epitome
of this kind of writing, points to an example of child-murder for
money as a sign of the times that sums up the spiritual state of the
modern world:

> At Stockport Assizes – and this too has no reference to the present
> state of trade, being of date prior to that – a Mother and a Father
> are arraigned and found guilty of poisoning three of their
> children, to defraud a 'burial-society' of some 3 l. 8 s. due on the
> death of each child: they are arraigned, found guilty; and the
> official authorities, it is whispered, hint that perhaps the case is
> not solitary, that perhaps you had better not probe farther into
> that department of things. . . . It is an incident worth lingering
> on. . . . Such instances are like the highest mountain apex
> emerged into view; under which lies a whole mountain region
> and land, not yet emerged.   (x.4)

Such an incident of grotesque horror leads Carlyle to raise the question, once again, of what wealth means and to whom it does any good in the modern world. In other words, Carlyle does not, in the manner of the reporter on the modern tabloid, use such incidents purely to arouse jaded or sick appetites. Rather, like so many recent writers, he finds in such grotesqueness a symbol of the Condition of England, a symptom of his age's spiritual and mental state. Carlyle's citation of the Stockport murder, Arnold's mention of similar crimes a decade later, and similar examinations of crime by Truman Capote, Norman Mailer, Joan Didion and Kate Millett all force the reader to confront hideous evil and attempt to determine if these horrors are truly signs of the times.[17]

In contrast to Symbolical Grotesques created from phenomena the sage interprets, there are those that take the forms of extended analogies, metaphors and parables. Given Carlyle's major emphasis upon fact, most of his Symbolical Grotesques, such as the Morrison's Pill (x.23–7), Workhouse Bastille (x.2), Amphibious Pope (x.138–40) and 'that great Hat seven-foot high, which now perambulates London streets' (x.141), in *Past and Present*, obviously derive from contemporary phenomena, but he occasionally employs the invented form of the Symbolical Grotesque, which appears, for example, in *Chartism*'s Sanspotatoe (xxix.136) and *Past and Present*'s 'baleful fiat as of Enchantment' (x.1). Such invented grotesques play a greater role in the sagistic writings of Arnold and Ruskin, and Arnold's analysis of England's Barbarians, Philistines and Populace in the third chapter of *Culture and Anarchy* and Ruskin's 'Goddess of Getting on' in 'Traffic' (xviii.450–1) exemplify some of the most brilliant satiric emblems of the sage. In his writings on political economy Ruskin makes major use of them and they effectively replace the word-painting that characterised his art criticism as his favourite rhetorical device. Ruskin's invented Symbolical Grotesques, which take several chief forms, are particularly useful in summing up the flaws in opposing oppositions. These little satiric narratives and analogies of course owe much to neoclassical satirists, particularly Swift, whose *Tale of a Tub* and *Gulliver's Travels* make extensive use of elaborate analogies to cast an opposing view in a poor light.

In 'Traffic' Ruskin mocks his audience's conception of an ideal life by presenting it in the form of what is essentially a dream-vision. Arguing that his listeners' worship of the Goddess of Getting-on implies that they also condemn others to miserable lives, he presents a picture of their ideal that enforces corollaries or implicit points they would willingly leave out of their sight and consciousness:

> Your ideal of human life then is, I think, that it should be passed in a pleasant undulating world, with iron and coal everywhere beneath it. On each pleasant bank of this world is to be a beautiful mansion, with two wings; and stables, and coach-houses; a moderately-sized park; a large garden and hot-houses; and pleasant carriage drives through the shrubberies. In this mansion are to live the favoured votaries of the Goddess; the English gentleman, with his gracious wife, and his beautiful family; he always able to have the boudoir and the jewels for the wife, and the beautiful ball dresses for the daughters, and hunters for the sons, and a shooting in the Highlands for himself. At the bottom of the bank, is to be the mill; not less than a quarter of a mile long, with one steam engine at each end, and two in the middle, and a chimney three hundred feet high. In this mill are to be in constant employment from eight hundred to a thousand workers, who never drink, never strike, always go to church on Sunday, and always express themselves in respectful language.[18]

As Ruskin points out, this image of human existence might appear 'very pretty indeed, seen from above; not at all so pretty, seen from below' (xviii.291), since for every family to whom the Englishman's deity is the Goddess of Getting-on, one thousand find her the 'Goddess of *not* Getting-on' (xviii.291). By making the implications of such a vision of life based upon the ideal of competition explicit, this Symbolical Grotesque serves a powerful satiric purpose. Ruskin's expertise as an art critic here turns out to be particularly helpful, for he carefully explains the sketched-in elements of his supposedly ideal scene with the same skill that he used in setting forth his descriptions of Alpine landscape, the city of Venice, or Turner's paintings. In each case he proceeds by presenting visual details and then drawing attention to their meaning. Here he first presents, slightly tongue-in-cheek, an image of the English capitalist's Earthly Paradise, and then, once he has sketched it for his audience, he presents its dark implications by showing the world of the have-nots upon which it sits both literally and symbolically. By moving through his created word-picture from upper to lower, he endows each portion of his visual image with a moral and political valuation: the upper classes reside literally, spatially, above the industries that provide their wealth and also above the workers who slave to make their lives one of ease.

A second form of the sage's Symbolical Grotesque, those that take the form of brief narratives, also appears in 'Traffic'. When Ruskin argues against those who claim that they cannot afford to create beautiful surroundings for human life, he employs a characteristic parable to reduce such opposing claims to absurdity. Suppose, he instructs his listeners, that he had been sent for 'by some private gentleman, living in a suburban house, with his garden separated only by a fruit wall from his next door's neighbour's' (xviii.278) to advise him how to furnish his drawing-room. Finding the walls bare, Ruskin suggests rich furnishings, say fresco-painted ceilings, elegant wallpaper and damask curtains, and his client complains of the expense, which he cannot afford. Pointing out that his client is supposed to be a wealthy man, he is told:

> 'Ah yes,' says my friend, 'but do you know at present, I am obliged to spend it nearly all on steel-traps?' 'Steel-traps! for whom?' 'Why, for that fellow on the other side of the wall, you know: we're very good friends, capital friends; but we are obliged to keep our traps set on both sides of the wall; we could not possibly keep on friendly terms without them, and our spring guns. The worst of it is, that we are both clever fellows enough; and there's never a day passes that we don't find out a new trap, or a new gun-barrel, or something.'   (xviii.278)

Fifteen million a year, his client tells Ruskin, the two good neighbours spend on such traps, and he doesn't see how they could do with less, and so, Ruskin the room decorator must understand why he has so few resources to beautify his client's environment. Turning to his audience, Ruskin abandons the pose of the naïf and comments in the tones of the Old Testament prophet: 'A highly comic state of life for two private gentlemen! but for two nations, it seems to me, not wholly comic.' Bedlam might be comic, he supposes, if it had only one madman, and Christmas pantomimes are comic with one clown, 'but when the whole world turns clown, and paints itself red with its own heart's blood instead of vermilion, it is something else than comic, I think' (xviii.278).[19] Having first mocked with his satirical parable the intellectual seriousness of his listeners' self-justifications for failing to spend money on beautifying their environments, Ruskin next moves from mocking to damning them. In the manner of the Old Testament prophet he demonstrates that the actions of his contemporaries reveal that they have abandoned the ways of God and are inevitably heading toward a terrible destruction.

Like most other techniques of the sage, this Ruskinian parable serves multiple functions: it simultaneously interprets the dullness of English design in terms of the nation's political, economic and military choices and satirises England and the English; it diagnoses his nation's ills, explains how they came about and threatens worse disaster if proper actions are not taken; it contributes to Ruskin's position or pose as a wisdom-speaker and hence adds to his *ethos*; and it creates a self-contained section or episode which can convince the reader even if he rejects Ruskin's other points in 'Traffic'. Such self-contained parables, sections and arguments typify the writing of the sage and create its characteristic discontinuity.

Perceiving how the sage's characteristic techniques form an identifiable genre assists us in understanding both an individual writer's particular strategies and his relation to others who write as sages. Furthermore, by clarifying some of this genre's basic themes and techniques, this approach suggests how to relate sagistic prose to other genres, such as the novel and sermon.

Notes

1. Matthew Arnold, *Culture and Anarchy with Friendship's Garland and Some Literary Essays*, ed. R. H. Super (Ann Arbor: University of Michigan Press, 1965) p. 88. Hereafter cited in text. Arnold remarked that for his 'indifference to direct political action I have been taken to task by the *Daily Telegraph*, coupled, by a strange perversity of fate, with just that very one of the Hebrew prophets whose style I admire the least, and called "an elegant Jeremiah" '.

2. Walt Whitman, *Specimen Days*, in *Complete Poetry and Collected Prose*, ed. Justin Kaplan (New York: Viking, 1982) pp. 898, 893.

3. Alastair Fowler, 'The Life and Death of Literary Forms', *New Directions in Literary History*, ed. Ralph Cohen (London: Routledge & Kegan Paul, 1974) p. 79. According to Fowler, 'Johnson's blunder over *Lycidas* and the more recent and even more spectacular critical error of taking *Paradise Lost* as classical epic with Satan the hero are dreadful examples. Clearly, generic forms must rank among all the most important of the signal systems that communicate a literary work' (p. 79).

4. Recent years have seen a significant increase in attention to Victorian non-fiction as literature; and the individual essays in *The Art of Victorian Prose*, ed. George Levine and Lionel Madden (New York: Oxford University Press, 1968), have done much to advance these kinds of critical investigation, as have book-length studies of individual authors, such as G. B. Tennyson, *Sartor Called Resartus: The Genesis, Structure, and Style of Thomas Carlyle's First Major Work* (Princeton, N.J.: Princeton University Press, 1965); Albert J. LaValley, *Carlyle and the Idea of the Modern: Studies in Carlyle's Prophetic Literature and its Relation to Blake, Nietzsche, Marx, and Others* (New Haven, Conn.: Yale University Press, 1968); Gerry H. Brookes, *The Rhetorical Form of Carlyle's 'Sartor Resartus'* (Berkeley, Calif.: University of California Press, 1972); Richard L. Stein, *The Ritual of Interpretation: The Fine Arts as Literature in Ruskin, Rossetti, and Pater* (Cambridge, Mass.: Harvard University Press, 1975) and Elizabeth K. Helsinger, *Ruskin and the Art of the Beholder* (Cambridge, Mass.: Harvard University Press, 1982).

   Thus far, the best discussions of Victorian non-fiction as imaginative literature have taken two forms – those, such as George Levine's *The Boundaries of Fiction: Carlyle, Macaulay, Newman* (Princeton, N.J.: Princeton University Press, 1968), that place it in the context of the novel and those, such as Pierre Fontenay's 'Ruskin and Paradise Regained', *Victorian Studies*, XII (1969) 347–56, and other works listed above, that place passages from individual works within the context provided by mythological and iconological studies. John Holloway's pioneering *The Victorian Sage: Studies in Argument* (London: Macmillan, 1953), which discusses Carlyle, Disraeli, George Eliot, Newman, Arnold and Hardy, obviously places Carlyle and Arnold – it omits Ruskin – within the context of the novel and, despite its many suggestive hints and comments about the sage's non-logical form of argumentation, in practice concentrates almost exclusively upon skilful New Critical examinations of imagery.

5. Thomas Scott, *A Commentary on the Holy Bible, Containing the Old and New Testaments* . . ., 5 vols (Philadelphia: William S. and Alfred Martien, 1958) III, 79. (Subsequent quotations from Scott in this paragraph are taken from this same page.)

6. *A Commentary on the Holy Bible*, III, 81.

7. Three biblical traditions have a major effect upon this Victorian genre – Old Testament prophecy, New Testament apocalyptics and typological exegetics. As I have argued in *Victorian Types, Victorian Shadows: Biblical Typology in Victorian Literature, Art, and Thought* (Boston: Routledge & Kegan Paul, 1980) pp. 110–18, 166–76, Carlyle and Ruskin draw heavily upon typological exegesis in their characteristic works. None the less, their writing as sages derives far more importantly from late-eighteenth- and nineteenth-century attitudes toward Old Testament prophecy. Although scriptural typology accounts for both the sage's general attitude toward interpretation and the meaning of specific passages, Old Testament

prophecy is directly responsible for the overall nature of this literary form as well as for many of its crucial characteristics, such as the sage's contentious attitude towards his audience, his alternation of satire and vision and his use of discontinuous literary structure. Much basic work remains to be done on this subject of Victorian notions of Old Testament prophecy and their effect upon secular culture, but Leslie Tannenbaum's excellent chapter on prophetic form in *Biblical Tradition in Blake's Early Prophecies: The Great Code of Art* (Princeton, N.J.: Princeton University Press, 1982) pp. 25–54 provides an essential introduction to the subject by examining some late-eighteenth-century writings on prophecy that remained influential well into the Victorian period.

8. In the same way that the apparent disorder of sublimity allowed Augustan critics to compensate for the restrictions and omissions of neoclassical conceptions of beauty, biblical prophecy allowed them to consider forms of literary organisation outside the neoclassical canon. According to Campegius Vitringa's *Typus Doctrinae Propheticae* (1708), whom Tannenbaum quotes from John Gill's popular Bible commentary, prophecies often 'admit of resumptions, repetitions of sayings, and retrograde leaps and skips, or scattered or detached pieces . . . which are inserted into the text, for the sake of illustrating this or that part of the prophecy. . . . To these may also be rightly referred the excursions and digressions, in which the prophets, whilst they really have before their eyes some object of more remote time, suddenly leave it, and by way of excursion turn themselves to men of their own time, or the next; that from the subject of their prophecy, they may admonish, exhort and convince them.' Vitringa might be describing *Past and Present* or *The Stones of Venice*! See Tannenbaun, *Biblical Tradition in Blake's Early Prophecies*, pp. 30, 32–9.

9. George P. Landow, 'Ruskin as Victorian Sage: the Example of "Traffic",' *New Approaches to Ruskin*, ed. Robert Hewison (London: Routledge & Kegan Paul, 1981) pp. 89–110.

10. Thomas Carlyle, *Works*, Centenary Edition, ed. H. D. Traill, 30 vols (London: Chapman, 1896–9) xxix.119, 122 (emphasis added). (Hereafter cited in text by page and volume number as xxix.119, 122.)

11. Then again the sage appears as an Understanding Eye, as society's organ of understanding the mysteriously encoded, for, as he explains, 'Events are written lessons, glaring in huge hieroglyphic picture-writing, that all may read and know them: the terror and horror they inspire is but the note of preparation for the truth they are to teach; a mere waste of terror if that not be learned' (xxix.155).

12. Charles Kingsley, 'Religion not Godliness', *Village Sermons, and Town and Country Sermons* (London: Macmillan, 1886) pp. 11–12.

13. For example, he begins 'Self-Destruction', a sermon on 1 Kings 22.23, by directing the audience's attention to the way in which the appointed text provides 'an insight into the meaning of that most awful and terrible word, – temptation' (p. 59), and he begins, 'The Courage of the Saviour', a sermon on John 11.7–8, by defining 'fortitude' (pp. 184–5).

14. Henry David Thoreau, *Reform Papers*, ed. Wendell Glick (Princeton, N.J.: Princeton University Press, 1973) p. 94.
15. Another instance of such satiric definition appears in 'A Plea for John Brown', in which he mocks contemporary believers for not making their religion a part of their life. According to him, 'The modern Christian is a man who has consented to say all the prayers in the liturgy, provided you will let him go straight to bed and sleep quietly afterward. All his prayers begin with "Now I lay me down to sleep" ' (*Reform Papers*, p. 121).
16. Ruskin's discussions of the grotesque, a mode which he believed played a major role in symbolism, allegory, fantasy, sublimity and satire, appear in *The Stones of Venice* and *Modern Painters*, vol. III. For the place of the grotesque in the context of Ruskin's thought, see my *Aesthetic and Critical Theories of John Ruskin* (Princeton, N.J.: Princeton University Press, 1971) pp. 370–98, and Helsinger's *Ruskin and the Art of the Beholder*, pp. 111–28, 286–8. Wolfgang Kayser, *The Grotesque in Art and Literature*, trs. Ulrich Weisstein (Bloomington, Ind.: Indiana University Press, 1963), and Geoffrey Galt Harpham, *On the Grotesque: Strategies of Contradiction in Art and Literature* (Princeton, N.J.: Princeton University Press, 1982), offer important discussions on their subject.
17. Truman Capote's *In Cold Blood: A True Account of a Multiple Murder and Its Consequences* (1965), Joan Didion's *The White Album* (1979), Norman Mailer's *The Executioner's Song* (1979) and Kate Millett's *The Basement* (1976) stand out as four particularly important works that take such crimes as Carlylean signs of the times. Ronald Weber, *The Literature of Fact: Literary Nonfiction in American Writing* (Athens, Ohio: Ohio University Press, 1980), provides several other important examples.
18. John Ruskin, *Works*, ed. E. T. Cook and Alexander Wedderburn, 39 vols (London: George Allen, 1903–12) XVIII.291. Hereafter cited in text by page and volume number as XVIII.291.
19. Ruskin echoes, possibly consciously, Carlyle's close to 'Phenomena' in *Past and Present*, which comments that the sum of mammon-worship, 'visible in every street, market-place, senate-house, circulating library, cathedral, cotton-mill, and union-workhouse, fills one *not* with a comic feeling!'

3

Prodigals and Prodigies: Trollope's Notes as a Son and Father

DONALD D. STONE

Victorian literature contains many memorable father–son relationships. One thinks, for example, of Meredith's Harry Richmond and his charismatic father, Richmond Roy, or of Tom Tulliver and his obstinate, proud parent, the miller Tulliver. One recalls the affectionate interchanges between Roger Hamley and Squire Hamley (in Gaskell's *Wives and Daughters*), between Sam and Tony Weller or Wemmick and his Aged P, and between the heroes of the early Dickens novels and their various surrogate fathers: Pickwick, Brownlow, the Cheeryble brothers. However, one also remembers the various paternal incubi and sham patriarchs in the Dickens novels, not to mention the various revered father-figures who loom largely, and often devastatingly, in the work and lives of Carlyle, Arnold, Ruskin and Mill. The implied rebelliousness of the sons of Browning's Bishop ordering his tomb is carried to a vindictive extreme in Butler's *The Way of All Flesh*. 'A man first quarrels with his father about three-quarters of a year before he is born', declares Butler. 'It is then he insists on setting up a separate establishment; when this has been once agreed to, the more complete the separation forever after the better for both.'[1] Although Butler presumes to be speaking for the mid-Victorian generation in which he grew up, his defiant attitude links him rather with the first modernists, such as Edmund Gosse, James Joyce, D. H. Lawrence and Virginia Woolf, for whom repudiation of the father-figure was seen as a necessity if they were to achieve artistic freedom.

A more balanced voice of the mid-nineteenth century than Butler's is Anthony Trollope, born twenty years before Butler. Trollope's fictional protagonists live in and for a world of relationships; and in that world, accommodation between father and son is seen as a necessity if each is to attain maturity of vision. The kind of personal estrangement from family ties which is essential for an artist like Butler's Ernest Pontifex or Joyce's Stephen Dedalus leads, in a Trollope novel, to tragic isolation, sometimes to madness. Trollope's fiction – like Dickens's, Eliot's, Gaskell's, Meredith's – celebrates familial bonding as an ideal in a troubled world; yet just as Trollope has more direct experience as father and son to draw upon for his depictions, so too does his wonted sense of candour oblige him to look critically at these relationships. It is possible, hence, for Ralph Newton (of *Ralph the Heir*) to regard his father as 'of all things the most valuable and most impossible to replace, – a friend whose love was perfect'; but it is also possible for the narrator of *The Small House at Allington* to speak of Lord Porlock and his father hating 'each other as only such fathers and such sons can hate'.[2]

Trollope's fiction contains richly detailed and subtly analysed depictions of every kind of family relationship.[3] Yet just as Verdi in his operas and Dickens in his fiction are especially stimulated by the father–daughter relationship, so Trollope is particularly inspired when he considers the bonding between Plantagenet Palliser and his son or (in a darker mood) between Mr Scarborough and his progeny. At times he invokes those antithetical – and, for nineteenth-century-trained minds like Kierkegaard and Freud, *primal* – myths of the father–son relationship: Abraham prepared to sacrifice his son in the name of a higher paternal authority; Oedipus unwittingly murdering his father and taking over his position. Father and son compete for power in many a Trollope novel: Archdeacon Grantly threatens to disinherit his son, the Major, if he marries against his will (in *The Last Chronicle of Barset*); while President Neverbend, of *The Fixed Period*, looks back wistfully to the days when 'the old Romans could punish filial disobedience by death' (ch. 7). Daniel Caldigate, in turn, considers it 'no more than natural' that his son, waiting to inherit the parental estate, should wish for his death (*John Caldigate*, ch. 3). The younger Caldigate, meanwhile, is one of many versions of the Prodigal Son who turn up in Trollope. (These include the delinquent young Anthony, as described in the *Autobiography*.) Occasionally Trollope joins Dickens in presenting images of the Prodigal Father taking advantage of his son. Yet despite the negative portraits – of domineering, devouring or absent fathers and of greedy, venal or inattentive sons – Trollope also presents positive images of loving fathers, of fathers learning to

love and to yield, and of sons learning to understand their parent
and forming strong bonds of friendship with him. Daniel Caldigate,
Archdeacon Grantly, President Neverbend and Plantagenet Palliser
all join, eventually, in responding to that 'heart in [a father's] bosom
which is more powerful than law or even custom' (*The Fixed Period*,
ch. 7) – something more potent than primal myth – and their sons
respond in kind.[4]

Trollope's remarkably full and candid treatment of the father–son
theme stems from his understanding of both sides of the generation
gap. His *Autobiography* displays considerable powers of loving
discernment directed toward an unusually difficult father, while his
letters are filled with solicitousness and affection towards his
frequently troublesome sons. Trollope's childhood was no less
traumatic than Dickens's. For example, at the same age that the
twelve-year-old Dickens was condemned to the blacking warehouse
for several months, Trollope was deprived of his mother's company
for nearly four years when she went to America, taking with her
most of the family.[5] Ostracised by his schoolmates, Trollope lived
mainly in the company of his fearsome father. Passages in Trollope's
Autobiography (written in the mid-1870s), dealing with the father's
misconceived efforts to educate a hopelessly idle son, read almost
like a parody of Mill's descriptions in his *Autobiography* (published
1873) of his relationship with James Mill.[6] But Trollope was
incapable of taking Dickensian revenge: he found Forster's
biography of Dickens 'distasteful'. 'Forster tells of him things which
should disgrace him, – as the picture he drew of his own father, &
the hard words he intended to have published of his own mother.'[7]

Both Anthony and Thomas Adolphus Trollope have left vivid
sketches of their father, Thomas Anthony Trollope; but the older
brother's portrait is at once fuller and more negative than
Anthony's: 'a disputatious man', always believing himself in the
right; a failed barrister, who quarrelled with his potential clients; a
sufferer from 'bilious headache', whose irritable temper eventually
'reached a pitch that made one fear his reason was, or would
become, unhinged'; a well-meaning, 'affectionate and anxiously
solicitous' father and husband, whose family shrank from his
presence. (Frances Trollope admitted that one reason for her going
to America was to escape her husband's company.) 'Happiness,
mirth, contentment, pleasant conversation, seemed to fly before
him as if a malevolent spirit emanated from him.' Tom opposes to
this pitiable, though hardly tragic, figure of a father afflicted by

some sort of curse the charming and cheerful figure of Frances Trollope, 'one of those people who carry sunshine with them'.[8] Anthony's assessment of his parents is more balanced: in contrast to his brother, he emphasises his mother's romantic, flighty nature to show that she had minor weaknesses as well as great strength of endurance; but he also sees the father's career in tragic rather than merely pathetic terms. 'I sometimes look back, meditating for hours together, on his adverse fate', Trollope writes in a memorable passage:

> He was a man, finely educated, of great parts, with immense capacity for work, physically strong very much beyond the average of men, addicted to no vices, carried off by no pleasures, affectionate by nature, most anxious for the welfare of his children, born to fair fortunes, – who, when he started in the world, may be said to have had everything at his feet. But everything went wrong with him. The touch of his hand seemed to create failure. He embarked in one hopeless enterprise after another, spending on each all the money he could at the time command. But the worse curse to him of all was a temper so irritable that even those whom he loved the best could not endure it. We were all estranged from him, and yet I believe that he would have given his heart's blood for any of us. His life as I knew it was one long tragedy.

Trollope admits that with the lapse of forty years he 'can tell the story' of his family's misery 'almost as coldly as I have often done some scene of intended pathos in fiction'. Yet despite this typical burst of self-deprecation, he adds that the scenes witnessed during his childhood were 'full of pathos', and that while he could dimly appreciate 'the misery of the blighted ambition of my father's life' and 'the strain which my mother was enduring', he could himself do little other than leave and provide one less 'burden' for them.[9]

Trollope ascribes to his lonely childhood the habit of creating fictions in his mind and thereby living 'in a world altogether outside the world of my own material life', a habit useful to the future novelist.[10] However, the years spent scrutinising, and later meditating on, his father helped sharpen his gifts as a psychological realist. He never drew upon his father in the manner of George Eliot, idealising her father in the portraits of Adam Bede and Caleb

Garth; nor did he exaggerate his father for comic or melodramatic effect, as Dickens did in the cases of Wilkins Micawber and William Dorrit. Nevertheless, bits and pieces of his father's 'adverse fate' and difficult, unyielding character turn up in several Trollope novels. In George Bertram, Trollope describes a brilliantly endowed, overly proud young man – possessing 'a high spirit, a good heart, and a bad head' for pursuing his own interests (*The Bertrams*, ch. 21) – who offends his wealthy uncle, as the elder Trollope did his uncle, thereby losing his inheritance. This melancholy novel, dealing with blighted hopes and ambitions, may owe something to Thackeray's *The Newcomes*, but there is surely also a personal motive on Trollope's part for dealing with the psychology of failure. The determination of Lady Mason's self-righteous son Lucius, of *Orley Farm*, to be an experimental farmer probably derives from the elder Trollope's fiasco in that endeavour. But the two characters who most closely resemble Thomas Anthony Trollope are the Reverend Josiah Crawley, in *The Last Chronicle of Barset* (1866), and Louis Trevelyan, of *He Knew He Was Right* (1868), both of whom share (along with George Bertram, Lucius Mason and Plantagenet Palliser) the elder Trollope's morbid sensitivity and his 'aptitude to do things differently from others'.[11]

In description after description of Mr Crawley, Trollope touches on aspects of his father's character: 'an unhappy, moody, disappointed man, upon whom the troubles of the world always seemed to come with a double weight'. 'He was morose, sometimes almost to insanity. There had been days in which even his wife had found it impossible to deal with him otherwise than as with an acknowledged lunatic' (*Last Chronicle*, ch. 1). 'Her husband's mind would not act at all times as do the minds of other men' (ch. 4). To his children he is a well-intending pedagogue. To a sympathetic outsider, Mr Crawley's 'crushing pride' lurks behind his mask of humility: 'It was, perhaps, after all, a question whether the man was not served rightly by the extremities to which he was reduced. There was something radically wrong within him, which had put him into antagonism with all the world, and which produced these never-dying grievances' (ch. 21). And Mr Crawley sees himself as a tragic figure – as the blinded Samson, 'sensible of the injury that has been done to him! The impotency, combined with his strength, or rather the impotency with the memory of former strength and former aspirations, is so essentially tragic!' (ch. 62).

Louis Trevelyan also sees himself in a tragic guise, but Trollope allows him to play out his tragic part to the end. Mrs Crawley fears that if her husband is mad, then 'he was incapable of managing the affairs of himself or his family' (*Last Chronicle*, ch. 4); nevertheless, Trollope enables him to be restored to mental health and prosperity and, in consequence, to rejoin the Barsetshire community. Trevelyan, whose obsession with having 'his own way' (*He Knew*, ch. 1) eventually drives him away from the human community and toward madness, is described as being 'absolutely unfitted by nature to have the custody or guardianship of others'. Some of the traits of Trollope's favourite character, Plantagenet Palliser, are presented in Trevelyan in extreme form: 'he was jealous of authority, fearful of slights, self-conscious, afraid of the world, and utterly ignorant of the nature of a woman's mind' (ch. 27). In the end he comes to realise 'that he had brought his misery upon himself by being unlike to other men' (ch. 84). Although Trollope thought he had failed in his intention of creating 'sympathy for the unfortunate man',[12] he did in fact create in Trevelyan the most imposing of his tragic figures, as well as the most harrowing of the psychological studies inspired by a son's brooding on his father's tragic destiny. Like the elder Trollope, he begins with 'all the world before him where to choose' (*He Knew*, ch. 1) and ends a raving lunatic, maddened by intermittent flashes of dreadful self-knowledge.

In *He Knew He Was Right* Trollope inserts one of his very rare portraits of a young child. For a writer so adept at illustrating the endless variety of human relationships, this avoidance of scenes of early childhood is odd. He may, perhaps, have been following Thackeray's lead in this respect: 'Only to two or three persons in all the world', declares the author of *The Newcomes*, 'are the reminiscences of a man's early youth interesting'.[13] But it is also possible that Trollope felt that the events of his own childhood were too painful to be drawn upon or recounted for fictional purposes. When he did deal fully with childhood, it was in the case of his own autobiography, published posthumously. Like Trollope in his adolescent years, the infant Louis Trevelyan is deprived of the company of his mother and forced, for a time, to live alone with his brooding father: 'the former woman-given happinesses of his life were at an end' (ch. 79). The child fears 'his father from the bottom of his little heart, and yet was aware that it was his duty to try to love papa' (ch. 84). The elder Trevelyan, like the elder Trollope, means well. He desires 'to bring [his son] up so that he may be a happier man than his father' (ch. 67); he tries

his best to be soft and gentle to his child. . . . He had spared no
personal trouble, he had done all that he had known how to do,
he had exercised all his intelligence to procure amusement for the
boy; – but Louey had hardly smiled since he had been taken from
his mother. And now that he was told that he was to go and never
see his father again, the tidings were to him simply tidings of joy.
'There is a curse upon me,' said Trevelyan; 'it is written down in
the book of my destiny that nothing shall ever love me!'   (ch. 84)

'He was a man', Thomas Adolphus Trollope similarly notes of his
father, 'who would fain have been loved, and who knew that he was
not loved, but knew neither how to manifest his desire for affection
nor how to conciliate it.'[14] The fate of little Louey is almost as sad as
that of his father: first glimpsed as 'a strong, hearty, happy infant,
always laughing' (ch. 11), he is later seen as a melancholy, reserved
'cowed' child (ch. 86). Among the other portraits of young sons in
Trollope are the child of Alaric Tudor (in *The Three Clerks*), born
during the father's imprisonment in jail, and the young Florian
Jones (of *The Landleaguers*, Trollope's last novel), who is murdered
while trying to assert his loyalty to his father's values and hoping, in
vain, to gain back his father's affection.

The young Anthony, observing his father, grew into a parent
worrying about his two difficult sons, as well as into the prodigious
creator of countless literary progeny. The claims of youth interested
him no less than the claims of parenthood, although he had no
illusions concerning the superior virtues of youth. Writing to Alfred
Austin in 1870, he contended that the noble qualities often
attributed to young people are rarely actually to be found. In fact,
'We hardly expect the young to be other than selfish.'[15] The
youthful male protagonists of his fiction are generally callow, idle,
selfish – until they are redeemed by labour and love, and sometimes
not even then. Among the 'hobbledehoys' in Trollope's work are
Charley Tudor, of *The Three Clerks*, Johnny Eames, of *The Small House
at Allington* and Trollope himself, as he appears in the *Autobiography*.
Eames's father is a brief sketch of Trollope Senior: 'a man of many
misfortunes, having begun the world almost with affluence, and
having ended it in poverty'. (Like the elder Trollope, he 'lost much
money in experimental farming'.) Eames himself means well, but,
having been cut off from decent society, he lives to and by himself,
wandering 'about in solitude, taking long walks, in which he
dreams of those successes which are so far removed from his powers

of achievement' (ch. 4). He models himself after Don Juan in his imagination, but in reality he is prey to the wiles of women. Trollope, in the description of himself at Eames's age, is more censorious. During his lonely years as a London postal clerk, Trollope felt himself cut off from respectable company; he was idle, constantly giving way to temptation, 'entirely without control, – without the influences of any decent household around me'.[16] Reflection on his unhappy youth made him tolerant of the weaknesses of others. Trollope is invariably forgiving when he describes the large company of prodigal sons in his novels, extending from Lord Kilcullen, of *The Kellys and the O'Kellys*, and Bertie Stanhope, of *Barchester Towers*, to Mountjoy Scarborough of *Mr Scarborough's Family*.

This tolerance and understanding are also displayed in his relations with his sons Henry and Frederic. They were born in Ireland, where Trollope had established himself as a responsible official in the postal service, where he had married his wife Rose and where, in the year of Fred's birth, he published his first novel, *The Macdermots of Ballycloran* (1847, written 1843–5). Unlike James Mill or Thomas Anthony Trollope or, for that matter, Charles Dickens, he freely expressed his affection for his boys, worried about their health, was solicitous about their future, was indulgent toward their mishaps. Like many a Trollope protagonist, Harry first considered a career in the law; dissatisfied, he then (with his father's aid of £10,000) became a partner in the publishing house of Chapman and Hall. Finally he turned author himself, writing on Molière and other French authors and subjects. Mrs Oliphant, who commissioned a biography of Racine and Corneille, was unhappy with the results and considered the son a poor copy of the father; but Trollope defended Harry's efforts, always providing encouragement. When Harry became involved with a French actress ('A woman of the town', as Trollope's friend George Henry Lewes called her), the father promptly packed him off to Australia to visit his younger brother, who had left school in his late teens in order to become a sheep farmer.[17] (Perhaps this incident in Harry's life, occurring in 1872, found literary expression in the Paul Montague–Mrs Hurtle relationship in *The Way We Live Now*, which Trollope commenced writing not long afterwards.) In later years Trollope worried about his son's ability to manage; yet he was also overjoyed when Harry was elected to the Athenaeum Club.

Fred's case was even more difficult. Of more headstrong

disposition than his older brother, he managed a sheep station for a while. Trollope, perhaps hoping that his son might prosper in Australia as he had in Ireland, offered every encouragement, but he deeply missed his 'shepherd son'. He made the long voyage to Australia twice in order to see him and was 'miserable' at the second parting, feeling that at his age his days of voyaging were over. Trollope admitted that the energetic sheep farmer hero of his Australian novel, *Harry Heathcote of Gangoil*, was 'very much the same' as Fred.[18] It has been suggested that the book can be read as 'a kind of sermon' to his son celebrating 'courage, industry, and independence', traits that Trollope felt that 'Fred had not quite attained'. Despite his hard work, Fred lost money, which his father made good. 'It is a kind of misfortune which I can bear', Trollope declared in the magnanimous style of his Plantagenet Palliser, who settles *his* sons' various debts. (*The Duke's Children* was begun later in the same year, 1876, in which Trollope came to Fred's financial rescue.) Perhaps his son's difficulties made him think of his father's: he 'seems to me to have more troubles on his back', Trollope declared of Fred, 'than any human being I ever came across'.[19]

Dickens, by contrast, was far less generous toward his sons. A recent biographer has commented on Dickens's habit of reminding his sons of their financial burden to him: he 'harbored the nagging fear that his sons would turn out to be like [Dickens's feckless] father, who constantly needed to be rescued from financial crises'.[20] Another observer has suggested that Dickens did not 'find enough enduring paternal instinct in himself to give life to the father and son theme in his books, except very occasionally'. Children of geniuses have the problem of having to live up to their parents, and the result is all too often failure: Dickens's daughter Kate suggested to George Bernard Shaw that 'Men of genius . . . ought not to be allowed to have children.'[21] Trollope, to be sure, obstinately maintained that he was no genius; but in the portraits of Palliser and his sons, he movingly describes both the Duke's and their sense of having disappointed one another – and yet, in terms of emotional ties, of not having failed at all. Trollope's sons were not notably successful in their careers, but they were spared the severe psychological problems of Dickens's children. Both followed in their father's footsteps: Harry maintained an authorial career, while Fred ended up in the civil service. Both copied their father in a number of other ways – adopting, for example, an exaggerated version of his political conservatism. (In this, too, they attained only a single aspect of his multiple talents and views.) The strength of the emotional bonds can be seen in their letters, including those written after Trollope's death. Fred thought the *Autobiography*, which Trollope had presented as a parting gift to Harry, 'a most charming piece of writing'. And, as Thomas Adolphus Trollope wrote his elder nephew, following his brother's death: 'Yes! my dear Harry no man as you say ever had a better father. . . . And as you also truly say he had a heart capable of loving much.'[22]

It has been said of romantic writers, such as Byron or Dickens, that their custom of living with imaginative creations 'totally unfitted [them] for domestic habits'.[23] Trollope, by contrast, treated his fictive progeny with the same affectionate concern that he treated his sons. During the creative process, he found himself 'crying at [his characters'] grief, laughing at their absurdities, and thoroughly enjoying their joys'. Once having been summoned into being, they retained a lifelong intimacy with their creator: major and minor figures return in book after book, and those who die in his fiction, like Mrs Proudie, haunted his memory as ghosts. The practice of living in a world of the imagination stemmed, as Trollope claims in the *Autobiography*, from the habitual solitude endured during his childhood; but, paradoxically, in that imaginative world a romance of order and domesticity, which the friendless and disorderly youth hungered after, was allowed to flourish.[24] Not until he himself was flourishing in Ireland, however, was Trollope able to transform day-dreams into books. The subject of his first book, *The Macdermots of Ballycloran*, might seem an unlikely Trollope project: a nightmarish chronicle of domestic disorder and personal victimisation of which the Ireland of the hungry 1840s afforded all too many real-life counterparts. Yet Trollope's immersion in Ireland and Irish literature presented him with themes and characters which reappear in the English novels. His 'celebration', for example, of the caring 'resident landlord who knows and cares about his tenants' is repeated in his sympathetic descriptions of English landlords[25] – and also in his depictions of caring fathers.

The most successful of Trollope's sons of Ireland, Phineas Finn, benefits from the paternal pride and encouragement of Dr Finn. But Trollope began and ended his writing career with tragic accounts of a son sacrificed to father and fatherland: *The Macdermots* and *The Landleaguers*.[26] In the first work, Thady Macdermot has from 'a very early age had to bear the weight of the family', finding 'only in his dreams' (ch. 6) the possibility of an orderly existence. The impoverished Macdermots are heavily stylised versions of Trollope and his father, living in continual 'debt to his landlord and to the tradesmen he employed'. 'Our table', Trollope recalls, 'was poorer . . . than that of the bailiff who still hung on to our shattered fortunes.'[27] Thady is the first and most extreme example of a well-intending Trollope hero thwarted by circumstances, but there is no sweetheart or benefactor to come to his aid, as there is for Charley Tudor or Johnny Eames. And, unlike Trollope's hobbledehoys, Thady is both industrious and unceasing in his pursuit of the goodwill of his elders. 'Few men in any rank of life had known so little joy as he had done, or had so little pleasure; his only object in life had been to drive the wolf from his father's door and to keep a roof over him and his sister' (ch. 31). The novelist's first protagonist lives out the adolescent Trollope's worst fantasies of being abandoned and helpless, living with a deranged father who hates him. There are few moments in his fiction so terrible as that in which Larry Macdermot casts off his son, cursing him and hoping the police 'might catch him and hang him' (ch. 21).

If Trollope's first work of fiction focuses on a devouring father and a sacrificial son, his second introduces a character, modelled after the Prodigal Son, who talks back to his father. In *The Kellys and the O'Kellys* (1847), Lord Kilcullen is a worthless, idle gambler whom his father, Lord Cashel, wishes to reform by inducing him to marry an heiress. It is the first version of a stock Trollope situation. 'So wild, so mad, so ruinous', as his father calls him (ch. 30), Lord Kilcullen nevertheless manages to elicit Trollope's sympathy. The comic scene in which he drily agrees to act the 'considerate and . . . dutiful son' (ch. 13) by marrying Fanny Wyndham prefigures the better-known scenes in *Barchester Towers* (1857), in which Bertie Stanhope agrees to do as his family decrees. These unregenerate prodigals lack a heart and principles, yet they possess a sense of humour and a code of honour which prevents their acting in a mean manner. The scene in which Kilcullen parts from his disappointed father and sister, in order to live in permanent exile from Ireland, is oddly moving. Bertie's farewell scene with his exasperated father, Dr Stanhope, is, by contrast, a moment of high comedy, an impudent parody of the paternal-curse scene of melodrama. Bertie doodles sketches of the denizens of Barsetshire while his father tries to cast him off:

> 'Would it suit you, sir,' said the father, 'to give me some idea as to what your present intentions are? What way of living you propose to yourself?'
>
> 'I'll do anything you can suggest, sir,' replied Bertie.
>
> 'No, I shall suggest nothing further. My time for suggesting has gone by. I have only one order to give, and that is that you leave my house.'
>
> 'To-night?' said Bertie, and the simple tone of the question left the doctor without any adequately dignified method of reply.
>
> 'Papa does not quite mean to-night,' said Charlotte; 'at least I suppose not.'
>
> 'To-morrow, perhaps,' suggested Bertie.
>
> 'Yes, sir, to-morrow,' said the doctor. 'You shall leave this to-morrow.'
>
> 'Very well, sir. Will the 4.30 p.m. train be soon enough?' said Bertie, as he asked, putting the finishing touch to Miss Thorne's high-heeled boots.
>
> 'You may go how and when and where you please, so that you leave my house to-morrow. You have disgraced me, sir; you have disgraced yourself, and me, and your sisters.'
>
> 'I am glad at least, sir, that I have not disgraced my mother,' said Bertie. (ch. 45).

Trollope's habit of finding innumerable variations on, and sometimes reversals of, a theme is reflected in his various accounts of prodigal sons and prodigal fathers in his fiction. The biblical story of the son who leaves his father and wastes 'his substance with riotous living' has a considerable personal attraction for him. Some prodigals, like Lord Silverbridge and John Caldigate, leave off their riotous ways and return, reformed, to their fathers house, while others, like Mountjoy Scarborough, are incapable of reformation – are indeed liable, as in Mountjoy's case, of selling off the father's house to pay gambling debts. *John Caldigate* (1877), which Trollope began three months after completing *The Duke's Children*, is directly based on the parable, although the novelist may also be thinking of his own childhood when he depicts Daniel and John Caldigate, living (as the novel opens) in hostile proximity, the younger believing himself to be unloved and the older accepting as 'natural' that his scapegrace son must desire his death. Like the biblical Prodigal, John asks his father for his inheritance in advance so that he can pay his debts and journey to a 'far country' – in his case, the gold-mines of Australia. But, as in *The Duke's Children*, Trollope's theme is reconciliation between the generations: the emotional climax of the book occurs when father and son realise and express their affection for one another. However, in a tale written a decade earlier, 'The Misfortunes of Frederic Pickering' (1866), Trollope inverts the ending of the parable. His protagonist defies his father's wishes in order to become an author. Unlike the elder Caldigate or the Duke, the elder Pickering has no affectionate heart concealed beneath a stern exterior: he is 'not given at any time to softness with his children'. When the chastened and impoverished son returns home, with a sickly wife and child, there is 'no fatted calf' awaiting him; the unforgiving father refuses even to see him.[28]

Although such unyielding fathers as the elder Pickering are rare in Trollope, there are a number of devouring parents who follow in the wake of Larry Macdermot. George Bertram, hero of *The Bertrams* (1859), seeks out his long-unseen father; but Sir Lionel Bertram when found turns out to be a prodigal father who chooses to sponge off his son. The motif of the prodigal father ignoring, preying upon or casting off his son, returns in *The Belton Estate* (1865), with that book's opening description of the 'idle, thriftless' Bernard Amedroz, whose son commits suicide as a result of a 'state of things . . . brought about . . . chiefly due to the father's neglect' (ch. 1); in *The Vicar of Bulhampton* (1868), with Colonel Marrable, one of those men who 'indulge every passion, though the cost to others might be ruin for life' (ch. 33), and who robs his son of his inheritance; and in *Avala's Angel* (1878), in the figure of Isadore Hamel's reprobate father who rejects his son for daring to hanker after a conventional and moral way of life. Trollopean fathers often threaten to curse their progeny for following their own wishes, but none copies Larry Macdermot's example. When Sir Marmaduke Rowley vows to 'cast . . . off [his daughter] if she be disobedient' (*He Knew*, ch. 85), his wife responds. 'On the stage they do such things as that . . . and, perhaps, they used to do it once in reality. But you know that it's out of the question now. Fancy your standing up and cursing at the dear girl, just as we are all starting from Southampton!' (ch. 90).

Daniel Caldigate's assumption that his son's desire for his death would be 'no more than natural' is underlined in the various Trollope novels in which the hankering after dead men's shoes is treated. It is ever the way of Vanity Fair, Thackeray observes, that whoever has a patrimony to bestow will find himself wished out of the way by the beneficiary. 'If you were heir to a dukedom and a thousand pounds a day, do you mean to say you would not wish for possession? Pooh! And it stands to reason that every great man having entertained this feeling towards his father, must be aware that his son entertains it towards himself; and so they can't but be suspicious and hostile.'[29] The Honorable John de Courcey, in *Doctor Thorne* (1858), provides this 'lesson' to young Frank Gresham, who is, however, horrified to hear of the premature death of one's father regarded as 'a stroke of luck'.

> What! was he thus to think of his father, whose face was always lighted up with pleasure when his boy came near him, and so rarely bright at any other time? . . . He loved his father truly, purely, and thoroughly, liked to be with him, and would be proud to be his confidant. Could he then listen quietly while his cousin spoke of the chance of his father's death as a stroke of luck?

When reproached by Frank, the Honorable John pardons his cousin for being so green, but notes that if his own 'governor were to walk, I think Porlock [the elder son] would console himself with the thirty thousand a year' (ch. 4).

Trollope, 'surprised' by the enormous popularity of *Doctor Thorne*, guessed that the book had succeeded because of its unusually good plot (supplied him, incidentally, by his brother). But the plot arouses, to an unusually transparent degree in Trollope, the wishes of both the reader and the sympathetic protagonist, Doctor Thorne, that Sir Roger and Sir Louis Scatcherd, dissolute father and son, die as quickly as possible so that the heroine can come into the inheritance which is conveniently unknown to her and her fiancé, Frank. It is with the greatest of difficulty that the good doctor keeps himself from desiring the 'incubus' Scatcherd son's death, 'the earlier it might be . . . the better' (ch. 37). In the late novel, *The Fixed Period* (1881), Trollope draws upon the plot of the Massinger, Middleton and Rowley play *The Old Law* in which a decree is passed dooming to death all men who reach the age of eighty. The law, however, is not meant to be enacted: 'It is simply a device that brings pity and greed into the open.'[30] So too, in Trollope's novel set in the future, Neverbend, President of the former English colony of Britannula, has passed, thanks to 'the covetousness and hurry of the younger men' (ch. 8), a bill enforcing euthanasia for its older citizens. The bill is never carried out, for President Neverbend finds himself opposed by his own son, Jack, who wants to save the life of his fiancé's father. There is some strained humour in the combat between father and son: the young man opposes the elder by defending the elderly, while the progressive Neverbend laments a modern father's liability to inflict death or disinheritance as a punishment for 'filial disobedience' (ch. 7).[31]

The testing of a son's character, using the motif of the waiting on dead men's shoes, is most fully treated in *Mr Scarborough's Family*. But the most astonishing use of the theme appears at the beginning of *Barchester Towers*. We are introduced to Archdeacon Grantly waiting beside his dying father and aware that his chance to succeed him as Bishop of Barchester depends on the old man's immediate decease. The old man's calm is contrasted to the worldly son's anxiety:

> He knew it must be now or never. He was already over fifty, and there was little chance that his friends who were now leaving office would soon return to it. No probable British prime minister but he who was now in, he who was so soon to be out, would think of making a bishop of Dr Grantly. Thus he thought long and sadly, in deep silence, and then gazed at that still living face, and then at last dared to ask himself whether he really longed for his father's death.

It is an extraordinary moment in Trollope: his characters are so prone to self-dramatisation (sometimes, as in Trevelyan's or Mr Crawley's case, to tragic or near-tragic effect) that the moment of self-confrontation can be shattering rather than exhilarating. In the Archdeacon's case, the result is 'salutary': 'The proud, wishful, worldly man sank on his knees by the bedside and, taking the bishop's hand within his own, prayed eagerly that his sins might be forgiven him' (ch. 1).

In his awareness of his worldly weakness, and his attempt (like Doctor Thorne's) to overcome it, Dr Grantly demonstrates a moral consciousness denied to the Proudies, Stanhopes and Slopes. But if his desire to 'play first fiddle', as Trollope puts it, is a human weakness, it will interfere with the Archdeacon's ability to be a loving father no less than it interfered with his filial sentiments. In *The Last Chronicle of Barset* (1866), we find him, while prepared in

time to accede to his son Major Grantly's desire to marry Grace
Crawley, nevertheless wishing 'that his son should recognize his
father's power to inflict punishment' (ch. 56). Dr Grantly relishes
the paternal *role*, that of outraged father in the melodrama
threatening to disinherit his son; but the Major is attached to his
role too, and he histrionically looks forward to renouncing his
patrimony. 'There is, perhaps, nothing so pleasant', Trollope says
of the son's grievance, 'as the preparation for self-sacrifice' (ch. 58).
Yet neither the Oedipus nor the Abraham–Isaac story tells the whole
truth about father–son relations. Like Plantagenet Palliser with Lord
Silverbridge, Dr Grantly is obliged to let his better instincts subdue
his weaker ones. It is impossible, as he realises, for him to sustain his
paternal anger for very long. Although initially resolved not to
forgive his headstrong son, he remembers 'that the evening would
come, and that he would say his prayers; and he shook his head in
regret, – in a regret of which he was only half-conscious, though it
was very keen, and which he did not attempt to analyse, – as he
reflected that his rage would hardly be able to survive that ordeal'
(ch. 33).

Despite his wish to exert paternal power, Dr Grantly belongs to
the company of Trollope's loving rather than devouring fathers:
with Squire Gresham in *Doctor Thorne*, who regrets the injury he has
done his son by mortgaging the family property; with Squire
Newton in *Ralph the Heir* (1869), who regrets the injury he has done
his son by not providing for his legitimacy; and, above all, with
Palliser, who regrets that he has 'failed to indoctrinate his children
with the ideas by which his own mind was fortified and controlled'
(*The Duke's Children*, ch. 65), but who submits to all their individual
choices. It may seem odd to place Mr Scarborough, of *Mr
Scarborough's Family* (1881), in this company of affectionate fathers;
but, according to Trollope, 'in every phase of his life [Scarborough]
had been actuated by love for others. He had never been selfish,
thinking always of others rather than of himself' (ch. 58). At the very
beginning of the novel, he is described as having been 'affectionate
to his children, and anxious above all things for their welfare, or
rather happiness' (ch. 1). Yet the relationship between the dying
Scarborough and his sons Mountjoy and Augustus is quite the
reverse of that between Palliser, Dr Grantly, Squire Newton and
Squire Gresham and their sons. Even the most loving of
relationships, Trollope observes in *The Last Chronicle of Barset*, lead to
bitter oppositions: 'It would be wrong to say that love produces

quarrels,' he notes, 'but love does produce those intimate relations of which quarrelling is too often one of the consequences' (ch. 49). In *Mr Scarborough's Family* the most negative aspects of the father–son relationship predominate, and paternal affection turns into unforgiving hatred.

Near the end of his writing career, Trollope summoned up many of his favourite father–son motifs and played a last, dazzling set of variations on those themes: an affectionate albeit a devouring father is matched by his two sons, one a prodigal given to bad company and riotous ways, the other so selfish that he openly wishes his father dead so that he can step into his shoes. Even the comic sub-plot of the book deals with the antagonism between the generations: between an uncle determined to exert power and his headstrong nephew expecting the other's wealth as his due. (Once again, Trollope invokes the situation of his father, disowned by the uncle whose inheritance he had counted on.) If the nephew proves victorious – in the manner of one of the seventeenth-century English plays which Trollope drew upon from time to time – the main plot provides a more ambiguous resolution. For the struggle between Scarborough and his younger son Augustus produces a mutual animosity which exceeds anything articulated or hinted at in Trollope's earlier novels. They become 'absolute enemies' (ch. 21), each determined to destroy the other.

Augustus tells his father to his face 'that the world would be no world for him till his father had left it' (ch. 38), and in revenge Scarborough husbands his last ounces of physical strength and cunning for the purpose of ruining his younger son. 'Who could have expected that a man in such a condition should have lived so long, and have been capable of a will so powerful?' Augustus marvels. 'He had not dreamt of a hatred so inveterate as his father's for him.' The 'gleam of victory, and the glory of triumph, and the venom of malice' with which the dying man confronts Augustus in the end (ch. 56) brings us back to the scene of Larry Macdermot cursing his son Thady – yet Scarborough is both clear-headed and justified in his malice. One can scarcely sympathise with the disinherited Augustus, who is not only cruel-minded but too stupid (as Scarborough points out) to have concealed his cruelty. It may be 'natural' for sons to want their father's goods, but civilisation depends on the masking of those sentiments. And while the older son, Mountjoy, is afforded some measure of sympathy, there is no hope for his future reformation: Scarborough realises that by having spoiled his favourite son, he only encouraged that weakness of character which has turned him into a self-destructive gambler. Despite all his scheming to leave his property intact for his sons, despite the affection and solicitude lavished upon them, the sons prove to be (in Scarborough's lawyer's words) 'gambler and beast', respectively (ch. 39); and the novel ends with the prospect of the vanishing of the property to pay off gambling debts. Looking over his father's valuable library, Mountjoy muses that 'three or four days [of card-playing] at the club might see an end of it all' (ch. 53).

Scarborough's ultimate, Lear-like recognition of the nature of his offspring is also a dreadful admission of his own failure: 'I have tried them both, as few sons can be tried by their father, and I know them now' (ch. 56). For each son is a dim reflection of aspects of his own nature: 'Augustus was very like his father in his capacity for organising deceit, for plotting, and so contriving that his own will should be in opposition to the wills of all those around him' (ch. 21); while the headstrong Mountjoy's gambling (as Robert Tracy suggests) 'is a minor version of Mr Scarborough's continual gamble with his own ability to survive and scheme'. Tracy's view is certainly correct: Scarborough's 'sons are his pawns, and they are also his victims'.[32] But if the sons take after the father, the father takes after Trollope's father, in terms of his solicitousness and thwarted affection, and he takes after Trollope too: in his determination to exert control over his life, even in his failing moments, he replicates the ageing novelist's determination 'to assert his own artistic power' in the face of all the conventionalities and adversities of life.[33] And perhaps, too, there is a poignant realisation on Trollope's part that despite all his love for his sons and concern for their careers (dim reflections of his own), he might somehow have failed them and they him.

Yet Trollope is no Mr Scarborough; and if in *Mr Scarborough's Family* he considers the worst possibilities of the father–son relationship, in *The Duke's Children* (1876) he surveys the more genial possibilities. Trollope may identify, to a certain extent, with Mr Scarborough as an artist, an ingenious plotter, but he is emotionally closer to Plantagenet Palliser, the Duke of Omnium, than to any of his other characters. This marvellous novel is constructed as a double *Bildungsroman* in which the Duke's older son, Lord Silverbridge, gives up his prodigal son ways, while the initially obstinate and distant father learns to yield to the wishes of the younger generation and, in the process, becomes more human.

Early in the book it is said of Palliser that he 'does not much care about young people' (ch. 4), and indeed, the Duke initially reveals the morbid sensitivity and seeming inflexibility of one of Trollope's tragic figures. He realises, to his pain, 'that he was not as are other men' (ch. 1). 'He was a man so reticent and undemonstrative in his manner that he had never known how to make confidential friends of his children' (ch. 5). He has never felt proud of his sons, and with good reason, and now, with the death of his wife, Lady Glencora, 'in the solitude of his life, as years were coming on him, he felt how necessary it was that he should have someone who would love him' (ch. 66).

The Duke's Children was written immediately after the *Autobiography*, and in these plaintive descriptions of Palliser, Trollope echoes the account of his father, solitary and craving affection.[34] Yet in the depiction of the growing bonds of friendship between Palliser and Silverbridge, Trollope conveys something of his deep affection for Harry and Fred. As, one by one, his children defy or disgrace him, Palliser claims that they 'will bring [him] to the grave' (ch. 18). The older son switches political allegiance, choosing instead to follow, for a time, the orders of a fictionalised version of Disraeli, whom Trollope detested. He also plans to marry an American girl rather than the aristocratic lady approved by the Duke. Palliser's daughter falls in love with a commoner, and the younger son is plucked from Oxford and momentarily becomes a gambler. The children, for their part, respect their father, but feel they can never live up to him. Silverbridge 'had it at heart "to be good to the governor", to gratify that most loving of all possible friends, who, as he knew well, was always thinking of his welfare. And yet he never had been "good to the governor"; – nor had Gerald.' Nevertheless, as Silverbridge reflects, 'there were certain changes going on in the management of the world which his father did not quite understand. Fathers never do quite understand the changes which are manifest to their sons' (ch. 61). Gerald, for his part, does not sin on the grand level of his brother; yet he is also headstrong enough to withstand his father's advice. In one of the book's memorable comic moments, Palliser chides the young scapegrace for gambling: ' "Facilis descensus Averni!" said the Duke, shaking his head. "Noctes atque dies patet atri janua Ditis." No doubt, he thought, that as his son was at Oxford, admonitions in Latin would serve him better than in his native tongue. But Gerald, when he heard the grand hexameter rolled out in his father's grandest tone, entertained a comfortable feeling that the worst of the interview was over' (ch. 65).

If, in the last of the Palliser novels, the Duke learns to accommodate himself to his children and to a world less noble and generous-minded than himself, he also gains from the sacrifice. There is real anguish for Palliser in his discovery that his 'opinion is to go for nothing, – in anything!' (ch. 71). This echoes Dr Grantly's lament to his wife in *The Last Chronicle of Barset*, 'I am to yield in everything. I am to be nobody' (ch. 58). But Trollope and the Duke realise that there is often a greater reward in yielding to the young than in holding firm. In yielding, he proves his affection, and he demonstrates the strength of his Liberal views in which the interests of others take precedence over one's 'own individual interests' (ch. 7). 'There is so much which I should only be too ready to give up to you!' the Duke tells Silverbridge in the wonderful scene between them at the son's club, the Beargarden. Like young Frank Gresham, Silverbridge protests that he won't hear of his father's 'giving up anything', a statement which clearly moves Palliser in the light of his next act. 'Then the father looked round the room furtively, and seeing that the door was shut, and that they were assuredly alone, he put out his hand and gently stroked the young man's hair. It was almost a caress, – as though he would have said to himself, "Were he my daughter, I would kiss him" ' (ch. 26). In his last line in the novel the Duke learns to 'accept' – not just his new son-in-law and daughter-in-law, but also the new generation he has decisively embraced.[35]

In *The Duke's Children* Trollope accepts the fact that 'perfect love' between child and parent is rarely attainable, and that it is probably just as well that an element of 'fear' is mingled with the affection (ch. 61). Filial regard for the father-figure has been a basic part of Western and Eastern societies until fairly recently – until, one might postulate without too much exaggeration, the Romantic repudiation of the father and the concomitant rejection of a sense of parental responsibility toward the child. Rousseau's self-confessed depositing of his children at the foundling hospital, on the one hand, and Shelley's and Stendhal's lifelong campaigns against the paternal tyrant, on the other – these acts exemplify that strain of Romantic rebelliousness which seeks to liberate the individual from obligations to past and future alike. This extreme version of Romanticism places its emphasis on the detached self and the present moment. For a child of the Romantics, such as Arnold, 'We mortal millions live *alone*' rather than in relationships. And a recent critic has characterised the nineteenth-century novel in a manner which combines Romantic and modernist biases: 'In the realistic universe people have to recognize that their identity depends upon themselves and their actions, rather than on family, class, or some such "mark" of identity that has nothing to do with their wills or self-consciousness.' In a world of perpetual movement, 'the natural family often is a center of stillness and a source of paralysis for its offspring'.[36] This applies to Joyce more than to Trollope: in Stephen Dedalus's description, the artist is one who, like Shakespeare, fathers himself. Having defied religious and physical fathers, not to mention fatherland and God-the-father, Stephen dismisses paternity as 'a legal fiction. Who is the father of any son that any son should love him or he any son?' And in Samuel Butler's case, the son can only regard his parents, especially his father, as his 'most dangerous enemies'. (Like Rousseau, Ernest Pontifex disposes of his illegitimate progeny.) Why, asks Dimitri Karamazov of his father, 'Why is such a man alive?'[37]

Trollope's handling of the father–son relationship is, by contrast, exceptional in its mixture of candour and fairness to both sides. Occasionally his reflections on the hostility and rivalry between the generations strike a 'modern' note. However, in novels such as *The Duke's Children*, he reaffirms attitudes which Mikhail Bakhtin locates in the eighteenth-century 'family novel': works in which sons seek to re-establish a domestic idyll after having passed through a phase of homelessness. Bakhtin looks back fondly to a Renaissance humanist such as Rabelais who 'connects the growth of generations with the growth of culture, and with the growth of the historical development of mankind as well. The son will continue the father, the grandson the son – and on a higher level of cultural development.'[38] Reconciliation between father and son is a 'Classic' (as opposed to Romantic) theme, one more likely to be articulated by a Montaigne than a Rousseau, a Tolstoy than a Stendhal. In Montaigne's essay, 'Of the Affection of Fathers for their Children', the bond of mutual love and responsibility is seen as deriving from nature. Montaigne's moving account of the Marshal de Monluc, regretful following the death of his son at never having demonstrated 'the extreme affection that he bore him',[39] might be set alongside Trollope's description of Palliser's discovery of the need to reveal his own love for, and need to be loved by, his children. However, it is with the Russian novelists, above all, that Trollope stands in his capacious treatment of the theme: with Dostoevsky, who chronicles the neglectfulness of the fathers and the revenge of the sons (*The Possessed, The Brothers Karamazov*), but who also sees the need for mutual acceptance (*A Raw Youth*); with Tolstoy, whose masterpiece is built on a series of father–son relationships (Count Bezuhov and his son Pierre, Prince Bolkonsky and his son Andrei, Count Rostov and his son Nikolai, General Kutuzov and his army); with Turgenev, whose *Fathers and Sons* ends with the belief in 'everlasting reconciliation'.[40] Such a theme lay beyond Dickens's powers, or was anathema in the case of Joyce and Butler. Yet for Trollope the acceptance of the past, embodied in the son's love for the father, and the acceptance of the future, as seen in the father's yielding to the son, were vital and necessarily inter-related themes. As 'an advanced, but still a conservative Liberal', as he fairly called himself,[41] Trollope embraced the cause of the fathers and of the sons in deeply personal as well as memorable fictional terms.

Notes

1. Samuel Butler, *The Way of All Flesh*, ch. 79. Butler worked on the novel between 1873 and 1885, the same period in which Trollope wrote *The Duke's Children* and *Mr Scarborough's Family*.
2. *Ralph the Heir*, ch. 34; *The Small House at Allington*, ch. 17. Further references to Trollope's novels are in the text. The dates given for the novels (noted only when deemed important) refer to the year they were completed rather than published.
3. Trollope was also adept at depicting relations between husbands and wives (e.g., the Palliser novels, *The Claverings, He Knew He Was Right*), mothers and sons (*Orley Farm, The Way We Live Now*), mothers and daughters (*The Small House at Allington, Rachel Ray, Lady Anna*), fathers and daughters (*The Warden, The Vicar of Bulhampton, Sir Harry Hotspur of Humblethwaite*), and so on.
4. The finest study of the importance of interpersonal relations in Trollope (and other Victorian novelists) is J. Hillis Miller's *The Form of Victorian Fiction* (Notre Dame, Ind.: University of Notre Dame Press, 1968) esp. pp. 93–140.
5. Frances Trollope, with part of the family, was away from England from November 1827 until August 1831. Trollope's father and older brother Tom joined her, for a time, in 1828; for at least eight months

Anthony was completely separated from parents and siblings. In her biography of Frances Trollope, Helen Heineman describes the details of the American trip (pp. 37–58) and argues elsewhere (e.g., pp. 196–8, 255–7) that Mrs Trollope was a loving parent (her letters to and about Anthony support this claim): *Mrs Trollope: The Triumphant Feminine in the Nineteenth Century* (Athens, Ohio: Ohio University Press, 1979).

6. The following passage from John Stuart Mill's *Autobiography* might have come from Anthony or Thomas Adolphus Trollope's descriptions of their father: 'He resembled most Englishmen in being ashamed of the signs of feeling, and, by the absence of demonstration, starving the feelings themselves. If we consider further that he was in the trying position of sole teacher, and add to this that his temper was constitutionally irritable, it is impossible not to feel true pity for a father who did, and strove to do, so much for his children, who would have so valued their affection, yet who must have been constantly feeling that fear of him was drying it up at its source.' Like Anthony, Mill considered himself 'rather backward in [his] studies', and neither of their fathers saw the need for 'amusement' for his son. Mill, *Autobiography and Other Writings*, ed. Jack Stillinger (Boston, Mass.: Houghton Mifflin, 1969) pp. 32, 21, 22–3; Trollope, *An Autobiography*, ed. Michael Sadleir and Frederick Page, with Introduction and notes by P. D. Edwards (Oxford: Oxford University Press, 1980) e.g., pp. 14–15.

7. Trollope, *Letters*, ed. N. John Hall, 2 vols (Stanford, Calif.: Stanford University Press, 1983) II, 557. The first volume of John Forster's *Life of Dickens* appeared in late 1871. James R. Kincaid has discerned a 'Dickensian parallel' in the structure of Trollope's *Autobiography* ['Trollope's Fictional Autobiography', *Nineteenth-Century Fiction*, 37 (Dec. 1982) pp. 340–9]. When writing about his father, Trollope might well have considered how other Victorians, e.g. Mill and Dickens, had described their patresfamilias.

8. Thomas Adolphus Trollope, *What I Remember*, ed. Herbert van Thal (London: William Kimber, 1973) pp. 26–7, 98–9, 77. Michael Sadleir's largely negative view of the elder Trollope tallies with Thomas Adolphus's description [*Trollope: A Commentary* (London: Oxford University Press, 1961 repr.) pp. 51–5, 81, 96–7].

9. Trollope, *Autobiography*, pp. 31–2, 34.

10. Ibid., p. 43.

11. Ibid., p. 2. James Pope Hennessy links Trollope senior with Mr Crawley: *Anthony Trollope* (Boston, Mass.: Little, Brown, 1971) p. 274.

12. *Autobiography*, p. 321. Henry James praised the tragic quality of *He Knew He Was Right* in his 1883 tribute to Trollope [reprinted in *Partial Portraits* (Ann Arbor: University of Michigan, 1970 repr.) pp. 129–30].

13. *The Newcomes*, ch. 4. In this respect, Thackeray is following eighteenth-century tradition (as did Jane Austen, in her avoidance of portraits of children).

14. *What I Remember*, p. 99.

15. *Letters*, I, 516.
16. *Autobiography*, pp. 51–2.
17. See Vineta and Robert A. Colby, *The Equivocal Virtue: Mrs Oliphant and the Victorian Literary Market Place* (Hamden, Conn.: Archon Books, 1966) pp. 159–61; Trollope, *Letters*, II, 856–7, 575. P. D. Edwards relates Fred's life in *Anthony Trollope's Son in Australia: Life and Letters* (St Lucia, Qld: University of Queensland Press, 1982).
18. *Autobiography*, p. 341; *Letters*, II, 659, 693. Trollope, interestingly, named the sheep farmer of his novel after his older son (who became an author), while he named his would-be author, Frederic Pickering, after the sheep farmer son.
19. Robert Tracy, *Trollope's Later Novels* (Berkeley, Cal.: University of California Press, 1978) p. 150; *Letters*, II, 679, 659.
20. Arthur A. Adrian, *Dickens and the Parent–Child Relationship* (Athens, Ohio: Ohio University Press, 1984) p. 65. See Dianne Sadoff's *Monsters of Affection: Dickens, Eliot, and Brontë* (Baltimore: The Johns Hopkins Press, 1982) for an intriguing Freudian perspective on the revenge taken by Dickens against his father in his novels.
21. Eleanor Rooke, 'Fathers and Sons in Dickens', *Essays and Studies*, ed. Geoffrey Tillotson (London: John Murray, 1951) pp. 56, 69 ('The subject did not stir his imagination'); Adrian, p. 63. As Mill notes, 'the children of energetic parents, frequently grow up unenergetic, because they lean on their parents, and the parents are energetic for them' (*Autobiography and Other Writings*, p. 23).
22. Edwards, p. 40; *Letters*, II, Appendix D, p. 1039.
23. Lady Blessington, *Conversations of Lord Byron*, ed. Ernest J. Lovell, Jr (Princeton, N.J.: Princeton University Press, 1969) p. 49.
24. *Autobiography*, pp. 176, 276. See Andrew Wright, *Anthony Trollope: Dream and Art* (Chicago: University of Chicago Press, 1983) esp. pp. 1–12.
25. Robert Tracy, ' "The Unnatural Ruin": Trollope and Nineteenth-Century Irish Fiction', *Nineteenth-Century Fiction*, 37, p. 374.
26. In *The Landleaguers*, which was unfinished at Trollope's death in 1882, Trollope's sympathies have shifted from the son to the father; but Florian's insubordination is perhaps intended to parallel Irish insubordination (in Trollope's eyes) to England.
27. *Autobiography*, p. 13. Lucy P. and Richard P. Stebbins find a 'resemblance' between the Macdermots and the Trollopes [*The Trollopes: The Chronicle of a Writing Family* (New York: Columbia University Press, 1945) p. 117], and N. John Hall, more cautiously, detects 'some truth to the speculation', although he adds that 'the degree of correspondence is beyond demonstration' [see N. John Hall, Introduction to *The Macdermots of Ballycloran* (New York: Arno Press, 1981) n.p.].
28. Trollope, *Complete Short Stories*, ed. B. J. S. Breyer, 5 vols, (Fort Worth: Texas Christian University Press, 1979–83) II, 194, 212.
29. *Vanity Fair*, ch. 47. In his chapter entitled 'Father and Son', A. O. J. Cockshut concentrates on the negative father–son relationships in Trollope, those involving the transmission of property: *Anthony*

Trollope: A Critical Study (New York: New York University Press, 1968 edition) pp. 52–66.

30. Tracy, *Trollope's Later Novels*, p. 286.

31. 'Jack,' Neverbend protests, 'who did not, as far as I could see, care a straw for humanity in the matter, had vehemently taken the side of the Anti-fixed-Periodists as the safest way to get the father's consent' (ch. 4).

32. Tracy, *Trollope's Later Novels*, pp. 300, 299.

33. See Donald D. Stone, 'Trollope, Byron, and the Conventionalities', in *The Romantic Impulse in Victorian Fiction* (Cambridge, Mass.: Harvard University Press, 1980) esp. pp. 72–3.

34. The Stebbinses see in Palliser Trollope's romantic refashioning of his father's unhappy fate (*The Trollopes*, pp. 221, 287).

35. See Robert M. Polhemus, *The Changing World of Anthony Trollope* (Berkeley, Calif.: University of California Press, 1968) p. 231; George Butte, 'Ambivalence and Affirmation in *The Duke's Children*', *Studies in English Literature*, 17 (1977) 709–27; Lowry Pei, '*The Duke's Children*: Reflection and Reconciliation', *Modern Language Quarterly*, 39 (1978) 284–302. Two critics who take a darker view of the book's end are John Halperin, in *Trollope and Politics: A Study of the Pallisers and Others* (New York: Barnes and Noble, 1977) e.g. p. 268 ('If the future of England is to depend in any measure upon the labors of Palliser's two sons, then *The Duke's Children* paints a rather bleak picture of that future'); and James R. Kincaid, in *The Novels of Anthony Trollope* (Oxford: Oxford University Press, 1977) e.g. p. 233.

36. Elizabeth D. Ermarth, *Realism and Consensus in the English Novel* (Princeton, N.J.: Princeton University Press, 1983) pp. 55–6.

37. Joyce, *Ulysses* (New York: Vintage Books, 1961) p. 207; Butler, *The Way of All Flesh*, ch. 69. See Jerome Hamilton Buckley's fine chapter on Butler in *Season of Youth: The Bildungsroman from Dickens to Golding* (Cambridge, Mass.: Harvard University Press, 1974) pp. 116–39. [Joyce's account of the artist being his own father echoes, incidentally, Meredith's comment in *The Egoist* (ch. 39): 'the Egoist is the son of Himself. He is likewise the Father.']. Dostoevsky, *The Brothers Karamazov*, ed. Ralph E. Matlaw, trs. Constance Garnett (New York: W. W. Norton, 1976) p. 65. Two dogma-ridden studies of father–son relationships in nineteenth-century English literature are Bruce Mazlish's *James and John Stuart Mill: Father and Son in the Nineteenth Century* (New York: Basic Books, 1975), and, even worse, Howard R. Wolf's 'British Fathers and Sons, 1773–1913: from Filial Submissiveness to Creativity', *The Psychoanalytic Review*, 52 (Summer 1965) 197–214. For Wolf, the father represents (as he does for Butler) the greatest danger to the son's creative and psychological health. A more balanced view of the topic is Wendell Stacy Johnson's *Sons and Fathers: The Generation Link in Literature, 1780–1980* (New York: Peter Lang, 1985).

38. Bakhtin, 'Forms of Time and Chronotope in the Novel', *The Dialogic Imagination*, ed. Michael Holquist, trs. Holquist and Caryl Emerson (Austin, Tex.: University of Texas Press, 1981) pp. 231–2; 204. From

Romanticism on, Bakhtin argues, events are seen as 'unrepeatable', not part of an interconnected human cycle (p. 199).

39. Michel de Montaigne, *Complete Essays*, ed. and trs. Donald M. Frame, 3 vols (Garden City, N.Y.: Doubleday Anchor Books, 1960) II, 69.
40. Ivan Turgenev, *Fathers and Sons*, trs. George Reavy (New York: New American Library, n.d.) p. 207. Chekhov drew upon the theme of 'Fatherlessness' for a play written in his teens.
41. *Autobiography*, p. 291.

4

Ruskin, Arnold and Browning's Grammarian: 'Crowded with Culture'

DAVID J. DeLAURA

> *I've put in so many enigmas and puzzles that it will keep the professors busy for centuries arguing over what I meant, and that's the only way of insuring one's immortality.*[1]

One alert early reader, speaking of Browning's faculty of 'sympathising with artist-natures of singular aims and secluded merit', pointed to 'A Grammarian's Funeral' as a poem 'which, in spite of extreme oddity of thought and imagination, is a noble elegy of one of the indefatigable seekers after learning such as lived shortly after the revival of learning'.[2] Most readers, then and since, have accepted the poem as an 'elegy' of some almost indefinable variety;[3] but that troubling element of oddity – indeed, of the 'grotesque', as W. C. DeVane calls it – has given almost all recent readers pause, and has caused a handful to find the poem a satire, a caricature or an exposé.

Richard Altick, in an influential if perhaps 'humorous' argument, finds self-delusion on the disciples' part, but no divergence of sentiment between the grammarian and the students. Altick is careful to say that Browning 'probably was of two minds' regarding the grammarian's 'alleged virtues', and he adds that 'Browning's condemnation . . . is tempered by sympathy'; but the bulk of the article is designed to show that the grammarian's 'progressive detachment from life' is a rejection of the premises of Renaissance humanism and of Browning's view that 'life is to be used for living'.[4]

Martin Svaglic's widely-accepted response attempts a balanced view: 'Browning did mean the grammarian to be viewed with respect, even if he was not in every way a man after [Browning's own] heart.'[5]

But while some have profited from Svaglic's sense of complexity of effect,[6] the bulk of later readings seek to pile up evidence that Browning meant to praise the grammarian, and tend to be deaf to precisely those problematic and 'unresolved' elements in the poem that have led to an almost unprecedented range of incompatible interpretations.[7] I want to suggest a more complex matrix for the poem, which accounts for the 'surplus' elements on which critics continue to break their teeth, and finally to move toward a more inclusive reading of the poem.

I

That proposed matrix centrally involves John Ruskin, an already acknowledged source, and dating is important. *The Stones of Venice* II appeared in July 1853, and volume III in October. The Brownings had met Ruskin in London in September 1852; they read his works regularly (though English books were often delayed in getting to Florence), and a correspondence seems to have begun by late 1853.[8] Volume II would have been of intense interest to both readers, containing as it does the crucial chapter 'The Nature of Gothic', and within that the 'inconsequent' note praising Elizabeth's 'noble poem', *Casa Guidi Windows*, for its 'just account of the incapacities of the modern Italian'.[9] It is reasonable to assume that both volumes were in the Brownings' hands by late 1853; and Elizabeth's words to Miss E. F. Haworth, on 27 December 1853 – 'I shall write to Mr Ruskin'– may well refer to Ruskin's encomium.[10] DeVane judges that 'A Grammarian's Funeral' owes its 'inspiration to Browning's residence in Rome from December, 1853, until May, 1854', and was probably written, in a burst of activity, after his return to Florence from Rome.[11] And so the evidence strongly supports the long-held view that Browning's reading of 'The Nature of Gothic', ch. v of *Stones* II, played a role in the genesis of 'A Grammarian's Funeral'. But priority on Ruskin's part, and the fact that Ruskin's powerfully suggestive chapter may have acted as a partial stimulus or occasion, do not settle the causalities in Browning's poem so simply as critics have assumed or half-implied.

Long ago, Cook and Wedderburn cited lines 113–16 of Browning's poem,

> That low man seeks a little thing to do,
>   Sees it and does it:
> This high man, with a great thing to pursue,
>   Dies ere he knows it,

as tied to a key passage in *Stones* II:

> And therefore, while in all things that we see, or do, we are to desire perfection, and strive for it, we are nevertheless not to set the meaner thing, in its narrow accomplishment, above the nobler thing, in its mighty progress; not to esteem smooth minuteness above shattered majesty; not to prefer mean victory to honourable defeat; not to lower the level of our aim, that we may the more surely enjoy the complacency of success.   (x.191)[12]

Perhaps even more inspiriting to a Browning seeking popularity through a new poetry that would 'get people to hear and see' were the qualities that Ruskin found in Gothic architecture (in Curtis Dahl's summary):

> Vigor, irregularity, love of fact and detail, interest in detail, interest in character and historical period, prizing of spirit over form, humor, fancifulness, grotesqueness, tenderness, flexibility, contempt for smooth correctness, originality, discord interrupting harmony, playfulness but underlying seriousness, aspiration, changefulness and variety, a doctrine of imperfection and aspiration, a strong faith in God.

Even if we smile at the notion of Browning accepting the analogy between himself and a Chartres Cathedral or a York Minster, there is a legitimate sense in which these qualities may 'define Browning's poetry even better than they do actual Gothic architecture'.[13] But Dahl's inconclusive formulation – 'Browning is thoroughly Ruskinian Gothic – or is it Ruskinian Gothic that is thoroughly Browningesque?' – suggests just how confused the notions of influence remain in these matters.

A similar indeterminacy hovers over Lawrence Poston's intriguing claim that Browning 'conforms . . . to' Ruskin's stirring portrait, later in the same chapter, of the great Naturalist artist – of the order of Michelangelo, Giotto, Tintoretto or Turner – who 'takes the human being in its wholeness, in its mortal as well as its spiritual strength' (x.226).[14] Browning might have hesitated to rank himself so loftily, but he would certainly have been responsive to Ruskin's bold and refreshingly unmoralised description of this, 'the greatest class', who 'render all that they see in nature unhesitatingly, with a kind of divine grasp and government of the whole, sympathizing with all the good, and yet confessing, permitting, and bringing good out of the evil also' (p. 222). Browning might have accepted as well the more 'Victorian' (and probably more typically Ruskinian) caveat that follows: 'sounding and sympathizing' with all of a 'human being's' passions,

> he brings one majestic harmony out of them all; he represents it fearlessly in all its acts and thoughts, in its haste, its anger, its sensuality, and its pride, as well as in its fortitude or faith, but makes it noble in them all: . . . with all that lives . . . he claims kindred, . . . yet standing, in a sort, afar off, unmoved even in the deepness of his sympathy. . . .   (pp. 226–7)

This almost divine universality, at once tolerant and mysteriously detached, is not unlike the qualities attributed to the Shakespeare mythologised repeatedly by English and German Romantic critics; it was an elevated mode also often attributed to Goethe in the period, sometimes benignly as in Carlyle, but often with more sinister moral implications.[15]

But while 'The Nature of Gothic' may thus have stimulated Browning as he launched a new set of 'dramatic' monologues, it is worth noting that in all these matters Ruskin was reinforcing already well established tendencies of Browning's art, as well as the principles of character drawing found throughout the *Men and Women* volumes. Most importantly, Browning's philosophy of the imperfect clearly antedates 'The Nature of Gothic', and is found in its fully developed form in poems written earlier, especially in the painter-poems like 'Old Picture in Florence', 'Fra Lippo Lippi' and 'Andrea del Sarto'.[16] Browning's repeated exploration of the doctrine is a reflex of his return to a nearly orthodox Christianity in the late 1840s, under his wife's tutelage; and thus DeVane is right in calling it, a bit loosely, 'essentially a medieval philosophy'.[17]

Similarly, in Ruskin's exuberant portrait of the Naturalist artist who sympathises with good but 'permits' evil and draws good from it, Browning may well have found encouragement for his own 'mixed' art, a dramatic mode foreshadowed in his dramas, from the 1830s on. But again, his defence of such an art had come earlier, in 1851, when he wrote his 'Introductory Essay' to the spurious Shelley letters. There he had defined a Shakespearean 'objective poet' whose work is 'projected from himself and distinct', one whose motives may range from his 'soul's delight in its own extended sphere of vision' to 'an irresistible sympathy with men'. This 'Fashioner' poet, whose work is done 'in abstraction from his personality' and tends to the dramatic, deals with 'the noisy, complex, yet imperfect exhibitions of nature in the manifold experience of men around him'. Even more predictive of Ruskin's divinely tolerant Naturalist artist is Browning's portrait of the 'whole poet' – nominally Shelley, but really the Robert Browning of his own desire – who combines the objective and the subjective. His function is to behold 'with an understanding keenness the universe, nature, and man, in their actual state of perfection in imperfection; and his balancing virtue is that he is 'untempted by the manifold partial developments of beauty and good on every side, into leaving them the ultimates he found them' – by which involuted phrase Browning seems to mean, 'looking higher' than any actual beauty and good to some ideal future state of man.[18] And so the right image seems to be that of two men often on parallel tracks, shouting occasional advice and encouragement to each other, but not quite as 'sources' and 'influences' in the usual sense of those terms.

More incidentally, it helps to clarify the limits of this stimulus–irritant relationship if we note that Ruskin almost certainly did not (as some treatments come perilously close to implying) actually have Browning or Browning's poetic practice in mind when he wrote 'The Nature of Gothic' in 1853. For Ruskin, who knew Mrs Browning's poetry fairly well in this period, seems not to have made any serious effort to read Robert's poetry until he received the two volumes of *Men and Women* in November 1855. He spent the night of 2 December puzzling over the poems, with Dante Gabriel Rossetti's help, and sent a long letter to Browning, full of 'objurgations', the next morning. Rossetti, who was asked to forward the letter though he was not allowed to read it, reported to William Allingham on

8 January 1856: 'Ruskin, on reading *Men and Women* (and with it some other works he didn't know before) declared them rebelliously to be a mass of conundrums, and compelled me to sit down before him and lay siege for one whole night. . . .'[19]

One of those 'other works', almost certainly not previously known to Ruskin, was 'The Bishop Orders His Tomb at Saint Praxed's Church'. For in late January 1856, Ruskin wrote that he would discuss Browning's poems in *Modern Painters* IV, which he was then preparing: '. . . I don't know even yet what to think or say about you. What I *am* going to say will be about your wonderful understanding of painting & mediaevalism, unique amongst poets, and some reference to St Praxeds under coloured stones.'[20] This was the famous passage, to be looked at more closely below, in which Ruskin praised Browning's poem (first published in 1845) for its depiction of the worldly Renaissance spirit: 'It is nearly all that I said of the central Renaissance in thirty pages of the *Stones of Venice* [III] put into as many lines, Browning's being also the antecedent work' (VI.449). The praise is generous, and the priority real; but if, as it seems clear, Ruskin did not know 'Saint Praxed's' until late 1855, not only was Browning not a 'model' for Ruskin's treatment of the Gothic in *Stones* II, but Browning's poem was only after-the-fact corroboration of Ruskin's famous denunciation of 'the central Renaissance' in *Stones* III.

The deeper irony, as we shall see, is that both men had for years being reacting, complicatedly but for the most part independently, to a common body of new and challenging thought. There is amusement and instruction enough, for the moment, in hearing Browning respond on 10 December 1855 to Ruskin's elaborate bewilderment: 'A poet's affair is with God, to whom he is accountable, and of whom is his reward: look elsewhere, and you find misery enough.'[21] Here Browning, the supposed beneficiary of Ruskin on the 'imperfect' (in *Stones* II), feels obliged to lecture Ruskin on precisely that doctrine, in a formulation directly applicable to 'A Grammarian's Funeral' – a poem not mentioned, however, anywhere in the rapid flurry of lengthy expostulations between the men during this period. In the same letter, there is a similar irony in Browning's description of poetry in a now famous phrase as 'a putting the infinite within the finite', and he reminds Ruskin that 'in asking for more *ultimates* you must accept less *mediates*'. The terms hark back to the Shelley essay (which, suppressed soon after publication, there is no evidence that Ruskin ever read), where Browning warned the higher poet to seek ideal meanings and not be content to regard 'particular developments' as 'ultimates'. But Browning is also lecturing Ruskin in language not incompatible with Ruskin's own remarks on the Naturalist who seeks a higher 'harmony', distilled from the good and evil particular 'acts and thoughts' of men. Like many prophets and other 'strong' creative personalities, both writers had enormous difficulty in acknowledging (even to themselves) possible 'influences' and 'sources' – even when their feet were tangled in them.

II

I have been trying to establish, more precisely than has been done before, the ways in which Ruskin's treatment of the doctrine of the imperfect in 'The Nature of Gothic', in *Stones* II (July 1853), may have acted as an impetus in the writing of 'A Grammarian's Funeral', although each writer had been developing his views in independence of the other. But I want to show also that Ruskin's role in the complicated push–pull of emotion and ideology that works through Browning's poem extended well beyond general attitudes toward life, to the poem's actual subject-matter. For the striking chapter, 'Roman Renaissance' (in *Stones* III, in October), which Browning would have read almost simultaneously with 'The Nature of Gothic', is also essential for understanding this prolonged creative 'moment' in Browning's career from late 1853 into the early summer of 1854. But 'Roman Renaissance', as will appear, acted less as a corroboration than as a 'provocation' – of the sort that often triggered Browning's most complex responses.

'Roman Renaissance' is momentous in Ruskin's career, as his first developed statement of agreement with the substance of Alexis Rio's *De la poésie chrétienne, dans son principe, dans sa matière et dans ses formes: Forme de l'art: Peinture* (1836), a defence of 'Christian Art', a subject widely debated in England from the early 1840s on.[22] Rio, an outspoken Roman Catholic polemicist, argued that the medieval linkage between the arts and piety had been broken in the fifteenth century by a new pagan 'naturalism', especially under the sponsorship of the Medici in Florence. Though as we shall see Rio had English followers, the thesis – which was easily extended, especially in the religiously volatile 1840s, to a critique of 'modern' civilisation as a whole – was regularly associated with Rio, until it was appropriated by the powerful personality and style of Ruskin. The process began in *Modern Painters* ɪɪ (1846), but despite passing 'hits' at the Renaissance – itself a new term at mid-century in history and in cultural polemics – Ruskin's full-fledged attack waited until 'Roman Renaissance'. That Ruskin was in fact already having *doubts* about Rio's 'pious' reading of cultural history would not be evident to a reader in 1853; on the other hand, Ruskin – always eager to repel the imputation of Catholic or High Church sympathies – had already in 'The Nature of Gothic' questioned the excess of 'grace, and life, and light, and holiness', unshadowed by 'evil passions', in the Purists, artists like Fra Angelico and the early Raphael (x.221–2), and in *The Stones of Venice* ɪ (1851) he had launched a vehement attack on the architect A. W. Pugin and modern Romanism.[23]

Browning's responses to this tangle of new and controversial ideas, though largely negative, are at least as ambivalent as Ruskin's, and only recently have they begun to be sorted out. Distinctions are in order. Browning, for all his fascination with the vitality of the strongly marked individuals thrown up by the Italian Renaissance, centrally *shared* some of Ruskin's doubts about the Renaissance spirit. In his lavish tribute in *Modern Painters* ɪv (1856), Ruskin asserted: 'Robert Browning is unerring in every sentence he writes of the Middle Ages; always vital, right, and profound; so that in the matter of art . . . there is hardly a principle connected with the mediaeval temper, that he has not struck upon in those seemingly careless and too rugged rhymes of his.' And he concludes his discussion of 'Saint Praxed's' by summarising his own views in 'Roman Renaissance': 'I know no other piece of modern English, prose or poetry, in which there is so much told, as in these lines, of the Renaissance spirit – its worldliness, inconsistency, pride, hypocrisy, ignorance of itself, love of art, of luxury, and of good Latin' (vɪ.449). In short, Ruskin legitimately found in Browning, the predecessor in these matters, weight and authority for his own views. Certainly Browning is not, as some careless and anachronistic modern readers of 'Fra Lippo Lippi' have assumed, the simple defender of a 'worldly' Renaissance as against an otherwordly medievalism.

In fact Browning, though in many ways suspicious of 'Catholic' and reactionary religious readings of history, had himself begun, around 1850, to admire and collect the Italian 'primitives', the literal pre-Raphaelites, for whom Ruskin was simultaneously becoming the chief advocate. Browning's delight in the combined boldness and piety of the 'early' Italian painters was already evident in 'Old Pictures in Florence', apparently written in the spring of 1853.[24] Similarly, Browning might well have recognised his own Duke (in 'My Last Duchess', published in 1842) – though Ruskin presumably did not know the poem – in Ruskin's scathing denunciation of the 'constant expression of individual vanity and pride' in Renaissance portraiture. These likenesses convey 'coldness, perfection of training, incapability of emotion, want of sympathy with the weakness of lower men, blank, hopeless, haughty self-sufficiency'. Such art is of a piece with Renaissance architecture, which is 'rigid, cold, inhuman; incapable of stooping, of conceding for an instant' (xi.74); Browning's Duke to the life ('I choose / Never to stoop'), though in a more moralised and unshaded form. The standard by which the Renaissance is condemned is precisely that of the spontaneity – 'life' as opposed to 'system' – endorsed in 'The Nature of Gothic'.

Thus far would Browning have been likely to follow Ruskin into the labyrinth of 'Roman Renaissance'. But not, I think, all the way to the end. And a closer look at Ruskin's praise for Browning's 'wonderful understanding of painting & mediaevalism', especially in 'Saint Praxed's', helps explain why. For as early as the mid-1840s, and above all in that poem, Browning had consciously used poems as vehicles to attack – not primarily, as Ruskin's language would imply, Renaissance worldliness – but precisely the neo-medievalism, both Romanist and High Church, then reaching a crescendo in both religion and the arts.[25] Even as late as early 1853, when writing 'Fra Lippo Lippi', Browning would have known the polemical view of Christian Art directly from Rio, or as mediated by such cautious English disciples of Rio as Mary Shelley and, above all, the Brownings' close friend Anna Jameson.[26] But by the time he wrote 'A Grammarian's Funeral' in 1854, Browning had run up against the troubling views as now applied by Ruskin, in powerful and highly assertive new forms.

The specific question becomes, how Browning – already, like his wife, disturbed by Ruskin's habitual extravagance and overstatement – reacted to Ruskin's blazing version of the Christian Art argument, and especially the contrast between medieval and Renaissance. Of course, both men, essentially 'protestant' and Evangelical personalities, fiercely resisted the blandishments of Catholic piety, especially in its revived, nineteenth-century forms.

But Ruskin, at least into the mid-1850s, openly embraced the Rioesque 'disaster' reading of post-Renaissance and even post-Reformation history, as the loss of a 'healthy' unified culture, caused by the rise of modern rationalism and anarchic individualism. Browning, with perhaps greater consistency, was reluctant to write off 'modern' history so peremptorily, and was much more willing to bear the cultural 'costs' entailed in the rise of striking modern personalities and the fullness of self-awareness.

And (I will argue) it is precisely Browning's well-founded *doubts* about the medievalism that Ruskin insisted on praising him for, that governed his reading of 'Roman Renaissance' and that acted as a central part of the occasion for 'A Grammarian's Funeral'. That much-admired but also much-disputed poem thus joins, if somewhat more peripherally, the network of Browning poems of the 1840s and 1850s whose purport and emotional energies cannot be fully understood except in the light of the widespread debates over the issues of Christian Art. My hope, perhaps chimerical, is to stabilise efforts at interpretation.

III

In 'Roman Renaissance', which Browning was reading during the very period in which he wrote his poem, Ruskin's most sustained argument against Renaissance 'pride of learning' and in particular Renaissance grammar was set within a broader statement about the place of knowledge in life. The provocation and the strategy of response are illuminatingly like those in 'Fra Lippo Lippi', written the year before. For both 'Fra Lippo Lippi' and 'A Grammarian's Funeral' proceed from the entanglement of issues regarding the relations of medieval and Renaissance which around mid-century exercised, not only Ruskin and Browning, but thoughtful English readers generally. In both cases, Browning's forceful reaction to the new aggression led him, not to direct denunciation, but to a virtuoso display of sheer exuberance and a 'larky' whimsicality – an appropriate *kind* of reply to an asceticism which Browning found highly threatening. To be sure, the overt issues in 'A Grammarian's Funeral' are not earth-shaking, while the matters engaged in 'Fra Lippo Lippi' are of great moment for Browning's views of the arts and indeed of modern history. But in both poems, Browning applies as a norm the doctrine of the imperfect, a doctrine central to his own theory of character. And especially in 'A Grammarian's Funeral', Ruskin's ferocious, overstated moralism is met by a counter-argument of equal force, Browning's sportive, 'perverse' defence of a kind of paradoxical heroic pedantry.

Ruskin had dogmatically asserted, 'We no more live to know, than we live to eat', and it is 'the old Eve-sin' to assume that 'the trees of knowledge and of life are one' (xi.63–5) – and then denounced Renaissance grammar by precisely these standards. The disciples of Browning's grammarian declare, 'This man decided not to Live but Know' (line 139), thus converting a charge made by the uncomprehending 'world' – and by Ruskin – into a defiant, capitalised affirmation. The Browning who loved to make a 'case' for an undervalued character, here almost quixotically seizes the challenge of rehabilitating a 'type' of character under current and conspicuous attack. And, as we shall see, Browning doubles the fun and the whimsy by refusing to 'smooth out' the embarrassments of a character who entirely lacks the racy charm and childlike ebullience of Lippo. Browning revels in the paradoxes and uncomfortable conundrums, triumphantly snatching spiritual victory from apparent failure.

Browning's main tactic, within this larger strategy, and the easiest part of his task, is to defend the grammarian by showing that in reality he *meets* the criteria of 'Gothic' vitality that Ruskin had established in both 'The Nature of Gothic' and 'Roman Renaissance'. The central tour de force of the poem is to take a grubbing and even physically repellent subject, recently attacked by Ruskin, and to say as much for him (even if with a confidential smile at the bemused but indulgent reader) as can be made consistent with Ruskin's – and Browning's own – philosophy of the imperfect. Browning does not deny the mixture of pride and seeming triviality in the grammarian – 'This unhappy and childish pride in knowledge', as Ruskin called it (p. 73); nor does he develop much of a case for the intrinsic value of his work, though it is no doubt important to argue that the grammarian did establish the workings of *Hoti, Oun* and *De*. Instead, Browning ingeniously – and I think with some conscious sophistry – develops the case that the ardour, as well as the oddities and anomalies, of the Renaissance grammarians in fact promote venturesome attitudes toward life that Browning regularly commended. Browning daringly puts his own (and Ruskin's) central doctrine in danger, playing with it, finding admirable risk-taking at work, quite unexpectedly, in a proud learning that Ruskin had just dubbed 'ridiculous and trifling' (xi.68). The poem thus in its own strategies exhibits the boldness which its argument commends.

Ruskin argued, in 'Roman Renaissance', that the truly 'precious and necessary knowledge' is of 'whatever is immeasurable, intangible, indivisible' (xi.55, 61). This fulness of 'perception' he sets against 'the paltry knowledge' gained in 'the Renaissance system', preoccupied as it is with 'the sciences of words and methods' (p. 69). The Renaissance forgot 'the old religious and earnest spirit' and 'the common majesty of the human soul' (pp. 70, 78). Above all, the renewed study of 'Pagan writers' turned 'all men to words instead of things':

> half the intellect of the age was at once absorbed in the base sciences of grammar, logic, and rhetoric; studies utterly unworthy of the serious labour of men, and necessarily rendering those employed upon them incapable of high thoughts or noble emotion. Of the debasing tendency of philology, no proof is needed beyond once reading a grammarian's notes on a great poet. (pp. 127–8)

Debasing! Browning in effect retorts: this grammarian is a man of 'Lofty designs', 'still loftier than the world' – or John Ruskin – 'suspects' (lines 145, 147). And the 'world' in nineteenth-century England regularly expressed numerous doubts about the 'dead' classicism and philologism of the schools and universities.[27] But even Ruskin had granted that 'There were, of course, noble exceptions' to the Renaissance pride in grammars of language, logic, ethics and arts, 'but chiefly belonging to the earliest periods of the Renaissance, when its teaching had not yet produced its full effect' (xi.70). And Browning understandably chose exactly the period 'Shortly After the Revival of Learning in Europe' as the arena for defending his own apparently *ig*noble pedant.

The 'real animating power of knowledge is only in the moment of its being first received', Ruskin asserts, and with 'wonder and joy' at 'something which [a man] cannot know to the full, which he is always going on to know'. And this is 'a state, not of triumph or joy in what [the intelligence] knows, but of joy rather in the continual discovery, of new ignorance . . .' (p. 65). Browning retorts that *his* grammarian, though in a less humble spirit, also has infinite yearnings, the experience of 'continual discovery':

> Let me know all! Prate not of most or least,
>   Painful or easy!
> Even to the crumbs I'd fain eat up the feast,
>   Ay, nor feel queasy.
>
>   (lines 61–4)[28]

(Ruskin, too, had used the food image: 'is the knowledge we would have fit food for us, good and simple, not artificial and decorated?' p. 63) 'No end to learning', says the awed disciple, as if he just read Ruskin, and that is the meaning of the grammarian's decision, 'That before living he'd learn how to live' (lines 78, 77). It is precisely the *high* man, 'with a great purpose to pursue, / [who] Dies ere he knows it', and who, 'aiming at a million'/Misses an unit' (lines 115–20). Ruskin had insisted that all knowledge, but especially 'Renaissance knowledge', deadens 'the force of the imagination and the original energy of the whole man', a burden or a weariness that 'binds' and 'cramps' the spirit (xi.65–6). The disciples seem to reply directly: 'Did not he magnify the mind . . .?' (line 105). And in the most explicit turning of Ruskin's words back on himself, Browning protests that the grammarian, far from giving up the old religious spirit, in fact displayed an almost reckless trust (line 81): 'did not he throw on God . . . / God's task to make the heavenly period / Perfect the earthen?' (lines 101–4). 'God surely will contrive/Use for our earning' (lines 79–80). This 'neck or nothing' daredevil 'throws himself on God, and unperplexed/Seeking shall find him' (lines 109, 123–4). As the allusion to Matthew 7.7 (and Luke 11.9) – 'seek, and ye shall find' – shows, Browning affirms that he is in a true if 'broad' sense a *religious* quester, a squint-eyed Lippo Lippi of the Greek particles.

IV

But it was a comparatively easy, if perhaps quixotic, task to argue the case for a sort of religious greatness ('Was it not great?', line 101) in an unapparent form – thus making the grammarian a true if unexpected exemplar of Ruskinian Gothic, rough of surface but noble, indeed a Pascalian risk-taker. The real accomplishment of the poem, as well as the source of much of the interpretative confusion, comes from Browning's almost reckless willingness to treat playfully the unsettling difficulties in Ruskin's attack on the Renaissance spirit and Renaissance grammarians. Whether or not Browning saw himself in Ruskin's account of rugged Gothic (in *Stones* II), I think he might well have caught an even clearer glimpse of himself and his art (at least half-consciously) in Ruskin's various contemporaneous attempts to define the grotesque mode. In 'Grotesque Renaissance', in *Stones* III, Ruskin had recently asserted that even the most elevated class of writers (his examples are Wordsworth and Plato), yielding to their healthy 'impulses', 'condescend often to playfulness' (the whole passage suggests Schiller's *Spieltrieb*, though it is highly doubtful that Ruskin had him in mind), but this 'sportive energy' will combine with 'their more earnest purposes', making 'its idlest fancies profitable, and its keenest satire indulgent'. The 'true grotesque' is 'the expression of the *repose* or play of a *serious* mind' (XI.152–6, 170). It was precisely Browning's own spirit of serious but reposeful play that led to a *surplus* of jangled signals, repugnant to most Victorian readers and still confounding interpretation.[29] Working in this grotesque mode, and provoked by Ruskin's denunciation, Browning goes out of his way to make things difficult for himself.[30]

Even small details suggest precisely how 'Roman Renaissance' helped provoke Browning to his display of 'perverse' ingenuity. Does Ruskin insist on acquiring only as much knowledge as will 'leave . . . our eyes clear', as opposed to the 'dim-eyed proprieties of the multitude' of scholars (XI.63, 118)? Then Browning's grammarian's 'eyes grew dross of lead' (line 87; 'eyes like lead': line 53). Does Ruskin mock their 'crabbed discipline and exact scholarship' (p. 118)? Then Browning's grammarian will have fiercely 'mastered learning's crabbed text' (line 59). Does Ruskin see, in 'a grammarian's notes on a great poet', 'the debasing tendency of philology' (p. 128)? Then Browning's grammarian will zestfully press on from the text to 'the comment' (line 60). The grammarian must be even more unattractive than Ruskin's figure, paralysed, bound and cramped by 'the Renaissance knowledge' (pp. 65–6): Browning's is 'cramped and diminished', bald, eyes like lead, racked by *calculus* (gallstones), attacked by *tussus* (bronchitis) and 'Dead from the waist down' (lines 38, 53, 86–8, 132).[31]

Browning's single most daring and unsettling transformation of

Ruskin's themes is shown in his willingness to sport at length with Ruskin's all-out attack on the *pride* of Renaissance learning. As we have seen, Browning is quick to pick up Ruskin's ideal of 'always going on to know', of 'continual discovery', and to find it exemplified even in those who grind at grammar. One might also expect that he would endorse Ruskin's view that such endless learning should be 'a state, not of triumph or joy in what it [the finite creature] knows, but of joy rather in the continual discovery of new ignorance, continual self-abasement, continual astonishment', and share Ruskin's judgement that 'this unhappy and childish pride in knowledge' such as syntax and syllogisms is ridiculous (pp. 65, 69, 71, 73). But instead, Browning's experiment in value-making-and-unmaking develops at length, and without overt criticism, the disciples' naïve, even childishly enthusiastic, sense of triumph and joy in knowledge as the chief object of life.

Again, it was comparatively easy to mediate the hard-driving mortal 'grappling' of the grammarian, whom we can admire for having 'stepped on with pride/Over men's pity' (lines 45, 43–4); and even the contempt for ordinary men implied in 'Leave Now for dogs and apes!' is softened by the elevation of 'Man has Forever' (lines 83–4). It was much more daring, however, to take up Ruskin's assault on Renaissance 'pride of learning' (xi.80) and in effect treat it as a legitimate claim on the part of the disciples.[32] For the disciples are very far from acknowledging with Ruskin that the joy of learning should be 'in the continual discovery of new ignorance, continual self-abasement, continual astonishment'. Instead, they seem to be the very illustration of Ruskin's agreement with St Paul that knowledge 'puffeth up' and with Francis Bacon that there is ' "venomousness" in the very nature of knowledge itself' (xi.67). Unlike the natural sciences, the sciences of words and methods – such as philology, logic and rhetoric – have a 'power of feeding pride' exactly in proportion to their own 'ridiculous and trifling' nature (p. 68). In the Renaissance, a contempt for ordinary speech followed: 'Falsehood in a Ciceronian dialect had no opposers: truth in patois no listeners' (p. 69). Working in the spirit of this childish pride, a typical Renaissance architect is made to proclaim, 'I do not work for the vulgar' (p. 75). Never in earlier forms of pride had there been 'a forgetfulness so total of the common majesty of the human soul, and of the brotherly kindness due from man to man, as in the aristocratic follies of the Renaissance' (p. 78). These 'students of phrase and syllogism', absorbed in the study of 'words instead of things', turned away from all things medieval, including the 'truth' and 'pathos' of the Bible and the religious spirit (pp. 127–8).

These disturbing elements condemned at length by Ruskin run through the entire self-presentation of the grammarian's disciples. Even their movement up to 'the top-peak' (line 137), where thought is 'Rarer, intenser' (line 10), is jarringly phrased. 'Leave we the common crofts, the vulgar thorps' (line 3), they boast, and even more pointedly, 'Leave we the *unlettered* plain its herd and crop' (line 13: my emphasis). Three times, crop and herd and darkling thorpe and croft are associated with 'tethered' *sheep* and *safety* (lines 4–5, 29–30) – implying timidity and an animalistic spiritual unawareness in the 'low life' (line 23) down below. This is not merely a display of pride of learning, but an open scorn for those who do not share their special passion, and indeed for ordinary consciousness. The chorus leader even pauses for an unpleasant slap at the people in 'the market-place/Gaping before us' (lines 73–4). Thus the pursuit of exact learning, which in the grammarian was 'a sacred thirst' (line 95), becomes in the disciples, who lack his achievement and bask rather passively in the light he sheds, their way of coldly measuring their distance – apart from and above – the 'herd'. Their saving grace is, of course, their unfeigned admiration for the grammarian's greatness, his trust in God, his magnifying the mind. But even this generous realisation is marred somewhat by their disdain for those who lack such 'fierce' resolution: 'He would not discount life as fools do here' (lines 94, 107). The reader's teeth are further set on edge by the disciples' forcefully disjunctive way of expressing the grammarian's 'trust' that death would complete what he leaves undone on earth (lines 81, 101–4) – a doctrine with which in itself Browning is plainly sympathetic. For they seem actually to point or at least nod contemptuously as they recite words that they may well be putting into the grammarian's mouth: *This high man* is repeatedly set over against *That low man*, who is plainly one of the 'multitude below', who 'Live, for they can, there' (lines 113–22, 137–8).

This disquieting mixture of tones comes to a sharp focus in two key terms. One is *world*, used with great deliberateness five times, as part of the disciples' vindication of the grammarian's – and their own – lives. The word, in its Pauline and Augustinian origins, had implied a sharp division between the regenerate and the unregenerate; in its increasingly secular and aesthetic uses in the nineteenth century, it tends to separate off a class of the specially percipient from the unenlightened – culminating in the 1860s and 1870s in Walter Pater's formulations of a 'higher' ethics for 'special souls'. When the disciples praise the grammarian's refusal to give up the struggle in old age – 'No, that's the world's way' (line 41) – they are close to Paul's rejection of 'the wisdom of this world' (I Corinthians 2.6). The least emphatic, though still suggestive, use is in the assertion that the grammarian 'stepped on with pride / Over men's pity; / Left play for work, and grappled with the world / Bent on escaping' (lines 43–5). For Lippo Lippi, the world meant the entirety of sensible reality: 'The world and life's too big to pass for a dream' (line 251); 'This world's no blot for us, / Nor blank; it means intensely, and means good' (lines 313–14). The grammarian's world is the microcosm of enclitics and parts of speech. (The two men are linked by images of gross feeding that suggest their 'soul-hydroptic' intensity. Lippo Lippi: 'To find its [the world's] meaning is my meat and drink' (line 315); the grammarian, more grotesquely: 'Even to the crumbs I'd fain eat up the feast, / Ay, nor feel queasy' (lines 63–4).) But piety and spiritual pride mix uneasily when the disciples, in their elaborate positioning of the 'high' grammarian, declare disdainfully that the man of 'low' ambition 'has the world here – should he need the next, / Let the world mind him!' (lines 121–2). And then, in the fireworks ending, a more straightforward use, though still with an angry flick of the lash: the grammarian had lofty designs and a lofty ending – 'still loftier than the world suspects' (line 147).

V

The other heavily charged term is the innocent-looking 'culture' (line 16): for a surprising number of the cross-currents of Browning's rapidly shifting allegiances in the 1850s wash over this word whose overtones are notoriously difficult to control. It is important to note that 'culture', in its absolute form, began to emerge only around 1850, to fill a long-felt need in English intellectual life. The word was common, in a figurative sense, from the 1820s on, but only – to take examples from Carlyle, the chief propagator of the term – in a prepositional usage (the culture *of* the mind, *of* the poet, etc.) and, more innovatively, in combination with qualifiers (human, moral, poetic *culture*). Only once, in 1827, does Carlyle rise to a broader generalisation and use the absolute form, when he announces that 'the first and last of all culture' is a 'harmonious development of being': 'the great law of culture is: Let each man become all that he was created capable of being; expand, if possible, to his full growth.'[33]

But also from the 1820s on, there was a widespread discussion of the notion of 'self-culture' and 'self-development', especially as English writers and critics came to terms with the disquieting example of Goethe, who had, supremely, lived the life of personal and artistic development, or *Bildung*. And so it is not surprising that a sort of 'puritan' reaction against the very idea of a modern and 'aesthetic' self-culture set in simultaneously with the wider use of the free-standing term *culture* at mid-century.[34] Punctually, in fact, in 1850, Emerson culminates a long debate among the American Transcendentalists, when, though paying tribute to his realism and effort, he harshly lashes out against a Goethe 'incapable of a self-surrender to the moral sentiment', a man whose devotion was not 'to pure truth; but to truth for the sake of culture'. [35] Carlyle, who had discussed these matters with Emerson in 1847, was in even more violent reaction against his earlier 'German' and Goethean views. In 1851, in *The Life of John Sterling*, he complains: 'It is expected in this Nineteenth Century that a man of culture shall understand and worship Art', one of the loudest of the modern 'windy gospels'. Browning would have noted both uses, which chimed in with the new conservative drift of this own thought.[36]

But quite as likely to attract Browning's attention was a notable *positive* use of the newly available term, by none other than Matthew Arnold, in his first published prose work, the Preface to the *Poems* of 1853, dated 1 October. There, Goethe and the liberal classical historian Barthold Niebuhr are praised as 'the men of strongest head and widest culture' of the present age.[37] Browning would have read the Preface with close attention, since in it Arnold explained why he was suppressing 'Empedocles on Etna', the key poem of his 1852 volume, and we know that Browning, already acquainted with Clough, was deeply struck by 'Empedocles' itself. Arnold – himself working toward a more 'moral' and public aesthetic, in which a comparatively benign sense of 'culture' was to play a central role – was repudiating a poetry replete with 'modern' doubts and discouragement, 'the dialogue of the mind with itself'.[38] Arnold's rejection of his own deepest poetic impulses, though radical, proceeded by gradual stages; certainly he remained rather stiff-

necked – and this Browning also would have noted, and perhaps
with some sympathy – in his cool disdain for the 'present age'
(*CPW*, I.13).[39]

Most illuminatingly, that Browning's 'Cleon' was written in
conscious reponse to Arnold's 'Empedocles', which appeared in late
1852, has been widely accepted. Long ago, A. W. Crawford noted
that in Cleon, who embodies in himself the highest reach of classical
civilisation, Browning depicts 'a full consciousness of the failure of
Greek culture to satisfy the longings and aspirations of the human
spirit, and yet too arrogant to receive a new doctrine from an alien
source'.[40] William C. DeVane has illuminatingly written of the
conflict in Browning between Evangelical Christianity and 'the
Greek revival'. Although Browning's 'full and formal repudiation of
Greece' does not come until the 1880s, the poems of *Men and Women*
also show a very un-Hellenic Browning – caught up 'in the spectacle
of contemporary humanity, in concrete and vivid actualities, in the
scrutiny of human motives, in the development of a soul from
weakness to strength' – forced into a distorting undervaluation of
the supreme achievements of Greek culture, in order to promote a
view of modern 'progress' in morality and religion.[41] Of course,
Browning may be said to reject, not so much ancient Greece and its
high attainments in arts and letters, as modern, self-consciously
'pagan' Hellenism – with origins as far back as Winckelmann and
Goethe, and gathering new strength in a Matthew Arnold – which
defines itself as an alternative to Christianity. And an even broader
Christian-Hellenic split, deep in English culture from at least
Milton's time, is undoubtedly a central source of the jangle of
motives and tones in some key Browning poems of the 1850s.[42]

This elaborate context may at first seem a heavy burden to rest on
the innocent-seeming word 'culture' in 'A Grammarian's Funeral',
but I hope it has become clear that the poem can only be properly
understood as part of Browning's attempt, in the years just after
1850, to apply the newly refurbished Evangelical standard and to
counter – most notably in 'Cleon' – a chief enemy of this point
of view, a resurgent 'pagan' Hellenism. Significantly, 'Cleon' was
written more or less simultaneously with 'A Grammarian's
Funeral', after the Brownings returned to Florence in June 1854
(DeVane, *Handbook*, p. 253). They are in effect companion-poems,
growing out of the 'culture' debates of the period. Two current and
polemical works – Arnold's pained treatment of a late, 'modern'
phase of ancient Greek culture, and Ruskin's fierce condemnation of

the most glamorous period of early modern classicism – had helped Browning plot the allowable range of his own ambivalence on the issues. Matters developed more gravely and subtly in 'Cleon', are dandled more jauntily and experimentally in 'A Grammarian's Funeral'; and the latter poem – though eluding a firm critical grasp – is not, I suggest, likely to wander far from the attitudes dramatised in 'Cleon'.[43]

When the grammarian's disciples leave the herd on the unlettered plain, they seek 'sepulture/On a tall mountain, citied to the top,/Crowded with culture!' (lines 14–16). That last is a puzzlingly breezy phrase; moreover, it is not easy to visualise what seem to be high mountain towns or cities, topped by a burial-site. The crowded culture is presumably evidence of past and present civilisation in its 'high' manifestations – one supposes, architecture, sculpture and perhaps exterior painting, mosaics and funerary art.[44] This 'crowded' scene is balanced by a more dignified reference to the grammarian's desire – though one apparently never fulfilled – to know the 'shaping' intentions of those ancient Greeks 'who most studied man, the bard and sage' (lines 48–9). Browning was preoccupied just then with that all-inclusive bard and sage, Cleon, who with easy self-congratulation – as writer of epics, sculptor, painter, philosopher and musician – announces: 'In brief, all arts are mine' (line 61). His self-vaunting is meant to unsettle the reader of the poem: 'I, Cleon, have effected all those things' (line 45); 'I stand myself' (line 151) – though, of course, 'all pride apart' (line 153)! And his contemptuous contrast of his own attainments with the incomprehension of 'vulgar souls', 'the vulgar' (lines 25, 36, 109), not only matches the more exuberant culture-snobbery of the grammarian's disciples, but ensures that our sympathetic identification with Cleon is severely limited.[45]

These linked poems most clearly diverge in the ways that they treat Browning's key doctrine of the imperfect. The disciples, like their master, are, as we have seen, sufficiently redeemed by their recognition – quite beyond the limits of their naïve pride – that the grammarian had thrown the burden of incompleteness on God, whose task it is 'to make the heavenly period/Perfect the earthen' (lines 101–4). Cleon, appropriately, develops the doctrine even more impressively, only to put it aside out of what one critic aptly calls 'the bigotry of culture'.[46] Cleon is fluent about 'progress' in self-understanding, as well as the 'synthesis' of Greek civilisation which he himself embodies (lines 92, 94). The binding image of the poem is that of 'the daily building' of the *tower* of one's life (lines 26, 36) – apparently a metaphorical structure strongly reminiscent of the much-deplored 'pyramid of my existence' that Goethe claimed to have spent his life in building.[47] But these images of growth through 'culture' (lines 114, 131) proved to be chimerical.[48] In a long and difficult meditation (lines 182–220), Cleon muses wistfully on the view that 'imperfection means perfection hid' (line 185) and that joy and happiness are the natural crown of 'intro-active' growth in the 'third thing', critical self-awareness. But in an abrupt shift this hope for a natural, joyous and endless 'progress' (line 222) is painfully and paradoxically denied, above all by the apparent finality of death. This high development of consciousness, the 'Watch-tower and treasure-fortress of the soul', that should be the crown of life: 'The soul now climbs it just to perish there!' (lines 225–36). In his proud denial of the possibility of revelation and further mystery, especially from 'a mere barbarian Jew' (line 343), Cleon is affecting in his despair and yet blamably inferior to the simple-hearted King Procus whom he presumes to instruct. (On Browning's attitudes toward Cleon, see Appendix III.)

This imagery of quest and ascent, as the answer to what constitutes 'the very crown and proper end of life', is even more central to 'A Grammarian's Funeral'. The poem is Browning's positive application of the doctrine of the imperfect to a 'difficult' case, in at least partially intentional contrast to 'Cleon', which also explores the periodic recurrence of classicism as a cultural ideal and alternative. (My guess, in the lack of any clearer evidence, is that 'Cleon' was conceived first, as a response to Arnold's 1852 poem, and that 'A Grammarian's Funeral' came soon after as Browning's half-approving, half-exasperated counter-statement to Ruskin's recent work – especially the pressure from the 'opposite' extreme, in 'Roman Renaissance', which provoked Browning, seeking a new middle ground, to an almost mischievous recasting of these entangled themes.[49]) Here, in sharp contrast to 'Cleon', there is buoyant, rhythmic, upward movement. The disciples carry up and convey aloft; they seek the appropriate country, the proper place – the top-peak, the citadel, the summit, the heights. The grammarian is the quintessential 'high' man, associated with the 'next' (and even higher) world, one who naturally consorts with 'high fliers'. The atmospherics of the finale – a joyous light and sound show of meteors, clouds and lightnings – convey the *reality* underlying the grim exterior of this fierce scholar's life. Lofty designs, and lofty effects, indeed. There are, then, two sorts of summits in the poems: the one, an ending, where we 'perish' alone in unfulfilled craving; the other, open to unlimited futurity, not in the fearful-sublime way, but in baroque, almost Handelian grandeur.

VI

The three-part dialectic established in *Christmas-Eve and Easter-Day*, initiates Browning's conscious and continuous 'positioning' of himself 'in the middle', between what he saw as ideological extremes. In that poem he had rejected the 'loveless learning' of German myth-critics of the Bible, like D. F. Strauss. From the same post-Christian side soon came a new, striking and more aesthetic paganism, embodied in Arnold's despairing but proud Empedocles – a challenge Browning countered in 'Cleon'. At least as distasteful, though technically not so far from Browning's own Christian norm, was the 'opposite' extreme of neo-Catholic piety, gaining ground in the High Church party and the 'aggression' of a newly recrudescent Romanism, seemingly risen almost from the grave. Deeply threatened by the sexual repressiveness and authoritarianism of the new Catholicism, in both life and art, the ultra-Protestant side of Browning's personality reacted strongly from the mid-1840s, in poems like 'Pictor Ignotus' and 'The Flight of the Duchess'.[50] There is a softer, more appreciative rejection of Rome in *Christmas-Eve*; but in the hectic 'Fra Lippo Lippi', as we have seen, the asceticism of the new 'Christian Art' thesis drew from Browning a 'wild' and almost boyish spirit of rebellion. When Ruskin soon after attacked Renaissance learning from the same reactionary point of view, a similarly 'freakish' mood carried Browning through the response embodied in 'A Grammarian's Funeral'.

The poems of ideas in the *Men and Women* volumes enact themselves in the space Browning cleared between these ideological extremes. And the *norm* of Browning's 'centre', it is important to reiterate, is precisely the Gothic standard – paradoxically both Evangelical and exuberantly vitalistic – just given powerful restatement in Ruskin's 'The Nature of Gothic'. What we now need to define is the form or mode Browning found suitable for his art of the centre, not least in order to give some stability to our interpretative efforts. That mode involves the continuous interplay of five or six distinguishable (though sometimes implicit) 'presences' that need to be teased apart: poet, reader, disciple(s), grammarian, 'world'.

To begin: the grammarian, though the *subject* of the poem, is 'a' grammarian. He remains strangely elusive, 'mediated', quoted (by the disciples), summarised, interpreted and eulogised; he is *not* (in Ralph Rader's phrase) the 'fully autonomous character' from whom we differ, found in the full-fledged dramatic monologue – he is in fact famous but dead.[51] Though 'grotesque', he is not 'exposed' in his blindness or evil, as are Browning's Bishop and Duke, nor is he granted – at the other extreme – the sympathetic, ironic self-insight of the speaker in 'Childe Roland'. On the other hand, the speaker, a more obvious candidate for a dramatic monologue, is not clearly dramatised and characterised either. As he puts a good face on the grammarian's life, what we become aware of is his 'strategy', which is sincere enough, but artful and rhetorical too – an example of legitimate special pleading. Recent defenders of the poem, eager to reject Altick's exposé reading, tend to overlook that the world – of the fifteenth century or of the 1850s – after all has a point, which 'we' (Browning and the reader) are fully aware of and partially concede. This shared awareness accounts for the smile and the slight but detectable and continuous condescension in the portrait that leaves our attitude hard to articulate. As with John Donne's most complex lyrics, we end at least *half*-convinced of a difficult 'case' (of which the disciples are almost wholly convinced); or at least we no longer raise objections, as the world might: the grammarian has *not* wasted his life, he *is* a genuine hero, to be understood and after a fashion even admired. What we are fully convinced of and exhilarated by (again, as in Donne) is the prestidigitation of the 'implied author', triumphantly managing seemingly intractable materials.

The voices of the chorus and the chorus-leader present problems that have even defied description – and that may be partially a defect of Browning's art. The leader at points encourages his fellow-disciples – 'Hearten our chorus!': line 76 – and the disciples are chanting together, perhaps a hymn ('Step to a tune': line 25), as they move rhythmically upward in a funeral cortège. But, unlike some readers, I do not see any part of the leader's discourse – that is, the actual words of the poem – as unmistakably vocalised by the group as a whole. For the 'argument' that constitutes the bulk of the poem seems unlikely to be addressed to hearers referred to as 'fools' and 'low' men – and even compared to apes and dogs! Even the most encomiastic section, the conclusion, openly disparages the 'world', presumably by this time below and well out of earshot. If such speech *were* to be heard (in the intervals, say, of the disciples' singing) it would be very deliberately insulting – and that would not comport with the directions to the disciples to be discreet in their conduct when near the beholders. Further, a 'defence' of the grammarian, if addressed to a sceptical and indifferent world, would be unlikely to include so extensive an account of the grotesque and unattractive aspects of the man; and thus I do not accept that the speaker in any way tailors his case for the ears of the gaping world. Indeed, the hypothesis that fits the circumstances most completely is, I suggest, that the poem is primarily the chorus-leader's formulation, for the encouragement of his fellow-disciples (he is likely to be in some sense a senior member of the group), of the reasons for their devotion to 'our' leader. It is spoken during pauses in their public 'Singing together' (line 2) and his own quieter directions as to their physical movements and demeanour.[52]

This hypothesis accounts, I think, for the various changes in the tone and volume of the speaker's voice, besides the breaks that Browning indicates after lines 28 and 72. Two parentheses (in lines 95 and 102), representing slight intensifications, are integral to the argument. Two others, in lines 41–2 and 90–1, are physical directions to his fellow-disciples, and thus while they interrupt the argument, they are not necessarily delivered in a lowered voice. But two more, on the 'gaping' market-place (lines 73–5) and 'Hearten our chorus!' (line 76), along with 'Ware the beholders!' (line 26), are instructions for impressing the onlookers, and thus *would* be delivered *sotto voce*. This reading also helps us put aside the attempt of one critic to separate 'public' sections, in which the disciples conform the grammarian to a medieval and pious myth of the uses of learning which they do not hold, from 'private' sections in which they satirise and denigrate him.[53]

This much, I suggest, remains of the division between public and private views. By the dignity of the ceremony and the heartiness of their singing, the disciples do attest to their own sincerely held views regarding the grammarian's distinction; but they 'conceal' two aspects of their sentiments from the onlookers. The chorus-leader (speaking to the other disciples and on their behalf, but in private), is startlingly, even amusingly frank (and yet uncritical) about the 'grotesque' realities of the grammarian's physical state and his mental struggle – or, to give him the benefit of the doubt, he is tolerant but clear-eyed about his master's limitations. More substantively, the elaborate 'case' for the grammarian's special and paradoxical merits is not, *cannot* be, delivered to the uncomprehending 'world'; it can only be rehearsed for the initiated and committed. From their point of view, and Browning's, such a double strategy is a legitimate rhetorical manoeuvre, not unlike the ancient doctrine of the 'economy', recently the focus of bitter controversy in Tractarian polemics: that is, conveying to the poorly instructed 'multitude' only so much of the truth as it is prepared to take in – in this case, the public 'chorus' or anthem we do *not* hear in the poem. But in any event, it seems fair to conclude, they do not express serious reservations regarding the grammarian's life and work.

In summary, much of the negative evidence collected by Altick and others *is* present: the disciples are culture-proud and scornful of the 'vulgar'; and to the extent that they uncritically anatomise the grotesque aspects of their master, they seem to share some of his uncouthness. Thus we, like Browning, maintain a distinct emotional and moral distance; indeed, we look down on them as naïve, not quite 'like us'. But, equally important, their very *naïveté* redeems them to a crucial extent; their youthful exuberance mitigates the repellent effect of their pride; and we smile at their seemingly extravagant panegyrics, but sympathetically, for they are, after all, essentially correct about the real merits of the grammarian – 'loftier than the world suspects'. And it is precisely the 'world', vividly present to the speaker throughout, that provides the counter-norm by which we can securely 'position' the disciples, who are of the party of those who comprehend.

VII

But the world – and two other vital figures, Robert Browning and the reader – are not yet fully accounted for. The relationships are made clearest if we see that two 'cases', closely parallel in method and purpose, are being made, a case within a case. The leader – in the very words of the poem – explicitly argues a brief for the master, underrated by an indifferent and uncomprehending world. Browning, as the implied author, simultaneously makes an implicit 'framing' case for the benefit of the reader, a broader but congruent argument. Both are examples of special pleading, in the service of a higher and more complex truth than meets the eye. And in both, an audience is being *tested*; the deeper drama of the poem lies in the question, will the reader be as successful as the disciples in rising to the challenge?

Browning wrote the poems of *Men and Women* with an acute awareness of his readers and their susceptibilities. He told Milsand on 24 February 1853: 'I am writing a sort of first step toward popularity (for me!) "Lyrics" with more music and painting than before, so as to get people to hear and see.' But readers and reviewers – most notably Ruskin – continued not to understand, finding the new poems 'careless' and 'reckless'.[54] Particularly provocative was Ruskin's complaint that reading the poems – bright and deep but full of clefts – was like crossing an Alpine glacier 'with ladder and hatchet'.[55] Browning replied, in now famous words: 'I don't make out my conception by my language; all poetry being a putting the infinite within the finite'; but he refuses to 'paint it all plain out'. He advises: 'You ought . . . to keep pace with the thought tripping from ledge to ledge of my "glaciers" '; 'poking your alpenstock into the holes' is suitable for *prose*, but in poetry, 'in asking for more ultimates you must accept less *mediates*'.[56] There is a dizzying irony – and an instinctive propriety – in Browning's lecturing Ruskin, since it was Ruskin himself who had earlier provided Browning with the very idiom and images for this rationale of reading and writing. For in 'Roman Renaissance', which struck Browning so forcefully, Ruskin attacked Renaissance 'system' and the 'base sciences' of method for leading people to disparage the Bible and Christ's teaching as lacking in rhetoric, logic and grammar: 'The stern truth, the profound pathos, the impatient period, leaping from point to point and leaving the intervals for the hearer to fill, the comparatively Hebraized and unelaborate idiom, had little in them of attraction for the students of phrase and syllogism' (xi.127–8).[57] Thus it is particularly sad that Ruskin failed to become one of Browning's 'few' ideal readers, since he at bottom *shared* Browning's view of poetry's leaping and tripping movement over the prose 'intervals', had in both 'The Nature of Gothic' and 'Roman Renaissance' helped Browning formulate his method in support of a higher, even religious, perception, and was moreover in the process of writing the most famous praise of a single poem that Browning received in his lifetime.

In speaking to Ruskin about 'my imaginary reader', Browning

insists that poetry has never been 'generally understood' – nor can it
be: 'A poet's affair is with God, to whom he is accountable, and of
whom is his reward: look elsewhere, and you find misery enough.'
Above all, 'It is all teaching, . . . and the people hate to be taught.'
He now seeks only 'a very few, who react upon the rest.'[58] The
contrast of the percipient few versus the unteachable many, as well
as the theme of seeking approval from God alone, suggest that 'A
Grammarian's Funeral' – whether or not Browning was half-
thinking of it at the time – may profitably be viewed as one of the
most self-reflexive poems, methodologically, of the *Men and Women*
volumes. Browning's 'elitist' dichotomy closely corresponds to the
two classes of readers detectable in the two cases made in the poem.
The world, which includes the bulk of actual Victorian readers and
reviewers, is scorned by both the disciples and Robert Browning.
Parallel to the appreciative disciples are the receptive 'very few',
individual readers who, while reading, are continually invited to
put aside 'worldly' and conventional judgement and join the select
company who participate in Browning's risky ventures. The
disciples' reading of their master is a supreme but challenging
illustration of the central Browningesque method of reading all
human situations. The drama of the poem lies in this struggle for the
'understanding' mind and heart of the reader, who is put to the test
in every encounter with the poem.

In his search for the ideal collaborative reader, what exactly could
Browning assume about the susceptibilities of his readers and what
demands did he make of them? It may help to view the issues in
three transparent 'overlays', of descending generalisation, which
comprise the complex reality of the poem. At the high ideological
level, the level of prose 'mediates'; Browning knew that the bulk of
his English readers in the 1850s shared his repugnance for the
neo-Catholic asceticism he had satirised in 'Fra Lippo Lippi', as
well as Ruskin's excessively 'medieval' rejection of Renaissance
classicism which (as I have claimed) was one of the provocations of
'A Grammarian's Funeral'. As for the opposite temptation, the new
'pagan' Hellenism represented by Matthew Arnold, Browning was
obviously at one with many of the early reviewers who, though not
unappreciative, had already assailed Arnold's sterile 'self-culture',
the hopelessness of his 'rehabilitated Hindoo–Greek theosophy',
and his deliberate positioning of himself '*ab extra* to Christianity'.[59]

Much more challenging to his readers were those issues 'in the
middle', less clearly labelled ideologically; in Browning's terms, it is

the world of unmediated ultimates, of those receptivities and inclinations that promote the fullest understanding of complex human situations. Browning requires of the reader an acquired disposition to be made to 'see through' or overthrow widely current views or received opinions – in short, an alert readiness for a certain kind of untraditional 'teaching'. 'A Grammarian's Funeral' challenged some specific, usually unquestioned, prejudices, as the well-known monologues written before *Men and Women* seem to me not to. We recoil finally from the Duke of Ferrara, with fascinated horror at his inhuman pride; but the basis of the recoil is not problematic: the poet and reader alike (Browning can safely assume) disapprove of murderous aristocrats – as well as morally defective connoisseurs like the Duke, or the Bishop who orders his tomb. But the anticipated response to 'A Grammarian's Funeral' is more complex: the average reader – indeed Browning and the ideal 'imaginary' reader too – may well have legitimate doubts about the disciples' narrow pedantry, culture-pride, contempt for ordinary people, and a curious indifference to the grotesquerie of the 'master'. The situation is instructively different in the other problematic dialogues of the period, such as 'Fra Lippo Lippi' or 'Bishop Blougram's Apology', where the speakers' personalities and personal values make us aware of their 'difference' from ourselves, but they are entrusted with some important but not essentially troublesome 'truths' to articulate. 'A Grammarian's Funeral' doubles the reader's difficulties by offering a none too appealing range of characters (speaker, fellow-disciples and grammarian), who champion a philosophy of life aggressively paradoxical and far from self-evidently true – as our continuing difficulties of interpretation show.

When Browning says he wishes to teach the reader to 'see and hear', he is promoting, and acting out before the reader, a special *method* or technique of perception, a word which nicely bridges on one side a sensory alertness, a sheer aliveness to possibility in a 'dramatic' situation, and on the other, a fullness of what he calls 'understanding'. When he further asks that the reader 'concede licenses' to him, he implies that such seeing and hearing is an act of *trust*, requiring tact and shared experience, keeping pace from ledge to ledge with the Alpine guide, and at the risk of losing one's footing. Seeing, in short, is an intensely value-making activity: seeing is believing as well as knowing.[60]

There is also a content or substance in this richly conceived phenomenology of reading that can to some extent be defined. Again, working below the high definition of Browning's much-discussed doctrine of the Incarnation, this mode of knowing has some claim to be called Browning's 'humanism', at its most balanced in the early 1850s. The best of the poems set the reader on a course of exploring moral and aesthetic complexity, in a way that Victorian Christianity – and for that matter, the more high-minded forms of Victorian free-thought – generally were unwilling to endorse. The premise is that of the difficulty of passing judgement, in deliberately chosen 'hard' cases; in this the Higher Casuistry, the only proper manner is not the judicial, but the informal, shrewdly sensory one of the 'poet' in 'How It Strikes a Contemporary': 'scenting the world', scrutinising, standing and watching, glancing, taking cognisance (but not 'staring'), taking account – in short, the 'recording chief-inquisitor' for 'our Lord the King', who is not the judge of men, but himself 'has an itch to know things, he knows why'. The method or tactic, in a surprising number of poems – and notably in 'A Grammarian's Funeral' – is to take some aspect of traditional or merely contemporary opinion, and encourage a 'delay' in coming to judgement: again, a careful balance, seen at its rare best in *Men and Women*, avoiding quick and easy resolutions on the one side, but on the other, stopping short of the deliberately maintained 'distance' worked for in later, more decisively modernist art. The counter-norm is precisely Ruskin's or Carlyle's denunciatory mode; and the contrast helps us see how far Browning, for all his decried boisterousness, consciously *avoided* the early-Victorian 'prophetic' mode, seen concurrently in even coarser form in Charles Kingsley's writings.[61] Browning's mode is a curiously 'negative' process – his own *via negativa*: gaining understanding and fresh ways of valuing through a steady resistance to premature judgement. Everyone will have a day in Browning's court, but Browning's role is less that of a judge than that of the 'scrutinising' gatherer of evidence, 'a recording chief-inquisitor', often almost a devil's advocate: final judgement can be left to another, more ultimate court of appeal.

The poems, and thus Browning himself, continually show that to read human motives and the larger meaning of lives – with Browning's care and sympathy and ironic distance and scrupulous 'delay' – is dangerous and unsettling to one's complacency. Unlike Tennyson, say, Browning regularly strives, I think (despite some still current views to the contrary) to *avoid* saying what oft was thought but ne'er so well expressed. This is not to deny that underneath his 'dark and elliptical modes of speech', and his manner 'abrupt, sketchy, allusive, and full of gaps', Browning's 'actual sentiments . . . are [usually] perfectly plain and popular and eternal sentiments'.[62] But the depth of simplicity he seeks, requires a *breaking through* the crust of conventional and careless prejudice, to seek a deeper and firmer ground, *not* by simply 'drilling' or 'digging' violently, but by a double process: half a habitual attitude of shrewd apperception and alert 'watching', half the trustful adoption of new and agile modes of mental kinesis – tripping (with light, quick steps) across a treacherous glacier, then suddenly leaping from point to point.

In 'A Grammarian's Funeral', we end more than half-approving of the grammarian's heaven-bent recklessness; but the larger point and purpose is to participate, once again, with Browning and the poem as a whole in a new kind of risky venture in the scrutinising of human choices and their significance. Hence, I suggest, the exact propriety of the monetary images that appear in the second half of the poem (lines 97–124): two attitudes about 'profit' and 'success' in life are antiphonally contrasted. The worldly man, 'greedy for quick returns of profit', makes a bad bargain in life; such fools 'discount life', and are paid by instalment (like Victorian coupon-holders). The 'low man' adds one to one, and soon hits his goal of a hundred; he 'has a world here' and gives up all claim to the next. By contrast, the grammarian is the 'high man' who seeks 'far gain': he 'ventured' everything for 'heaven's success', and 'trusted' death to reveal any profit. Aiming at a million, he inevitably falls short: he 'throws himself on God' to make up the difference in his sums, and 'unperplexed/Seeking shall find him'.

That last, as we saw, is a New Testament allusion: and the standard throughout this section is plainly biblical, although systematically (if unobtrusively) secularised. 'For what is a man profited, if he shall gain the whole world, and lose his own soul?' (Matthew 16.26). 'Lay not up for yourselves treasures upon earth, where moth and rust doth corrupt, and where thieves break through and steal: But lay up for yourselves treasures in heaven' (Matthew 6.19–20). The one 'great thing' (line 115) the grammarian ventured all on is obviously close to the 'one thing needful', the *unum necessarium* (Luke 10.42). The low man's mode is a variety of hoarding treasures on earth, an additive and short-sightedly self-protective process. The grammarian's mode is a sort of cheerfully reckless gambling of everything on a single throw of the dice. 'Was it not great?' (line 101), the eulogist breaks out: the grammarian was in fact God's great venture-capitalist of the spirit, who made a Pascalian wager, to be admired now though its outcome of course, by definition, cannot now be known. And thus the meteors, lightnings and stars of the ending are the entirely appropriate, if whimsical, way to celebrate an act of fully human choosing, in a most unprepossessing form, appreciated in a shared act of 'understanding', spreading outward from grammarian to disciples to us. This humanism of patience and delay is, again, best seen as hovering in the middle, *below* a full-fledged nineteenth-century doctrine of 'warm' sympathy and emotional identification (as in Shelley or George Eliot), and *above* the heuristic technique I have described of highly sensate seeing and hearing. Thus, though they are conceptually separate, method and substance overlap, since both are modes that encourage moral openness and a certain (paradoxical) innocent shrewdness, a trust that honest and 'humorous' scrutiny will yield justice and the unapparent truth of things.

VIII

Much of the preceding discussion implies an unusually intense form of the poet's own presence in 'A Grammarian's Funeral', but it is not easily defined. The question is that of the manner and tone appropriate to Browning's sensory method and venturesome attitude towards life. Everyone recognises the spirit of 'play' pervasive in the poem: we delight in a tone humorously alert to absurdity, and hence unpredictable and a little dangerous. The poet, 'virtually' present and at the height of his powers, displays his supreme freedom and ease in dealing with problematic materials. But despite this strongly 'performative' quality in the poem, Browning himself remains exceptionally masked and impersonal, and in the absence of clearly discernible opinions and even sympathies, much more is left up to the reader than in most other poems of the period. And Ruskin (yet again!) had recently, in *Stones* III, coined a term in which Browning may have seen himself even more clearly than in the 'rude' and 'rugged' Gothic qualities usually assigned to him. In the chapter 'Grotesque Renaissance', as we have seen, Ruskin spoke approvingly, if too briefly, of 'the true Gothic grotesque' as 'the expression of the *repose* or play of a *serious* mind', as opposed to 'the base grotesque' of the Renaissance, 'the result of the *full exertion* of a *frivolous* [mind]' (xi.170).[63] The mode is close to that of Browning's favourite, David, who defiantly justified himself for shamelessly uncovering his body and doing a supposedly demeaning dance before the Lord, who had appointed him King: 'therefore will I play before the Lord' (2 Samuel 6:20–1).

Browning's elusive but unfrivolous presence is discerned most clearly in the very rhythms and rhymes of the poem. The rocking 4–2 measure is appropriate to the movement of the disciples, but the mood of the poem as a whole is far from solemn or funereal, filled as it is with 'surplus' energy. We continually register the virtuoso self-display of the poet in the bumpy rhythms, the far-fetched diction, the half-, near- and eye-rhymes, the colloquialisms, and the 'falling' line-endings – all suitable for light or comic verse. The most conspicuous rhymes form a long list, worth highlighting: cock-crow/rock-row; sepulture/culture; moment/comment; easy/queasy; learned it/spurned it; fabric/dab brick; live/contrive; racked him/attacked him; not he/narrowly; dragon/flagon; far gain/bargain; God/period; all meant/instalment; failure/pale lure; does it/knows it; to one/million; soon hit/unit; *Oun*/down; loosened/dew send – the last pair 'infecting' even the lofty ending. (The closest parallel occurs in 'Old Pictures in Florence', but there the impudent comic rhymes are more plainly appropriate to a light subject whimsically treated, in a poem delivered in the poet's own apparent voice. The most instructive contrast is with 'Fra Lippo Lippi', where, despite the even more vehemently 'Browningite manner of delivery', the unobtrusive blank verse does not *in itself* contribute to our awareness of the performing poet in the poem.[64])

Even more offensive to current standards of literary propriety were not, in general, Browning's liberal–Christian views in themselves, abstractly put, but his willingness to 'play' with the ultimates, with a freedom and gaiety of tone, that only Clough among his contemporaries approached – and even Clough, as we saw, rejected Browning's 'reckless, de-composite manner'. Readers readily responded to the denunciatory tone of the prophet, as well as the high-poetic displays of sentiment and a very English nobility – qualities notable also in English musical tastes from Handel through Mendelssohn to Elgar. Carlyle, Ruskin, Tennyson and Arnold are thus much more 'typically Victorian' in their alternations between bitter reprehension and set pieces of pathos and conscious elevation. Indeed, the Ruskin who in December 1855 found Browning's poems a mass of 'amazing Conundrums' and unconscionable ellipses, was on the verge of defining poetry ('after some embarrassment', to be sure) as 'the suggestion, by the imagination, of noble grounds for the noble emotions' – that is, Love, Veneration, Admiration and unselfish Joy.[65]

Browning's defiantly undignified and reckless manner, then, is, more than we have calculated, an affront to the readers he claimed he was trying to attract. The poet is implicitly revealed in the startlingly large range of troubling emotions; for the apparently healthy playfulness and exuberance carry with them a more unsettling wildness, suggesting an undercurrent of aggression and menace. To baffle and tease a confused reader can imply a certain malice: the poet's alternations of the antic and the celebratory can suddenly seem inconsiderately perverse and freakish. Asked to participate in a display of fun and energy, the reader can be chilled by a sudden sense of darting mischief and a disturbing manipulation, at his own expense. (Too little has been made, I think, of something even more deeply disturbing, the implicit chaos and nihilism lurking just under the 'wild' surface of Browning's playground.) Browning treats the disciples and the grammarian with a tone of gentle mockery and conscious superiority; but it is vital to see that he stands with the disciples in their scornful rejection of the 'world' – for the world easily elides into what he called a decade later, and not lovingly, the 'British Public, ye who like me not, / (God love you!)' (*The Ring and the Book*, 1.1379–80). We sense in both poems Browning's exasperation with mid-Victorian readers and reviewers, and his resentment of conventional judgement and complacent moralism, seen as the enemies of understanding. Throughout 'A Grammarian's Funeral', the reader can feel uncomfortably unsure of his or her identity and place in the poem's dynamics: treated, more or less simultaneously, as the privileged sharer of the poet's ironies and as an obtuse member of the British Public.

Again, the most illuminating parallel is with 'Fra Lippo Lippi', a poem that ranges even more widely, between exuberance and an exceptional emotional violence. The reader feels the searing rage of Lippo, who has been told by the Prior to 'rub . . . out' his too fleshly portraits; anger is his reaction – 'Hang the fools!' – even to the praise of one of his fellow-monks, who delightedly notes (combining opportunism and moralism) that Lippo's *Martyrdom of St Lawrence* causes the 'pious people' 'to say prayers there in a rage': 'pity and religion grow i' the crowd' (lines 323–35). We sense Browning standing closely behind Lippo here, sharing his irritation with his 'betters', who 'pull a face'; and even more so, I suggest, in Lippo's outburst:

> The world and life's too big to pass for a dream,
> And I do these wild things in sheer despite,
> And play the fooleries you catch me at,
> In pure rage!
>
> (lines 251–4)

which is at once an 'apology' (to ingratiate himself with the captain of the guard) and a defiant reiteration of his bold principle of representing things 'Just as they are, careless of what comes of it' (lines 293–4). As the grammarian is to the world and its judgement, and Lippo is to his conventional viewers, so is Browning to his readers. There is, after all, more than a touch of Browning in the grammarian himself, for Browning too was bitterly conscious of having his merits under-appreciated; he too was 'loftier than the world suspects'; and he was regularly assailed as a 'crabbed', obscure word-grinder. The bitterness is that of wounded pride and unrequited love – though Browning could not of course know the completeness of his failure to win a new, wider readership until the pained and puzzled and slightly offended reviews came in late 1855, culminating in his own outburst to Ruskin in December.

Ruskin! – his name has been threaded throughout this discussion of the ways in which 'A Grammarian's Funeral' emerges as a central poem in Browning's own self-conception: a poem about poets and readers, and a guide to reading the other poems of *Men and Women*. Repeatedly, Ruskin provided both the norms and the counter-norms as Browning clarified for himself his own new ideological and creative situation. The influence, as Lawrence Poston puts it, was 'reciprocal', as they responded to some identical currents of contemporary feeling and opinion, and often from similar premises – not surprisingly, considering their similar backgrounds.[66] (What Browning had not yet detected, however, was that in specifically religious matters they were on parallel tracks but moving in opposite directions: Browning, embracing his own childhood Evangelicalism, but on a new more 'liberal' basis; Ruskin in the painful process of turning away from the biblical literalism and the

puritanism of his family.[67]) But it is, finally, a rather confused
communication – if more abundant and significant than we have
suspected – between two strongly independent creative figures,
and the influence is not fundamental on either side. Rather they
tended to stimulate and even irritate each other into self-awareness
about the nature of art and poetry.

One is tempted to say that Ruskin in effect selected himself to
serve as Browning's ideal reader, and – by Browning's standards –
failed the test. (Browning may never have been fully aware that he
had found such a reader in Dante Gabriel Rossetti, who, ironically,
was more 'unbelieving' than the reader Browning probably
envisaged – but who was, perhaps as a result, unusually receptive to
learning how to read the new poetry. Rossetti can sound as
amusingly protective and defiantly chivalrous as the disciples
defending their master, when he angrily reflects on the 'complete
torpor' of the reviewers toward *Men and Women*, which for *him* was
'this my Elixir of life'. Until the unfortunate severance of the
friendship in 1872, Browning remained 'that stunner', Rossetti's
'own Poet' and one of his 'gods'.[68]) 'A Grammarian's Funeral' and its
context reveal that the education of such a reader ('my . . . reader',
as Browning yearningly says) is the focus of Browning's intentions.
The reader today can still feel challenged, asked to differentiate
himself from the case-hardened world, in an act of self-realisation
that simultaneously brings the poem to life. Browning openly
demands of his readers a 'trust' that few, finally, have been willing
to extend. ('The grammarian uncalculatingly grants such trust to *his*
ideal 'reader', God – who, unlike the world, will interpret rightly
and reward accordingly.) It is hard to think of another poet, before
the twentieth century, who both demands and gives so much, and
yet receives so little in return – and Browning feels the poor bargain
bitterly. Sometimes Browning seems more like the disciples,
harshly decrying the world's failure to read and interpret rightly,
than the neck-or-nothing grammarian, who *unperplexed* 'stepped
on with pride/Over men's pity'. And Browning's own refusal to
compromise sufficiently to create a 'remnant' of such desired
confidants and fellow-Alpinists, by meeting them halfway, itself
remains a mystery teasing one into further speculation.

But when the poems work best, the actual reader always begins
on the margins, outside the action and 'gaping' without
understanding. Browning, performing at the centre a reckless,
deliberate David's dance, beckons the reader to act as the counter-

presence necessary to animate the dialogue that is the poem. This joint performance, indefinitely repeatable in every re-enactment of the poem, both expresses the 'truth' of things (the world 'means intensely, and means good', as Lippo insists), and discloses the 'scrutinising' nature of its own activity. The norm of the ideal reader always begins as a nearly pure potentiality, powerfully seeking embodiment in our responsive selves: the reader, Browning and God are all finally 'centred' in a shared act of understanding. Life itself becomes a process of learning to read the world as a heap of texts awaiting interpretation; in that process we ourselves become texts that are continually read.

APPENDIX I
BROWNING AND ARNOLD'S 'EMPEDOCLES ON ETNA'

No one seems to have speculated on why Browning, who had used materials in Arnold's poem for his own attack in 'Cleon' on the limitations of Greek culture, and who was increasingly a critic of modern 'pagan' classicism, should in the 1860s urge Arnold to reprint the chief document of Arnold's own early classicist point of view, one consciously detached from Christianity. First of all, quite apart from issues of doctrine, Browning genuinely admired the poetic merits of the drama, as his prolonged savouring of the Cadmus and Harmonia section shows. (Moreover, Arnold's achievement of a 'calm' detached point of view, at least in the Callicles sections, held out to Browning an ideal not given sufficient play in his own poetics and personality – even if, as we saw, he could not know that *he* was in Arnold's mind a prime counter-example!)

More substantively, Crawford ('Browning's *Cleon*', see n. 40) helps to soften the apparent anomaly when he describes 'Cleon' as less a criticism than 'a companion picture and a supplement' to Arnold's poem (p. 487). 'Empedocles' was, most importantly, Arnold's honest facing up to a process of degeneration endemic to classical civilisation. Browning was able to imagine an even later stage of the process, and add a polemical, if implicit, comparison with Christian 'progress' and happiness. This, Browning implies, is what Hellenism – ancient and modern – *at its best* amounted to, and to this extent Arnold had 'made Browning's point' for him. (And in a more obscure but important sense, perhaps, Browning felt he had a stake in keeping Arnold's early and most alienated classicism before the public mind.)

In the Preface of 1853 Arnold had deplored the loss of 'the calm, the cheerfulness, the distinterested objectivity' of 'early Greek genius' (*CPW*, I.1), and this remained one essential note of his own rapidly evolving poetic ideal. Indeed, in a highly constrained way, the Preface itself, with its emphasis on action and objectivity of treatment, is a programme for attaining calm and detachment – though not exactly cheerfulness. The tamer sort of modern classicising 'culture' extolled in the Preface culminates in the more cheerful Hellenism developed in *Culture and Anarchy* in the late 1860s, though this too seemed premature and complacent to Arnold by 1869, as he turned directly to religious topics. Browning's later skittish attitudes toward the modern culture-ideal are focused on this very public and benignly Hellenic phase of Arnold's career (see Appendix II).

But I believe that – as the converging evidence shows – Arnold's more troubled Hellenism in his early poetry and in the 1853 Preface was more central than we have thought for Browning as he entered on his more openly Christian phase, and that it remained a kind of touchstone of elevated modern paganism to 'play off against'. What Browning almost certainly did *not* perceive was that Arnold in the early 1850s was already having a costly dialogue with the various phases of his own highly 'Germanised' and Goethean classical ideals. The *drift* of Arnold's career, in short, though his movement was far slower and his destination ultimately less traditional and unqualified, was not wholly unlike Browning's own. (On Goethe's role in Arnold's early career, see my 'Arnold and Goethe: the One on the Intellectual Throne', in *Victorian Literature and Society: Essays Presented to Richard D. Altick*, ed. James R. Kincaid and Albert J. Kuhn (Columbus: Ohio State University Press, 1984) 197–224.)

APPENDIX II
BROWNING AND CULTURE

A close scrutiny of Browning's uses of the word 'culture' would reveal a running thread of irony and doubt of the sort we saw emerging in 'A Grammarian's Funeral' and 'Cleon'. It is surprisingly seldom used in the favourable or even the neutral sense common from, say, the 1860s on. The term became the centre of public debate in the 1860s and 1870s – first in Matthew Arnold's writings, and even more intensely, after 1873, in those of Walter Pater – when critics often attacked its allegedly self-referential, impractical or irreligious character. Arnold's polemical use of the term first reaches high visibility in *The Study of Celtic Literature* (in instalments, March–July 1866; in book form, June 1867), and, above all, in *Culture and Anarchy* (instalments, July 1867–August 1868). Browning, then in fairly regular touch with Arnold, would have taken the closest note of the debate. The word begins to appear with some regularity in Browning's poetry only in the last four books of *The Ring and the Book*, most of which – according to DeVane's figures (*Handbook*, pp. 319, 324) – was written between April 1867 and October 1868. The causal connection seems evident.

In *Luria* (1846), II.220, in one of the first 'absolute' uses in England, 'new culture' and 'cultivated life' somehow refine the 'instincts' – and I detect no disquieting overtones. But in *The Ring and the Book* (IX.351), we hear that Caponsacchi is 'of culture', meaning well-bred (as Altick in the Penguin Edition reads it), which in the legal situation has a slightly disdainful tone. (The Pope uses 'Diligent culture' (x.431) in a similar sense, regarding Guido's upbringing, but with an apparent touch of irony – considering Guido's character.) A more ambitious, almost 'Arnoldian', sense emerges, for a moment only, when the Pope (x.2014–29) revolves the more expedient 'reasons to forgive' Guido. He is clearly ironic and disturbed when he prophesies, 'the spirit of culture speaks, / Civilization is imperative', as he is in giving a mock-welcome to a new Virgilian golden age: 'Civilization and the Emperor / Succeed thus Christianity and Pope'. This reading has been recently supported by the penetrating analysis of C. Stephen Finley, in 'Robert Browning's "The Other Half-Rome": a "Fancy-Fit" or Not?', *Browning Institute Studies*, 11 (1983) 127–48: 'With his [the Other Half-Rome's] refined and aesthetic sense, his worldliness, his moving easily between pagan and Christian mythology, he represents the very "spirit of culture" that the Pope spurns, a culture that is no longer interested in the "old heroism" of Christian piety and salvation.' And see p. 145 on his being no Christian, but a man of the 'next age', 'a master of all mythologies but an adherent of none'.

Thereafter, 'culture' is regularly and pointedly treated as superficial, as in *Parleyings* (1887), 'With Christopher Smart', lines

19–20, where 'decent taste' and 'Adequate culture' are linked – or, even more conspicuously, in *Fifine at the Fair* (1871), lines 292–3, where 'sheer strength' is amusedly set off against 'ineffectual grace, / Breeding and culture'. But two passages, in particular, more clearly reveal Browning's doubts about the contemporary ideal of a self-sufficient 'culture', as well as his appeal to a standard *above* individualistic self-cultivation. In *Prince Hohenstiel-Schwangau* (1871), lines 948–55, although originally 'man is made in sympathy with man', they end 'in dissociation, more and more / Man from his fellow, as their lives advance/In culture'. Humanity, 'fining' (i.e. refining) itself, 'ends in isolation, each from each'. Self-centred 'culture' as the breaker of the social bond is equally the target in *The Inn Album* (1875): 'safety' is the motivation for 'culture' (almost equivalent to 'Civilization' here, as in *The Ring and the Book*), but such 'progress means/What but abandonment of fellowship?' (lines 1709–13). In his context, Browning was in effect declaring his doubts about Arnold's insistence, in *Culture and Anarchy*, that social and moral motives *should* propel the culture-enterprise; indeed, Arnold's own turning, immediately afterwards, to the religious question, in effect acknowledged the deficiencies of 'culture' in this wider sphere.

The epithet 'cultured' was for Browning – as it has remained into our own time – somewhat embarrassing, and he tends to treat it with a lightly derisive tone: for example, the humorous use of 'cultured triumph' in *Inn Album*, lines 62–4; or the irreverent use of 'the cultured class' in *Jocaseria* (1883), line 700. More pointed disparagement occurs in 'Filippo Baldinucci' (1876), lines 390–2: 'cultured taste/Has Beauty for its only care,/And upon Truth no thought to waste'. The ironic point is even sharper in *Parleyings*, 'With Francis Furini', lines 251–2, where the painter is invited to 'preach', in 'actual London', to 'us the cultured, therefore skeptical'.

APPENDIX III
CLEON VERSUS EMPEDOCLES

The drift of 'Cleon', not one of Browning's 'problem' poems, has never been in doubt; and Browning, the 'simple-hearted casuist', clearly has designs upon us. But so full is the imaginary portrait of Cleon, and so generous is Browning in granting him real insight and real achievement, that while reading we tend to overlook the degree to which a pagan philosopher exhibits an improbably full insight into the 'natural' tendency of humanity toward a Christian – indeed, a Browningesque – vision of reality. The contrast with Arnold's 'Empedocles on Etna' helps measure just how thoroughly Browning has reduced and distanced Cleon. William Irvine, in 'Four Monologues in Browning's *Men and Women'*, *Victorian Poetry*, 2 (1964) 163, notes that 'Cleon lacks the inwardness of Arnold's Empedocles': both portraits are dark-hued, 'but whereas Empedocles longed for true virtue, happiness, and the consolation of Deity, Cleon seems to want chiefly perpetual youth and pleasure' – and his sensuality is entirely absent in Arnold's austerely intellectual figure.

Cleon in his intellectual pride – evident in his contempt for the 'vulgar' and his self-satisfaction: 'I, Cleon, have effected all those things' (line 45) – is plainly more chilling than Empedocles in his anguished assertion, 'I have not grown easy in these bonds': 'I have loved no darkness, / Sophisticated no truth, / Nursed no delusions, / Allowed no fear!' (ii.397–403). Roma King, Jr well observes ('Browning: "Mage" and "Maker" – A Study in Poetic Purpose and Method', *Victorian Newsletter*, 20 (1961) 22–5; cited here from *Robert Browning: A Collection of Critical Essays*, ed. Philip Drew (Boston, Mass.: Houghton Mifflin, 1966) 189–98) that 'Cleon undergoes no change, experiences no deepening insights which lead to purgative action', and that when in the finale he is confronted with a new challenge, 'he displays a proud, querulous, and provincial, if not petty, outlook' – failing to detect the 'ironic similarity' between the new religion and 'his own intuitive longings'. For these very reasons, I think King overstates the parallel with Arnold's later treatment of Marcus Aurelius (1863), who, though also presented as a figure of pointedly limited vision, is more elevated spiritually and evokes a greater pity. (Without referring to Irvine or King, Antony H. Harrison and Samia Dodin, 'Cleon's Joy-Hunger and the Empedoclean Context', *Studies in Browning and His Circle*, 9.2 (1981) 57–68, further simplify Cleon by an approach even harsher and less nuanced than Browning's: 'Cleon must be seen finally as an epicurean philosopher, a hedonist and aesthete who is concerned not with the development and fulfillment of the soul as it is normally [*sic*] conceived but with the perpetuity of the body and the expansion of every sensory pleasure man is able to enjoy': p. 58).

Browning's systematic 'reductions' in content, regarding two so apparently similar figures, also help to account for 'modal' changes, and the ways in which we are compelled to differentiate kinds of reading and degrees of identification. I use the terms developed by Ralph Rader (see n. 51). The monologue In Act ɪɪ of 'Empedocles' can best be read as a 'mask lyric', in which – as in Tennyson's 'Ulysses' or Eliot's 'Prufrock' – the speaker is 'an artificial person projected from the poet', expressing 'an emotion inwardly real' to the poet. The figure and the situation are more symbolic than real, and 'the reader, not a dramatic auditor', is addressed. Above all, we feel that 'the character's predicament is in essence our own' – an attitude enforcing a sense of similarity and identity. All of this fits the impatient but perceptive remark of an Oxford friend of Arnold's, who said, while the poem was being written: Empedocles' 'name and outward circumstances are used for the drapery of [Arnold's] own thoughts' (J. C. Shairp to Clough, 24 July 1849, in *The Correspondence of Arthur Hugh Clough*, ed. Frederick L. Mulhauser (Oxford: Clarendon Press, 1957) ɪ.270). Cleon, a speaker in a true dramatic monologue, is, in contrast, 'a simulated natural person in contrast with the poet', who addresses a specific auditor and who creates around himself a highly specific context, 'natural but not actual'. Moreover, a steady succession of unsettling details and attitudes forces the reader into a position of superior judgement, and keep Cleon at a variable but detectable distance from our full sympathy. His *dilemma* is indeed universal, as presented by Browning, and thus potentially the subject of a mask lyric: but attitude is all, and despite his brilliant gifts, his insight, and his personal suffering, every word that falls from his lips is to a significant extent invalidated by his chilling pride – the pride of culture.

I would add to Rader's distinctions a more controversial and even mysterious point, perhaps *implicit* in his argument. It follows from Rader's premises that we are forced to read 'Empedocles' sympathetically, and from the 'inside', *whatever* our judgement of Arnold's views. Conversely, we are compelled to see Cleon as detached from ourselves, with a strong and critical awareness of his deficiencies and of his falling short of an implied standard, even if the reader's views are not close to Browning's own. In this sense, the reader's prejudices and ideological biases are 'deferred' or bracketed in the mask lyric and belief suspended or put 'out of play'; whereas in the dramatic monologue we are, even when attentive and sympathetic, continuously aware of the difference of the speaker from ourselves – whatever our personal beliefs. (Herbert F. Tucker, in *Browning's Beginnings: The Art of Disclosure* (Minneapolis: University of Minnesota Press, 1980), stimulatingly treats Browning's art of 'disclosure' – that is, his resistance to premature closure and resolution. This ironic mode of 'deferment', which is the analogue of Browning's moral doctrine of incompleteness, would throw light on 'A Grammarian's Funeral', a poem Tucker does not treat at length.)

In 'A Grammarian's Funeral' we have – as a partial explanation of our difficulties in interpretation – two intertwined modes. The chorus-leader, speaking for himself and the other disciples, naïvely and yet fundamentally on the side of the angels, is kept at some emotional distance from the reader, by his unpleasant and not fully conscious 'give-aways'; whereas the grammarian, when quoted or being spoken about by the disciples, though physically repellent, is largely protected from such distancing overtones, and to that extent, though plainly not a mask for Browning, he participates in a mixed mode close to that of the mask lyric.

Notes

1. James Joyce, about *Ulysses*, to his translator, Jacques Benoît-Méchin, in Richard Ellmann, *James Joyce* (New York: Oxford University Press, 1959) p. 535. My thanks to Vicki Mahaffey for the identification.
2. William Stigand, in *Edinburgh Review*, Oct. 1864; cited here from *Browning: The Critical Heritage*, ed. Boyd Litzinger and Donald Smalley (London: Routledge & Kegan Paul, 1970) p. 252.
3. George Monteiro, 'A Proposal for Settling the Grammarian's Estate', *Victorian Poetry*, 3 (1965) 266–70, cites a letter of William James, in one of his hearty but still discriminating moods, of Jan. 1868: 'It always strengthens my backbone to read [the poem]' – a 'gallant' feeling, 'fit to be trusted if one-sided activity is in itself at all respectable'.
4. Richard D. Altick, ' "A Grammarian's Funeral": Browning's Praise of Folly?', *Studies in English Literature*, 3 (1963) 449–60; cited from *Robert Browning: A Collection of Critical Essays*, ed. Philip Drew (Boston, Mass.: Houghton Mifflin, 1966) pp. 199–211. Robert L. Kelly, 'Dactyls and Curlews: Satire in "A Grammarian's Funeral" ', *Victorian Poetry*, 5 (1967) 105–12, ingeniously, and I think exaggeratedly, argues – on the basis of diction, imagery and verse form – that the poem is satire, a 'deflation', especially directed at the self-deluding and 'vulgar' students. But he too, somewhat like Altick, sees the grammarian as the object of Browning's compassion and pity.

5. Martin J. Svaglic, 'Browning's Grammarian: Apparent Failure or Real?', *Victorian Poetry*, 5 (1967) 93–104.

6. James F. Loucks, 'Browning's Grammarian and "Herr Bultmann" ', *Studies in Browning and His Circle*, 2 (1974) 79–83, well if briefly recommends leaving 'ample room for ambivalence, on Browning's part': 'If there is any measure of identity between Browning and his scholar, it must have been painful as well as prideful on Browning's part.' Monteiro, *Victorian Poetry*, 3 (1965) 266–70, had even earlier argued, though briefly, that while the reader's judgement of the grammarian remains positive, the disciples' words are 'rife with ambivalence of tone and assessment'.

7. Ian Jack, *Browning's Major Poetry* (Oxford: Clarendon Press, 1973) p. 175, finds the movement of the poem 'celebratory and triumphant'. But his reading, and that of Mary W. Schnieder, 'Browning's Grammarian', *Studies in Browning and His Circle*, 6 (1978) 57–65, would have been stronger if they had tried to negotiate the 'negative' elements as well. The difficulties of seeing the poem as a whole are dramatically evident in S. M. Adamson, 'Seven Footnotes on "A Grammarian's Funeral" ', *Browning Society Notes*, 9 (1979) 6–8, which attempts in the last two 'footnotes' to reverse, by an unclear logic, the 'negative' evidence compiled in the first five. But one of those last two notes does adduce an illuminating passage, stanza 56 of *Fifine at the Fair* (1872), in defence of the 'forerunner' scholar.

8. See David J. DeLaura, 'Ruskin and the Brownings: Twenty-Five Unpublished Letters', *Bulletin of the John Rylands Library*, 54 (1972) 314–56, esp. 315–17.

9. *John Ruskin, Works*, ed. E. T. Cook and A. Wedderburn (London: George Allen, 1903–12) x.243. Hereafter cited by volume and page alone.

10. *The Letters of Elizabeth Barrett Browning*, ed. Frederick G. Kenyon, 2 vols (New York: Macmillan, 1897) ii.151. Hereafter cited as *LEBB*.

11. William Clyde DeVane, *A Browning Handbook*, 2nd edition (New York: Appleton, 1955) p. 270. DeVane also says (p. 271) 'we know the Brownings were reading [*Stones* ii and iii] in the early summer of 1854'. But the evidence he offers, Elizabeth's letter of 6 June 1854, does not in fact support this interpretation. Elizabeth thanks Miss Mitford for 'giving me that pleasure of Mr Ruskin's kind word at the expense of what I know to be so much pain to yourself': 'the words you sent me from Mr Ruskin gave me great pleasure indeed, as how should they not from such a man. . . . His "Seven Lamps" I have not read yet. Books come out slowly to Italy.' *The Letters of Elizabeth Barrett Browning to Mary Russell Mitford*, ed. Meredith B. Raymond and Mary Rose Sullivan, 3 vols (Waco, Tex.: Armstrong Browning Library of Baylor University, 1983) iii.411–14. Raymond and Sullivan note that the reference is to Ruskin's letter to Miss Mitford of 22–23 April 1854. See *The Friendships of Mary Russell Mitford as Recorded in Letters to Her Literary Correspondents*, ed. A. G. L'Estrange (New York: Harper, 1882) p. 318: Ruskin speaks, after reading a number of her poems 'for the first time. I only knew her mystical things . . . before':

'I have not had my eyes so often wet for these five years. I had no
conception of her poems before. I can't tell you how wonderful I
think them.' Elizabeth's arch recollection, as late as 17 March 1855, of
'a word dropped by you in one of your books, which I picked up and
wore for a crown' (*LEBB*, II.191), may indeed refer to *Stones* II, or to
Stones I (1851), where Ruskin had spoken of the 'spirituality of
Elizabeth Barrett' (IX.228).

12. All citations from Browning's poetry (except for *The Ring and the Book*)
    and his Shelley essay are from Robert Browning, *The Poems* (Penguin
    English Poets), ed. John Pettigrew and Thomas J. Collins, 2 vols
    (Harmondsworth, Middx.: Penguin Books, 1981). *The Ring and the
    Book* is also cited in the Penguin Edition, ed. Richard D. Altick
    (Harmondsworth, Middx.: Penguin Books, 1971).

13. Curtis Dahl, 'Browning, Architecture, and John Ruskin', *Studies in
    Browning and His Circle*, 6 (1978) 45. This reading of Browning's
    words is given in William S. Peterson, 'The Proofs of Browning's
    Men and Women', *Studies in Browning and His Circle*, 3 (1975) 25.

14. Lawrence Poston, III, 'Ruskin and Browning's Artists', *English
    Miscellany*, 15 (1964) 199.

15. See two articles by David J. DeLaura: 'A Background for Arnold's
    "Shakespeare" ', in *Nineteenth-Century Literary Perspectives*, ed. C. de
    L. Ryals (Durham, N.C.: Duke University Press, 1974) pp. 129–48;
    'Heroic Egotism: Goethe and the Fortunes of *Bildung* in Victorian
    England', in *Johann Wolfgang von Goethe: One Hundred and Fifty Years
    of Continuing Vitality*, ed. Ulrich Goebel and Wolodymyr T. Zyla
    (Lubbock, Tex.: Texas Tech Press, 1984) pp. 41–60.

16. Svaglic ('Browning's Grammarian', p. 99), who like DeVane squints
    a little on the Ruskin influence, also usefully suggests in the
    background Carlyle's 'doctrine of work' in *Sartor Resartus* – and, he
    might have added, the chapter 'Labour' in *Past and Present*.

17. DeVane, *Handbook*, 271; but as we shall see, he misses the larger
    context when he says, 'it fits a little strangely into ["A Grammarian's
    Funeral"] which obviously has as its inspiration the early
    Renaissance'.

18. The best treatment of the Shelley essay, and of its place in
    Browning's career, occurs in ch. 5 of Thomas J. Collins, *Robert
    Browning's Moral–Aesthetic Theory, 1833–1855* (Lincoln, Nebr.:
    University of Nebraska Press, 1967).

19. The episode, and both letters, are in DeLaura, 'Ruskin and the
    Brownings', pp. 322–7.

20. DeLaura, 'Ruskin and the Brownings', p. 329.

21. W. G. Collingwood, *The Life and Work of John Ruskin*, 2 vols (Boston,
    Mass.: Houghton Mifflin, 1893) I.234.

22. See David J. DeLaura, 'The Context of Browning's Painter Poems:
    Aesthetics, Polemics, Historics', *PMLA*, 95 (1980) 367–88.

23. The latter appears in Appendix 12. And there also (IX.36–40), Ruskin
    fiercely denies – though Rio's historical argument and the physical
    evidence scarcely sanction it – 'the incompatibility of Protestan-
    tism and art'. The growth of Ruskin's doubts is well described in

Richard Dellamora, 'The Revaluation of "Christian" Art: Ruskin's Appreciation of Fra Angelico, 1848–60', *University of Toronto Quarterly*, 43 (1974) 143–50.

24. DeVane, *Handbook*, p. 251. But after giving this date, DeVane perpetuates the confusions regarding Ruskin's influence by saying that the poem treats the philosophy of the imperfect, 'which John Ruskin had made famous in his chapter *On the Nature of Gothic*' – though it was not published until July, and not seen by the Brownings, it seems, until much later. DeVane illuminates Browning's essentially un-doctrinaire approach to these issues when (though still speaking with uncertain chronology) he groups all three of the painter poems of early 1853 as illustrative of the doctrine of the imperfect (p. 271): the poems effectively confound contemporary divisions of 'medieval' and 'Renaissance'.

25. See Robert A. Greenberg, 'Ruskin, Pugin, and the Contemporary Context of "The Bishop Orders His Tomb" ', *PMLA*, 84 (1969) 1588–94. See also sections v and x of 'The Flight of the Duchess' (1845); and I have added 'Pictor Ignotus' ('Browning's Painter Poems', pp. 371–3).

26. See DeLaura, 'Browning's Painter Poems', pp. 373–4.

27. The mirror image of Ruskin's Evangelical rejection of Renaissance verbalism was the powerful 'utilitarian' attack on Oxbridge classical studies. The most famous skirmishes were between writers in the *Edinburgh Review* and their Oxford opponents, in the years *c.* 1810; those passages at arms had just been vividly recalled by John Henry Newman, in *Discourses on the Scope and Nature of University Education* (1852). See Newman's *Idea of a University*, ed. I. T. Ker, Oxford English Texts (Oxford: Clarendon Press, 1970) pp. 136–9 and notes. An even more radical version of the charges is J. S. Mill's expression of disgust in 1834 at the universities' emphasising 'the mere niceties of language *first*'. *Essays on Philosophy and the Classics*, ed. John M. Robson and Jack Stillinger, in *Collected Works of John Stuart Mill* (Toronto, Ont.: University of Toronto Press, 1981) xi.39. On the Millite attack on 'the arid and usually fruitless studies of style, syntax, and language', see W. H. Burstin, *James Mill on Philosophy and Education* (London: Athlone Press, 1973) p. 79.

28. 'Let me know all!' inevitably suggests, I think, the equally fierce but more pessimistic and morally ambiguous yearning of Tennyson's Ulysses, 'To follow knowledge like a sinking star, / Beyond the utmost bound of human thought' (lines 31–2): *The Poems of Tennyson*, ed. Christopher Ricks (London: Longman, 1969) p. 564.

29. Without referring the notion to Ruskin, DeVane (*Handbook*, p. 272) speaks of Browning's use of 'the grotesque in the service of grandeur'. Walter Bagehot's 1864 essay, 'Wordsworth, Tennyson, and Browning; or, Pure, Ornate, and Grotesque Art in English Poetry', permanently linked Browning with the 'grotesque', though in a somewhat specialised (and elusive) sense: Walter Bagehot, *Collected Works*, ed. Norman St John-Stevas (London: Economist, 1965–78) ii.321–66.

30. Recent general studies, eager to repel a 'subversive' reading like Altick's, tend to neglect Browning's consciousness of having a difficult 'case' to make, an argument heavily laced with irony and humour as well as his mischievous handling of readers' expectations. C. C. Clarke, in 'Humor and Wit in "Childe Roland" ', *Modern Language Quarterly*, 23 (1962) 323–36, pausing to consider 'A Grammarian's Funeral' (pp. 324–5), is one of the few to catch the 'odd mixture of buffoonery and earnestness in the poem', one that forbids 'a conventional distinction between the ludicrous and the sublime'. But he also judges, too harshly, I think, that the poem has 'serious faults of tone', 'uncertain control' and (most puzzlingly) a lack of 'detachment'. Leonard Burrows, *Browning the Poet: An Introductory Study* (Nedlands, W.A.: University of Western Australia Press, 1969) pp. 120–30, is unusually alive to the 'ironies' in the treatment of both the grammarian and his disciples, but only briefly suggests the 'complex view' of the reader, torn between admiration and disquiet. Martin B. Crowell, *A Reader's Guide to Robert Browning* (Albuquerque, N.M.: University of New Mexico Press, 1972) pp. 194–206, valuably sees the poem as an example of Browning's 'case making' (p. 201). He is correct in seeing Browning's comparative detachment in this poem, but he seeks to resolve the discords by going to a new extreme, arguing in effect that Browning leaves the reader unable to make judgements.

31. It has been hard for post-Freudians not to see the implications of this last phrase as sexual – and hence particularly sardonic. But Browning's letter to Tennyson of 2 July 1863 suggests that for him, at least consciously, the reference is an innocent, indeed commendatory, reference to the grammarian's physical debility: 'There are tritons among minnows even, – and so I wanted the grammarian "dead from the waist down" – (or "feeling middling", as you said last night) – to spend his last breath on the biggest of the littlenesses: such an one is the "enclitic δε". . . .': Christopher Ricks, 'Two Letters by Browning', *Times Literary Supplement* (London), 3 June 1965, p. 464.

32. Loucks ('Browning's Grammarian', p. 82) is one of the few to single out 'the apparently overweening pride of the disciples', but he correctly rejects the temptation of reading the poem as simply satire or caricature.

33. *Thomas Carlyle, Works*, ed. H. D. Traill, Centenary Edition (London: Chapman, 1896–9) xxvi.19. This is a prophetic and benign usage, familiar later in J. S. Mill and Matthew Arnold, which the *Oxford English Dictionary* defines as not only the 'training, development, and refinement of mind, taste, and manners', but 'the intellectual side of civilization' itself.

34. The pre-1850 history of 'culture' I here summarise from my 'Heroic Egotism' (n. 15) 42–7.

35. Ralph Waldo Emerson, *Representative Men, Works*, ed. Edward Waldo Emerson, Concord Edition (Boston, Mass.: Houghton Mifflin, 1903) iv.284.

36. Carlyle, *Works*, xi.174. Browning had read *Representative Men* by Feb. 1851: see C. E. Tanzy, 'Browning, Emerson, and Bishop Blougram', *Victorian Studies*, 1 (1958) 255–66. And the publication of *Sterling*, late in the summer of 1851, coincided with the beginning of the period of the Brownings' most intimate personal relations with Carlyle: see Charles Richard Sanders, 'The Carlyle–Browning Correspondence and Relationship', *Bulletin of the John Rylands Library*, 57 (1974–75) 243–6, 430–6.

37. Matthew Arnold, *Complete Prose Works*, ed. R. H. Super (Ann Arbor, Mich.: University of Michigan Press, 1960–77) i.14. Hereafter cited as *CPW*. From 1857 on, 'widest culture' is applied to Niebuhr alone. Wordsworth's use in *The Prelude*, xiii.197–8 is prophetic, but lacks the philosophical and ethical burdens of '1850' and beyond.

38. *CPW*, i.1. Browning's intense involvement with 'Empedocles' is clear in Arnold's note in the 1867 *New Poems*, which restored the entire poem 'at the request of a man of genius . . . Mr Robert Browning'. *The Poems of Matthew Arnold*, 2nd edition, ed. Kenneth and Miriam Allott (London: Longman, 1979) p. 156. Arnold's fairly close personal friendship with Browning dates from the early 1860s: John Drinkwater, 'Some Letters from Matthew Arnold to Browning', *Cornhill Magazine*, Dec. 1923, pp. 654–64, and Browning's suggestion came no doubt during these years. Browning was touchingly flattered by Arnold's remark: see *Dearest Isa: Robert Browning's Letters to Isabella Blagden*, ed. Edward C. McAleer (Austin, Tex.: University of Texas Press, 1951) pp. 274, 278. Their 'affectionate intimacy', as Drinkwater calls it, continued until Arnold's death; but I also detect, clearly but with less direct evidence, that Browning felt slightly *intimidated* by the younger man's much cooler personality.

39. For Arnold's very gradual changes of front, see my 'Arnold and Literary Criticism', in *Matthew Arnold*, Writers and Their Background, ed. Kenneth Allott (London: G. Bell, 1976) pp. 118–48. How deeply the Preface of 1853 struck Browning is evident in the Preface to his 1877 translation of *The Agamemnon of Aeschylus*, which cites the Preface at length on the importance of *action* and on the Greek mastery of the 'simple and . . . subordinated' *grand style*. See *The Complete Poetic and Dramatic Works of Robert Browning*, Cambridge Edition (Boston, Mass.: Houghton Mifflin, 1895) p. 830; and *CPW*, i.5–6. Browning may well in 1853 have been impressed precisely by the degree to which Arnold's 'statuesque' ideal ran directly counter to his own exuberant, even reckless, experiments in style and voice during this *Men and Women* period. In fact, though Browning could not know it, he himself was already one of Arnold's prime negative examples, 'a man with a moderate gift passionately desiring movement and fulness, and obtaining but a confused multitudinousness'. And in May 1853, while storing up anti-spasmodic ideas for the Preface itself, Arnold judged that Browning's poetry 'loses itself' (see *The Letters of Matthew Arnold to Arthur Hugh Clough*, ed. Howard Foster Lowry (London: Oxford University Press, 1932) pp. 97, 136). Somewhat more favourably, Arnold told his

mother in 1869 that his own poetry had fused Tennyson's 'poetical sentiment' with Browning's 'intellectual vigour and abundance' (see *Letters of Matthew Arnold, 1848–1888*, ed. George W. E. Russell, 2 vols in one (New York: Macmillan, 1900)).

40. A. W. Crawford, 'Browning's *Cleon*', *Journal of English and Germanic Philology* 26 (1927) 488. Crawford further notes (p. 489) that in 'Old Pictures in Florence' (probably written in the spring of 1853), Browning also contrasted the Greek view of man's finitude with the Christian view of 'man as spiritual and infinite'. We now know that the Brownings were reading Arnold and Clough closely from the late 1840s on, even if not with entire approval. See *Letters of E. B. Browning to M. R. Mitford*, p. 286. As further evidence of the strong impression made by 'Empedocles', there runs, as a sort of flirtatious leitmotif throughout Browning's correspondence with Isa Blagden, from 1862 to 1871, a long series of allusions to 'the bright and aged snakes', in retirement, from the Cadmus and Harmonia section (i.ii.427–60). See *Dearest Isa*, Index, sub Matthew Arnold. But it is worth noting that the Cadmus and Harmonia passage was one of those actually reprinted in the 1853 *Poems*. On Browning's motives for urging Arnold to reprint the poem, see Appendix i.

41. William C. DeVane, 'Browning and the Spirit of Greece', *Nineteenth-Century Studies*, ed. Herbert Davis (Ithaca, N.Y.: Cornell University Press, 1940) pp. 179–98.

42. DeVane, 'Browning and the Spirit of Greece', usefully cites Christ's attack on the 'ancient sages' in *Paradise Regained*, e.g. iv.309–12. A number of these major themes of Browning's career first receive important definition in *Christmas-Eve and Easter-Day* (1850) – notably, besides the general endorsement of an Evangelical point of view, the philosophy of the imperfect: 'Making the finite comprehend/ Infinity' (*Easter-Day*, xxviii). More specifically, Browning develops the theme central to 'Old Pictures', 'Cleon' and (more obliquely) 'A Grammarian's Funeral', of the interplay of 'antique sovereign Intellect' and Christian Love, which 'Bade her scribes abhor the trick /Of [Greek and Roman] poetry and rhetoric' (*Christmas-Eve*, xi). He rather scoffs at modern classical scholarship, which, no longer content with its harmless quarrels over 'Our theory of the Middle Verb', 'anapaests in comic-trimeter' and the fragments of Aeschylus, now in a hateful spirit turns its methods on the sacred texts (xviii). Moreover, the none too respectful portrait of the Göttingen Professor, with his 'cranium's over-freight,/Three parts sublime to one grotesque' – his hawk nose, his spitting, his 'wan pure look' and his cough – looks like a first sketch for the Renaissance grammarian. In both cases, though with different tones, we see the humour of the man of bounding vitality looking with pity and some sympathy at the 'sallow virgin-minded studies/Martyr to mild enthusiasm' (*Christmas-Eve*, xiv) – or perhaps *ferocious* enthusiasm in the later case.

43. John Coates, 'Two Versions of the Modern Intellectual: "Empedocles on Etna" and "Cleon",' *Modern Language Review*, 79 (1984) 769–82,

has measurably advanced our understanding of the differences separating Arnold and Browning. He suggestively presents Callicles' songs as 'progressive sketches of man's developing consciousness' (p. 775), and – more to the present purpose – he complicates our understanding of Cleon by establishing the ways in which Browning modifies Cleon's 'arrogance and unpleasantness' by his 'wry, affecting, and subtle' treatment of the demeaning situation of the modern intellectual (p. 782). Equally interesting, but more suppositious, is Jane A. McCuskers's argument, in 'Browning's "Aristophanes' Apology" and Matthew Arnold', *Modern Language Review*, 79 (1984) 783–96, that 'Aristophanes' Apology' (1875) is Browning's disagreement with Arnold (Aristophanes in the poem) over the need for development in poetry, and the relationship of ideal poetic form to current reality. Her approach in effect extends to 'Aristophanes' Apology' the points established by DeVane regarding Arnold's central role in 'The Parleying with Gerard de Lairesse' (*Parleyings*, 1887), in his *Browning's Parleyings: The Autobiography of a Mind* (1927; repr. New York: Russell, 1964) ch. 6, esp. pp. 235–8.

44. Sections 46–84 of 'Roman Renaissance' (xi.81–114) treat the tombs of the fifteenth century – 'sepulchral monuments', 'sepulchral architecture' and 'statues' – as so many examples of Venetian 'Pride of State'.

45. Altick, in collecting evidence of 'removal from common life', is virtually alone in noting (if only in passing) not only the parallel with 'Cleon' but the significance of 'culture': '"Culture" may be interpreted as "artificial, decadent, sophisticated life" – the sort of civilization Browning disparaged through the complacent figure of Cleon' (p. 201). But this is, I think, plainly too pejorative a range of meaning to fit 'A Grammarian's Funeral', where the issues are kept admirably in suspension. The tone of Emerson's and Carlyle's then recent uses, given above, does approach this non-lexical 'puritan' sense.

46. Young C. Lee, 'The Human Condition: Browning's "Cleon" ', *Victorian Poetry*, 7 (1969) 61.

47. In Goethe's well-known letter to Lavater of 1780; cited here from G. H. Lewes, *The Life of Goethe*, 2nd edition (London: Smith, Elder, 1864) p. 260. For the widespread debate about Geothe's 'self-culture' from the 1820s on, see my 'Heroic Egotism' (n. 15). One is tempted to detect in Cleon Browning's acknowledgement of the widely held view of Goethe as the supremely 'many-sided' but problematic man.

48. 'Culture' here (line 131) is literally drawn from the cultivation of plants; it is used associatively to mean the comparatively untroublesome cultivation of the higher elements of 'natural life' (line 233). See Appendix ii for Browning's later uses of the term 'culture', most of them revealingly defensive and uncomfortable.

49. The topicality of Ruskin's 'ultra-Tory' views on economics, politics and religion, in *Stones* ii and iii, is illuminatingly explored by Robert Hewison, 'Notes on the Construction of *The Stones of Venice*', in *Studies in Ruskin: Essays in Honor of Van Akin Burd*, ed. Robert Rhodes and Del Ivan Janik (Athens, Ohio: Ohio University Press, 1982) pp.

131–50. To the numerous attempts to identify the historical prototype of the grammarian, I add the following from Carlyle's 'Varnhagen von Ense's Memoirs' (1838). Among the figures known to the young Varnhagen were 'Platonic Schleiermacher, sharp, crabbed, shrunken, with his wire-drawn logic, his sarcasms, his sly malicious ways . . . [and] Homeric Wolf, with his biting wit, with his grim earnestness and inextinguishable Homeric laugh, the irascible great-hearted man' (Carlyle, *Works*, xxix.93). Carlyle thus presents two great modern classicists with insistent paradox, the physically repellent qualities of the one (sharp, crabbed, shrunken), entirely like the grammarian's, as are the 'grim earnestness' and great-heartedness of the other: 'Fierce as a dragon'; 'Was it not great?'

50. See DeLaura, 'Browning's Painter Poems', pp. 371–3.

51. The terms are those used by Ralph W. Rader, in 'The Dramatic Monologue and Related Lyric Forms', *Critical Inquiry*, 3 (1976) 131–51.

52. But I speak with caution, since in his acute reading of the poem, Leonard Burrows (*Browning the Poet*, p. 125) sees the 'zealous followers' as demonstrating 'their beliefs to a surrounding audience'. Still this not uncommon view would have to meet the objections I raise.

53. Their own real ideal (and presumably Browning's) is that of the broader humanistic learning of the Renaissance, including both 'sexuality and intellectuality', as opposed to the grammarian's 'dehumanizing pedantry'. Thomas Frederick Scheer, 'Mythopoeia and the Renaissance Mind: a Reading of "A Grammarian's Funeral" ', *Journal of Narrative Technique*, 4 (1974) 119–28. This 'hypocritical' reading assumes in Browning far simpler and more 'modern' views than we know he held in the period; moreover, there is in my judgement no secure evidence that the disciples in fact seek goals – in 'life' or 'learning' – that in any way differ from those that guided the career of the grammarian.

54. For Browning's words, see Peterson, 'The Proofs of Browning's *Men and Women*' (n. 13). The latter terms were used, respectively, by William Morris and Arthur Hugh Clough; cited in Lee Erickson, *Robert Browning: His Poetry and his Audiences* (Ithaca, N.Y.: Cornell University Press, 1984) p. 133. Erickson's description of the reception of the poems, including the exchange with Ruskin (pp. 133–6), is suggestive; but where Erickson asserts (p. 136) that Browning had already, in *Men and Women*, abandoned his earlier hopes 'to reach a wider public and achieve a financial and poetic success', I would suggest that the *failure* of *Men and Women* to win the desired audience referred to in the letter to Milsand led Browning, retrospectively, to formulate the rationale he develops in the December 1855 letter to Ruskin. That rationale does indeed capture the actual method of some of the most recalcitrant pieces in *Men and Women*; but though (as he tells Ruskin) he is resigned to the fact that his poetry will 'act upon a very few who react upon the rest', and even though he ends by declaring himself 'apprehensive when the public, critics and all, begin to understand and approve me' (Collingwood, I.234–5), these statements (and the poems in *Men and*

Women) seem to me to fall well short of (in Erickson's words) Browning's later retreat into 'a doctrine of prophetic esoterism'.

55. Ruskin to Browning, 2 Dec. 1855, in DeLaura, 'Ruskin and the Brownings', pp. 326–7.

56. Browning to Ruskin, 10 Dec. 1855, in Collingwood, I.232–3.

57. I suggest that Carlyle's repeated efforts to describe the prophet's 'rough' and 'rude' speech lay behind these most interesting Victorian attempts to define poetry's proper inconsecutive manner. In *Heroes and Hero-worship* (1841), especially, Carlyle's own 'abrupt utterances thrown-out isolated, unexplored', are plainly parallel to 'the broken rude tortuous utterances' of a Cromwell, or even more Mahomet's 'unshaped', struggling words, without sequence or method. I discuss these matters in 'Ishmael as Prophet: *Heroes and Hero-worship* and the Self-Expressive Basis of Carlyle's Art', *Texas Studies in Literature and Language*, 11 (1969) 705–32. These best mid-century struggles to teach 'the British reader' (in Carlyle's phrase) a new and more adequate way of reading, in contrast to the 'respectable' and 'articulate' speech of traditional oratory, are the highly creative reality behind the usual simplicities about Victorian emotionalism and anti-intellectualism.

58. Collingwood, I.234.

59. *Matthew Arnold: the Poetry, The Critical Heritage*, ed. Carl Dawson (London: Routledge & Kegan Paul, 1973) pp. 42 (Kingsley), 76 (Clough), 111 (J. D. Coleridge). As we have seen, 'Cleon' was in effect the most sophisticated of the early disapproving responses to Arnold's poetry, and was almost certainly influenced, perhaps even inspired, by the reviews that began in 1849. Indeed, the evidence raises the real possibility that Matthew Arnold, who used the despairing Empedocles (as a friend said) 'for the drapery of his own thoughts', was himself, at least in his poetic persona and especially as characterised by the early reviewers, an actual *model* for Browning's portrait of Cleon.

60. Browning's implicit theory of 'speech acts' deserves to be drawn together. It is strikingly close to John Henry Newman's use of 'fiduciary' language in personal and religious saying and knowing – though Browning might not have been pleased to have the parallel pointed out. See John Coulson, *Newman and the Common Tradition: A Study in the Language of Church and Society* (Oxford: Clarendon Press, 1970).

61. The ironies should not go unremarked, because Ruskin did reinforce aspects of Browning's own changing views in the 1850s, and because Carlyle has been seen as the prototype of the 'poet' in 'How It Strikes a Contemporary' – though I for one think it a not very accurate portrait of Carlyle and his characteristic mode and manner. See Charles Richard Sanders, 'Carlyle, Browning, and the Nature of a Poet', *Emory University Quarterly*, 16 (1960) 197–209, and Susan H. Aiken, 'On Clothes and Heroes: Carlyle and "How it Strikes a Contemporary" ', *Victorian Poetry*, 13 (1975) 99–109.

62. The words are G. K. Chesterton's, in *Robert Browning* (1903; London: Macmillan, 1951) pp. 155–6.

63. In *Modern Painters* III (1856) Ruskin was soon to speak of the grotesque mode in visual art in ways strikingly (though unconsciously) applicable to some of Browning's key poems. In the grotesque there is 'a strange connection between the reinless play of the imagination, and a sense of the presence of evil'. The imagination 'in its mocking or playful moods . . . is apt to jest, sometimes bitterly, with under-current [*sic*] of sternest pathos, sometimes waywardly, sometimes slightly and wickedly, with death and sin'. In a 'fine grotesque', using symbols, 'the connection [of truths] is left for the beholder to work out for himself; the gaps left or overleaped by the haste of the imagination' (v.103, 131, 132). Even more pertinent is Appendix I of *Modern Painters* IV (1856), on 'Modern Grotesque': 'when the powers of quaint fancy are associated . . . with stern understanding of the nature of evil, and tender human sympathy, there results a bitter, or pathetic spirit of grotesque to which mankind at present owe more thorough moral teaching than to any branch of art whatsoever' (VI.471). Ruskin was thinking of Thomas Hood and George Cruikshank.

64. 'Browningite manner' is from Richard Holt Hutton, *Brief Literary Criticisms*, ed. Elizabeth M. Roscoe (London: Macmillan, 1906) p. 253.

65. In *Modern Painters* III (v.28). Arnold, rather disappointingly, soon after echoed: 'the noble and profound application of ideas to life . . . is the most essential part of poetic greatness' (*CPW*, I.211–12). Though Arnold would, I think, deny the connection, and he rather cruelly disparages Ruskin in these Homer lectures (I.101–2, 149), it is worth noting that Ruskin's chapter title is 'Of Received Opinions Touching the "Grand Style" ', and that Arnold is preoccupied throughout with precisely 'the grand style'. Carlyle is no doubt to an important extent an exception to my larger generalisation: John Sterling, accounting in 1835 for the small acceptance of *Sartor Resartus* 'among the best and most energetic minds in this country', spoke of the bewildering 'combinations' of tone: 'the startling whirl of incongruous juxtapositions, which of a truth must to many readers seem as amazing as if the Pythia on the tripod should have struck-up a drinking song, or Thersites had caught the prophetic strain of Cassandra' (see *Thomas Carlyle: the Critical Heritage*, ed. Jules Paul Seigel (London: Routledge & Kegan Paul, 1971) pp. 27, 31). Dickens also managed to offend the expectations of readers of his early novels, as in the reaction against the spirit of 'exaggeration' in *Martin Chuzzlewit* (1842).

66. I have sketched out the parallels in 'Ruskin and the Brownings', pp. 353–6.

67. Ruskin's religious doubts were in fact to be revealed with unusual frankness to Mrs Browning, from the late 1850s until her death in 1861 (see DeLaura, 'Ruskin and the Brownings', pp. 338–43).

68. The best account is that of Arthur A. Adrian, 'The Browning–Rossetti Friendship: Some Unpublished Letters', *PMLA*, 73 (1958) 538–44. There are additional details in Rosalie Glynn Grylls, 'Rossetti and Browning', *Princeton University Library Chronicle*, 33 (1971–2) 232–50.

5

The Comedy of
Culture and Anarchy

RICHARD D. ALTICK

*Mr Matthew Arnold. To him, Miss
Mary Augusta, his niece: 'Why,
Uncle Matthew, Oh why, will not
you be always wholly serious?'*
(caption of a Max Beerbohm
caricature in *The Poet's Corner*)

Banter, levity, raillery, superciliousness, badinage, facetiousness, playfulness: all these terms, as well as the less common 'coxcombry' and 'vivacities', have been used by Matthew Arnold's critics, contemporary and modern, to describe his comic manner in *Culture and Anarchy*. He himself spoke of it as 'chaff' and 'persiflage'. The broadest term he used, in a letter to his mother some months after the first instalment of the book appeared in the *Cornhill Magazine*, was 'irony', which, he explained, referred to 'the saying rather less than one means'.[1] But, as we shall see, his irony went far beyond mere understatement, and his choice of argumentative language included a number of comic effects not covered by the word. Perhaps the spirit and effect of Arnold's manner are best caught, not in any critical description, but in two caricatures: Beerbohm's of a rangy, carpet-slippered Arnold leaning negligently against a mantelpiece, his teeth exposed in a grimace that falls somewhere between a grin and a smirk, and an unsigned one in *Vanity Fair* (11 November 1871) of Arnold leaning on a furled umbrella, his face wreathed in an amiable smile, the whole figure suggesting, to one reader at least, a benevolent but not especially bright Nonconformist clergyman. The deceptive blandness of the latter picture is as sharp a satire of Arnold's public personality as one could wish.

The essence of the comedy in *Culture and Anarchy* is the persona that Arnold adopts with the assistance of his adversaries. Its development had begun as early as the preface to the 1853 *Poems*, with its 'delicate strokes of irony' and its 'slight but unmistakable air of superiority' (Coulling, pp. 45–6), and it had continued for the next dozen years as Arnold became embroiled in the several controversies which made him a well-known public figure. His opponents, seizing on such characteristics and mannerisms, baited him with them, and in response Arnold refined and exaggerated them. These elements of his forensic personality coalesced into the persona we see, in fully realised form, in *Culture and Anarchy*. How much of the image of Arnold that found its way into print was a natural reflection or extension of his private personality, and how much was deliberately assumed, was a matter of constant dispute among those who knew him. It is certain, however, that persona and personality overlapped; several of the terms cited at the beginning of this essay were used to describe the real Arnold as well as his fictive counterpart.

The running debate stirred by the publication of *Culture and Anarchy* in the *Cornhill* between July 1867 and August 1868 encouraged Arnold's strong inclination to argue in personal terms.[2] He delighted in casting himself as a nimble combatant in a clash of ideas. 'Here', he said at one point of his jousting, 'I think I see my enemies waiting for me with a hungry joy in their eyes. But I shall elude them' (p. 124, lines 2–4).[3] Their facetious characterisations of his gladiatorial manner provided further shape and coloration for the developing portrait, and their oracular utterances in print, Parliament, and elsewhere, along with those of other favourite butts, gave him 'golden opportunities', as he told his mother (Super, p. 410), to score points – not least, he might have added, through turning their personal aspersions on him to witty use. With such obliging adversaries, Arnold had little need of supporting troops.

Behind both the Beerbohm caricature and the *Vanity Fair* one of the benign middle-class man with the umbrella lay the most famous of the numerous labels that Arnold's opponents attached to him: the *Daily Telegraph*'s earlier (1866) description of him as an 'elegant Jeremiah' (p. 88, lines 9–21). Arnold had already accepted the characterisation, and though when he first revived it in *Culture and Anarchy* he deflected the shaft by the irrevelant observation that the paper had coupled him, 'by a strange perversity of fate, with just

that very one of the Hebrew prophets whose style I admire the least'
(ibid.), he later turned the epithet to his usual good account
by implicitly recalling the biblical tag about prophets going
unhonoured in their own country (or time). The preachers of
culture, he says, 'have, and are likely long to have, a hard time of it,
and they will much oftener be regarded, for a great while to come, as
elegant or spurious Jeremiahs than as friends and benefactors. That,
however, will not prevent their doing in the end good service if they
persevere' (p. 95, lines 30–4).

In the same spirit, Arnold welcomed the accusation in the
Illustrated London News (4 January 1868) that he had an 'effeminate
horror' of 'practical reforms' (p. 200, lines 11–12; p. 202, line 23).
Earlier, no fewer than four of his critics, Fitzjames Stephen in the
Saturday Review (3 December 1864), the *Daily Telegraph* (2 July 1867),
Henry Sidgwick (*Macmillan's Magazine*, August 1867) and Frederic
Harrison (*Fortnightly Review*, November 1867) had cast Arnold as a
latter-day parmaceti lord holding pouncet box to nose as he picked
his way through the cultural wasteland of mid-Victorian England.
At the outset of Chapter II (pp. 115, line 9–116, line 8) he recalled the
complaint, saying that its burden was that the 'religion of culture' he
espoused was 'not practical, or, – as some critics familiarly put it, –
all moonshine'. He enumerated several specific complaints to this
effect, in each case simplifying them in his paraphrase and, as he did
so, inviting sympathy for himself. A determined idealist and – as he
was to call himself later – one among the 'poor disparaged followers
of culture' (p. 222, line 13), he suffered a species of martyrdom,
mocked by 'objectors' in general, taunted by one paper and
upbraided by another. At the end of the essay, he portrayed himself
as continuing to smart under such persecution: 'It cannot but
accurately try a tender conscience to be accused, in a practical
country like ours, of keeping aloof from the work and hope of a
multitude of earnest-hearted men, and of merely toying with poetry
and aesthetics' (p. 135, lines 11–14). Let his opponents say their
worst: Arnold's withers were unwrung and his heart was pure.

To the image of an elegant Jeremiah crying (to adopt the phrase of
an earlier evangelistic Matthew) in the wilderness and that of a
trifler with 'aesthetics and poetical fancies' (p. 115, lines 24–5), one
of Arnold's principal disputants, Frederic Harrison, added another:
that of a would-be prophet, thinker, and reformer who was
incapable of philosophical thought, deficient, as Harrison said, in
'coherent, interdependent, subordinate, and derivative principles'.

Of the several contributions Arnold's critics made to his persona, this was the allegation he most relished for argumentative purposes. From the time of 'On Translating Homer' (1861) onward, in response to his critics' complaints of his air of superiority, of intellectual arrogance, he had occasionally adopted a pose of humility. Now, in *Culture and Anarchy*, he freely conceded that he was 'a man without a philosophy' (p. 137, lines 1, 10–11) and adroitly turned that seeming deficiency into a virtue. He could disclaim sophistication and put himself forward instead as a slow thinker who had to take pains to make things clear to himself: 'the simple unsystematic way which best suits both my taste and my powers' (pp. 88, lines 38–89, line 1). 'Knowing myself to be indeed sadly to seek, as one of my many critics says, in "a philosophy with coherent, interdependent, subordinate, and derivative principles", I continually have recourse to a plain man's expedient of trying to make what few simple notions I have, clearer and more intelligible to myself by means of example and illustration' (p. 126, lines 27–32). The apologetic posture, however, serves to mask a far from hesitant thrust at his critics. What Arnold really means is that they must have the truth spelled out for *them* in the simplest terms.

'What I know of my own mind and its poverty' (p. 160, line 2) forces him, he says, to avoid philosophising and to stick to practical issues, just as his critics urge: 'an unpretending writer, without a philosophy based on inter-dependent, subordinate, and coherent principles, must not presume to indulge himself too much in generalities. He must keep close to the level ground of common fact, the only safe ground for understandings without a scientific equipment' (p. 192, lines 1–5). 'We . . . having no coherent philosophy, must not let ourselves philosophize' (p. 194, lines 6–7).

On this point, however, the reader must feel that Arnold protests too much, although the effect may have been less grating on those who read *Culture and Anarchy* as it was serialised over a period of a year than it was on those who subsequently read it straight through in book form. Time and again he depreciates himself, regretting his 'want of coherent philosophic method' (p. 139, lines 35–6), his being 'a notoriously unsystematic and unpretending writer' (p. 143, lines 22–3), his 'confessed inexpertness in reasoning and arguing' (p. 192, lines 12–13). Here, by no means uniquely in his polemic prose, Arnold failed to recognise when a joke had worn thin.

The same affectation of humility leads him, following the picture of the pouncet-box lord beleaguered by his enemies, to declare his willingness to learn from his betters: 'It is impossible that all these remonstrances and reproofs should not affect me, and I shall try my very best . . . to profit by the objections I have heard and read' (p. 116, lines 9–13). And to this assumed receptivity Arnold adds another ingratiating quality, his willingness to present himself as a comic figure. He describes himself as a free spirit, 'delivered from the bondage of Bentham' (p. 111, lines 10–11), an unlikely allegiance indeed for an elegant Jeremiah, but useful for the implication that he has thus liberated himself from the philosophy which still holds the enemies of culture captive. At another place he represents himself as carrying about with him on his school-inspecting rounds in the East End, in the manner of a breviary, a particularly pompous (and wrong-headed) leading article from *The Times*, attributing the economic distress in that vicinity to 'Nature's simplest laws', and a complementary effusion by Robert Buchanan interpreting Malthus in the roseate light of William Paley (pp. 213, lines 26–214, line 33).

Both the self-mockery and the claim to possess homely virtues are meant, according to the ancient precepts of rhetoric, actually to enhance the writer's authority and diminish that of his opponents. In confessing his own fallibility, Arnold undercuts their own pretensions of superior wisdom. His candour regarding himself further implies that all that he says of them is equally lacking in guile. And who but such a clear-sighted person as he depicts himself as being can have the truth within his grasp? Since he harbours no illusions about himself, he is equally able, with respect to the society about him, to see things steadily and see them as they really are (p. 167, line 31; p. 172, line 1). By adopting such a posture, Arnold in effect turns the tables on his opponents. Now it is he, not they, who can claim final authority by virtue of his celebration of the clear light of reason.

'This sort of plain-dealing' with himself, as he puts it, which 'has in it, as all the moralists tell us, something very wholesome' (p. 138, lines 13–14), also enables him to score a specific point or two. In anatomising the failings of the middle class, he humbly offers himself as a 'representative man' who illustrates what he considers to be its 'defect' (i.e. deficiency).

The too well-founded reproaches of my opponents [he says] declare how little I have lent a hand to the great works of the middle class . . . and . . . 'the believers in action grow impatient' with me. The line, again, of a still unsatisfied seeker which I have followed, the idea of self-transformation, of growing towards some measure of sweetness and light not yet reached, is evidently at clean variance with the perfect self-satisfaction current in my class, the middle class, and may serve to indicate in me, therefore, the extreme defect of this feeling. But these confessions, though salutary, are bitter and unpleasant. (p. 138, lines 17–30)

By pleading guilty to the 'reproaches' Arnold makes for himself a fresh opportunity to emphasise his own earnest search for truth and at the same time to pin down the 'defect' of the middle class. As a seeker after his better self, he exemplifies what the middle class should be – and is not.

A few pages later, he reiterates his membership in the middle class. 'I myself am properly a Philistine', he confesses, '– Mr Swinburne would add, the son of a Philistine' (p. 144, lines 7–9). Or more precisely, a Philistine manqué. But he also admits that when, for example, he takes up a gun or fishing-rod or finds himself in one of the Barbarian's 'great fortified posts' he feels a strong, perhaps atavistic, affinity with the aristocracy (p. 144, lines 15–32). There, but for 'reason and the will of God' (p. 145, line 24), walks a true Barbarian, 'a very passable child of the established fact, of commendable spirit and politeness, and, at the same time, a little inaccessible to ideas and light' (p. 144, lines 25–38). But, the implication is, he *is* accessible to such ideas. Thus Arnold again eats his cake and has it too. He has established his sympathy with both the Philistines (from whom he sprang) and the Barbarians (toward whom he feels a powerful attraction), yet, by virtue of his shortcomings, as they would view them, he is a man without a class, an outsider. Because of this, as well as because he possesses the crucial faculty of perception and self-criticism they are without, he can exercise a disinterestedness of which truly involved members of a class are incapable. (It is noteworthy, incidentally, that Arnold makes no such attempt to associate himself with the Populace.)

Through his mask of benignity Arnold repeatedly manifests his lack of hostility and partiality and his 'disposition to see the good in everybody all round' (p. 127, lines 36–7). Mainly through his favourite device of ironic praise, he constantly stresses that no personal enmity taints the ongoing debate; on the contrary, he is eager to perceive and do homage to his adversaries' sterling qualities. His reluctant disagreement with them rests on exclusively ideological grounds. Disinterestedness could go no further. Witness

the generosity with which he alludes to his antagonists and the
other objects of his scorn: 'Mr Bright . . . said forcibly in one of his
great speeches' (p. 117, lines 18–19); 'a powerful speech from that
famous speaker, Mr Bright' (p. 200, lines 10–11); the *Nonconformist*
newspaper is 'written with great sincerity and ability' (p. 101, lines
19–20); *The Times* and the *Daily News* are 'authorities I so much
respect' (p. 156, line 18).

The essence of the irony often resides in the fact that the professed
respect is not only *pro forma* but is misdirected. The impact of such
thrusts lies in what they *fail* to praise. In a passage deleted when the
Cornhill articles were collected, Arnold expressed his admiration for
'vigorous language, as language' (p. 504, lines 28–9); and this proves
to be the basis on which he finds himself able, in a way, to praise
men whose ideas are repugnant to him. Whether or not his respect
is sincere – in most instances it is not – it is concentrated on matters
of style, the surfaces, manners and effects of the statement in
question, and not on the crucial question of its intellectual validity.
Nowhere in Arnold's generous distribution of brickbats
transparently disguised as bouquets is there any implication that the
recipients *think* correctly. Thus Charles Spurgeon the revivalist
(p. 194, lines 35–6), Hepworth Dixon, author of a book about
the Mormons (p. 206, line 29) and the *Daily News* (p. 152, line 36)
are all credited with 'eloquence', and another mixed bag of
writers and speakers with the gift of 'beautiful' utterance, as we
shall see.

Sometimes Arnold is not content to let the patent insincerity of his
epithets respecting style do its work unaided. Bringing down two
birds with one stone, he observes at one point that 'we seem to be
entering, with all our sails spread, upon what Mr Hepworth Dixon,
its apostle and evangelist, calls a Gothic revival, but what one of the
many newspapers that so greatly admire Mr Hepworth Dixon's lithe
and sinewy style and form their own style upon it, calls, by a yet
bolder and more striking figure, "a great sexual insurrection of our
Anglo-Teutonic race" ' (p. 206, lines 31–7). The 'bold' figure may be
judged on its own merits; what is not so apparent is that 'lithe and
sinewy style' is not Arnold's phrase but that of a magazine review,
quoted in an advertisement for Dixon's book (Super, p. 443). He
disposes of *The Times'* editorial prose with equal deftness: 'The
first-named melancholy doctrine is preached in the *Times* with great
clearness and force of style; indeed, it is well known, from the
example of the poet Lucretius and others, what great masters

of style the atheistic doctrine has always counted among its promulgators' (p. 156, lines 20–5).

Especially when contained in a mere word or two, without the elaboration that might clarify his intention, an ironist's praise is, by definition, dubious. In its very equivocation lies much of its effect. But in Arnold's case, it is sometimes hard to tell whether he is being ironic or not. The presence of so many instances of unmistakably ironic praise tempts the reader to believe that all his admiring epithets are delivered tongue in cheek, but a closer inspection, employing the aid of either context or external evidence (his letters sometimes provide a litmus test for suspected irony), reveals that several of them are not as hollow as they first sound. In the opening chapter, in a passage that most readers, not least modern Americans whose received views of Benjamin Franklin and Arnold would seem to place the two in spectacular ideological opposition, Arnold pays what seems to be excessive if not actually false tribute to Franklin – 'a mind to which I feel the greatest obligations, the mind of a man who was the very incarnation of sanity and clear sense, a man the most considerable, it seems to me, whom America has yet produced' (p. 110, lines 22–5). But an ironic interpretation is doubly unlikely: we have solid evidence of Arnold's genuine regard for Franklin and his 'imperturbable common sense' (Super, pp. 421–2), and this chapter originally was an Oxford lecture, a thoroughly sober discourse in which there are only the slightest flecks of comedy. He refers at another place to Frederic Harrison's 'very good-tempered and witty satire' of himself in 'Culture: a Dialogue' (p. 116, lines 1–2). In view of the spirit in which he alludes to Harrison elsewhere in *Culture and Anarchy*, one might justifiably assume that here, too, Arnold was being ironic. But the fact is that in one of his letters he wrote that he found the satire 'in parts so amusing that I laughed till I cried' (Super, p. 424).

The touchstone of context is not always reliable. At the opening of Chapter II, in the famous paragraph about the parmaceti lord, Arnold writes:

> That Alcibiades, the editor of the *Morning Star*, taunts me, as its promulgator, with living out of the world and knowing nothing of life and men. That great austere toiler, the editor of the *Daily Telegraph*, upbraids me – but kindly, and more in sorrow than in anger, – for trifling with aesthetics and poetical fancies, while he himself, in that arsenal of his in Fleet Street, is bearing the burden

and heat of the day. An intelligent American newspaper, the
Nation, says that it is very easy to sit in one's study and find fault
with the course of modern society, but the thing is to propose
practical improvements for it.   (p. 115, lines 19–29)

The irony is obvious – the more so when we become aware that, as
Dover Wilson points out, Alcibiades is 'the type of all that was
luxurious, cosmopolitan, brilliant, accomplished, fascinating and
unprincipled in the Athens of Socrates'.[4]

Arnold uses various kinds of deflationary techniques to qualify
or, indeed, negate what starts out to be praise. Mr Miall, he says, is
'a personage of deserved eminence' – 'among the political
Dissenters' (p. 128, lines 15–16). In an especially feline instance, he
describes Mr Odger as a working-class exemplar of the 'beautiful
and virtuous mean' – 'of whom his friends relate . . . much that is
favourable' (p. 133, lines 21–3). A sentence that begins amiably
enough (in a letter to his mother, Arnold praised Robertson's
biography as 'a most interesting, remarkable life': Super, p. 436)
takes a distinctly unamiable turn at the end:

> There is a sermon on Greece and the Greek spirit by a man never
> to be mentioned without interest and respect, Frederick
> Robertson, in which this rhetorical use of Greece and the Greek
> spirit, and the inadequate exhibition of them necessarily
> consequent upon this, is almost ludicrous, and would be
> censurable if it were not to be explained by the exigencies of a
> sermon.   (p. 164, lines 25–31)

There is a decidedly qualified compliment to be found, also, in
Arnold's reference to his 'old adversary, the *Saturday Review*,
[which] may, on matters of literature and taste, be fairly enough
regarded, relatively to the mass of newspapers which treat these
matters, as a kind of organ of reason' (p. 147, lines 29–32). He can
also invert the device, to praise with a faint ironic damn. Knowing
that his opponents are annoyed by his repeated admiring quotation
of Bishop Wilson, a man of wisdom of whom they have never heard
(Huxley accused Arnold of inventing him: p. 231, lines 9–11),
Arnold obliges them by referring to him as 'that poor old hierophant
of a decayed superstition' (p. 128, lines 34–5).

'Interesting' is one of the most equivocal words in Arnold's
argumentative vocabulary. In his private letters he used it as a

mildly laudatory epithet; there was no more irony in his application
of it, in conjunction with 'very well behaved', to describe
Swinburne's demeanour at a dinner party than there was in its
application to Robertson's 'deeply interesting' life (Super, pp. 432,
436). In print, the word could be interpreted as non-committal,
ambiguous or – possibly – even approving. There is probably a
difference in degree and pitch of ironic inflection in each of these
references: the 'interesting speakers' he heard during the Reform
debates in the House of Commons (p. 127, line 4); the 'interesting
productions of nature' who were the old Barbarians (p. 141, line 29);
Hepworth Dixon's 'able and interesting work' (p. 148, line 17);
'interesting explorers' (a motley crowd of ultra-Hebraists, called a
'noble army' in the same passage: p. 159, lines 24–6); 'that very
interesting operation, – the attempt to enable a man to marry his
deceased wife's sister' (p. 205, lines 20–2). One can find speakers,
writers, activists and their proposals 'interesting' for more than one
reason. At the very least, the word is a convenient one when a more
definite judgement is to be (conspicuously) withheld. The same dry
ambiguity may be detected in Arnold's several professions of
pleasure in hearing the debates in the Commons: 'Once when I had
had the advantage of listening . . .' (p. 127, lines 2–3); 'This
operation I had the great advantage of with my own ears hearing
discussed in the House of Commons, and recommended by a
powerful speech from that famous speaker, Mr Bright' (p. 200, lines
8–11); 'I was lucky enough to be present when Mr Chambers
brought forward . . . his bill for enabling a man to marry his
deceased wife's sister' (p. 205, lines 25–7).

'Great' is another useful multi-purpose word in Arnold's
vocabulary. He normally uses it with plainly ironic intent, applied to
a variety of subjects from Robert Lowe's fatuous speech at
Edinburgh (p. 126, line 36) to the works – despised by Arnold – of
the middle-class liberals (at least eight times, e.g. p. 137, line 22,
p. 151, line 34 ['great and heroic']). Once, however, it is used both
descriptively and ironically, in repeated reference to 'Mr Spurgeon's
great Tabernacle' (p. 198, lines 3, 4, 8). Earlier, Arnold had spoken of
the 'bigness' of Spurgeon's church (p. 108, line 36), a fact well
known to every Londoner. 'Great' in the latter passage not only
contains the idea of imposing physical dimensions but draws irony
from the immediate context, the mention of Bright's being 'so
ravished with admiration' as he beheld the building. But twenty
lines farther on, Arnold transfers the epithet to the Church of

England, where no irony can possibly be meant. Its force is diminished, if not actually compromised, by the preceding application.

A similar effect occurs in connection with the phrase 'man of genius'. There is no reason to believe that Arnold's application of it to Carlyle is anything but sincere, even though it is hedged by a form of praise by which Arnold avoids expressing any judgement of Carlyle's ideas ('a man of genius to whom we have all at one time or other been indebted for refreshment and stimulus': p. 124, lines 19–20). We are thus prepared to accept the phrase as meant in the same spirit when it is later applied to Bright (p. 130, lines 4–5), but in view of the terms in which Arnold elsewhere professes his admiration of that politician (e.g. 'that great man': p. 228, line 9), its use there can only be ironic.

In Arnold's usage at least two other words are equally or even more unstable, to the detriment, surely, of his steady purpose. They are witness to the elementary truth that the connotations of a repeatedly used value word cannot be turned on or off at will but, once established, persist across many pages, to strike a false note when introduced in a context markedly different in spirit from earlier ones. Arnold's surprising neglect of this fact may doubtless be attributed to his having written *Culture and Anarchy* in 'piecemeal' fashion (Super, p. 411), as separate magazine articles, over a period of some six months. One such troublesome word is 'affecting', which first appears in a heavily ironic context, that of Alderman-Colonel Wilson's facile rationalising of his inaction in the face of civil disturbance in the streets of the West End: 'Honest and affecting testimony of the English middle class to its own inadequacy!' (p. 132, lines 12–13). The second occurrence is even more emphatically comic, related as it is to Arnold's self-mocking persona: 'And although, through circumstances which will perhaps one day be known if ever the affecting history of my conversion comes to be written, I have, for the most part, broken with the ideas and the tea-meetings of my own class' (p. 144, lines 9–12). Yet in the word's third appearance it is meant in utter seriousness: 'boundless devotion to that inspiring and affecting pattern of self-conquest offered by Jesus Christ' (p. 166, lines 7–9).

But the prime instance of Arnold's tone-deafness, so to speak, is provided by the words 'beauty' and 'beautiful'. These are words that possess especially glowing resonance in the language of a Post-Romantic poet and literary critic, and by virtue of that circumstance they demand to be handled with the utmost tact. In the first chapter, 'Sweetness and Light', they occur often, in celebration of the desire for 'beauty and sweetness' nurtured by the Oxford Movement (p. 107, lines 21, 30) and, more prominently, in connection with Arnold's exposition of the ideal of perfection. Such uses are purely serious, and their intention – the presentation of a lofty moral idea in aesthetic terms – is underscored by the occasional appearance, as counterpoint, of the antonyms 'hideous' and 'hideousness', as in: 'I say boldly that this our sentiment for beauty and sweetness, our sentiment against hideousness and rawness, has been at the bottom of our attachment to so many beaten causes, of our opposition to so many triumphant movements' (p. 106, lines 6–10; another example is on p. 107, lines 21–4).[5] But the coming ambiguity is foreshadowed early on, by the use of 'beautiful' in an essentially comic context. Arnold remarks that readers of *The Times'* smug articles on the steady increase of the population 'would talk of our large English families in quite a solemn strain, as if they had something in itself beautiful, elevating, and meritorious in them; as if the British Philistine would have only to present himself before the Great Judge with his twelve children, in order to be received among the sheep as a matter of right!' (p. 98, lines 13–19). No doubt more than one reader of *Culture and Anarchy* has found pleasure in the 'beautiful' notion of a complacent Victorian paterfamilias lining up his full dozen inside the pearly gates. Every subsequent occurrence of 'beauty'/'beautiful' is tinged, to some degree, by that initial tincture of irony.

Henceforth, serious applications of the words abound. Arnold writes of 'the beautiful and virtuous mean', one of his catch-phrases (p. 127, lines 17–18; p. 130, lines 27, 34, etc.), of Wilhelm von Humboldt as 'one of the most beautiful souls that have ever existed' (p. 161, lines 5–6), of the Hellenist's ideal of 'seeing things in their essence and beauty' (p. 168, line 35), and of 'the difference in force, beauty, significance, and usefulness, between primitive Christianity and Protestantism' (pp. 174, line 38–175, line 2). (There are additional examples at p. 167, lines 32, 37; p. 168, line 19; p. 178, line 21; p. 179, lines 14, 26.) Meanwhile, however, these unquestionably serious uses have been interspersed with an equal number in which Arnold's intention is patently ironic. He alludes to Mr Murphy's appeal to the Mayor of Birmingham to defend his right to free speech: 'Touching and beautiful words, which find a sympathetic chord in every British bosom!' (p. 120, 11–12). Shortly thereafter, Arnold speaks with equally explicit irony of 'That beautiful sentence Sir Daniel Gooch quoted to the Swindon workmen', his mother's advice, 'Ever remember, my dear Dan, that you should look forward to being some day manager of that concern!' (p. 122, lines 7–14). By now, the reader probably is prepared to find 'beauty' and 'beautiful' playing a recurrent role in Arnold's game of ironic praise, and so they do: 'As Mr Bright beautifully says, "the cities it has built, the railroads it has made, the manufactures it has produced, the cargoes which freight the ships of the greatest mercantile navy the world has ever seen" ' (p. 142, lines 20–3). Beauty is far to seek in so prosaic an utterance, as it also is, supposedly, in the 'dexterous command of powerful and beautiful language' Arnold attributes to political philosophers (p. 194, lines 2–3), in an M.P.'s 'formula of much beauty and neatness for conveying in brief the Liberal notions. . . . "Liberty"', said he, "is the law of human life" ' (p. 206, lines 3–5), and in *The Times*' claim that the 'indefinite multiplication of poor people' is 'the result of divine and beautiful laws' (p. 214, lines 11–14).

The fact is that once a highly charged word like 'beauty' is used in a memorably ironic way, as in Arnold's tribute to Mother Gooch's Golden Rule, it is irremediably compromised for use later on; subsequent non-ironic occurrences are inescapably coloured by the reader's recollection of the preceding usage. The reader is conditioned to expect irony where, in fact, irony is farthest from the author's intention. The ironic resonance cannot be dispelled, no matter how opposed to irony the new context is.

Those who regret seeing the word 'beauty' falling victim to Arnold's ill-calculated use of emotive language may be pleased to behold him hoist with his own petard. At one place, ironically proposing that 'we Hellenise a little with free-trade, as we Hellenised with the Real Estate Intestacy Bill', he urges that we 'see whether what our reprovers beautifully call ministering to the diseased spirit of our time is best done by the Hellenising method of proceeding, or by the other' (pp. 209, line 31–210, line 4). He has clearly forgotten that three times earlier, the last as close as the beginning of the preceding paragraph, it was not Arnold's 'reprovers' but he himself who had (beautifully?) written, in contexts innocent of any ironical design, of 'minister[ing]' to the diseased spirit of our time' (p. 191, lines 27–8; p. 199, line 34; p. 209, lines 1–2).

To his various devices for establishing, however suspectly, his goodwill, Arnold adds the age-old rhetorical trick of extending the clammy hand of friendship to his opponents. 'Our Liberal friends' tolls like a slightly defective bell through the last pages of *Culture and Anarchy*. Its chief connotation has already been prepared for. The note of condescension inherent in the device was struck in the first essay, where Arnold alludes to the 'well-intentioned' and 'well-meaning' friends of the people (p. 108, line 4; p. 109, line 17). Their purpose, he implies, is more to be admired than their ideas; moreover, whatever their altruistic motives, they are dangerous. Arnold expands this argument in the middle of ch. III. The 'guides and governors' of Victorian society, namely the journalistic opinion-makers and legislators (p. 156, lines 14–16), are flatterers of the people: 'the voice which makes a permanent impression on each of our classes is the voice of its friends' (p. 151, lines 37–8). The upshot is that by the end of *Culture and Anarchy*, 'our Liberal friends', well-meaning and eloquent though they may be, are presented as being in truth enemies of the people.

Sometimes, as one or two examples have already shown, Arnold removes the glitter from his epithets by quick strokes of qualification. Writing of Lord Elcho, he seems to heap up praise. He begins: '. . . in the brilliant lord, showing plenty of high spirit, but remarkable, far above and beyond his gift of high spirit, for the fine tempering of his high spirit, for ease, serenity, politeness, – the great virtues, as Mr Carlyle says, of aristocracy. . . .' But in completing the predication he defaces the portrait with a delicate but crushing understatement: 'in this beautiful and virtuous mean, there seemed evidently some insufficiency of light' (p. 127, lines 13–19) – a defect shared, Arnold would later point out, by Mr Odger, idol of the working class (p. 133, line 25). In such passages, ironical purpose is served by a kind of anticlimax, which, in its various forms and degrees, Arnold found a most congenial weapon. In its simplest form, it might be contained within a phrase ('Thyesteän banquet of claptrap': p. 227, lines 32–3), or in an unobtrusive declension of values (Englishmen believe that 'the having a vote, like the having a large family, or a large business, or large muscles, has in itself some edifying and perfecting effect upon human nature': p. 108, lines 17–20; the Barbarians' precious legacy of 'vigour, good looks, and fine complexion': p. 141, line 13).

Or anticlimax might require two sentences: 'London, with its unutterable external hideousness, and with its internal canker of *publicè egestas, privatim opulentia*, – to use the words which Sallust puts into Cato's mouth about Rome, – unequalled in the world! The word, again, which we children of God speak, the voice which most hits our collective thought, the newspaper . . . with the largest circulation in the whole world, is the *Daily Telegraph*!' (pp. 103, line 37–104, line 7). An anticlimax worthy of a Mencken[6] brings the pretentious structure of this sentence crashing to the ground:

> And if we are sometimes a little troubled by our multitude of poor men, yet we know the increase of manufactures and population to be such a salutary thing in itself, and our free-trade policy begets such an admirable movement, creating fresh centres of industry and fresh poor men here, while we were thinking about our poor men there, that we are quite dazzled and borne away, and more and more industrial movement is called for, and our social progress seems to become one triumphant and enjoyable course of what is sometimes called, vulgarly, outrunning the constable.   (pp. 210, line 37–211, line 9)

A surprise of a different sort, anticlimax of idea rather than of language, awaits the reader of this artfully wrought sentence:

> Who, I say, will believe, when he really considers the matter, that where the feminine nature, the feminine ideal, and our relations to them, are brought into question, the delicate and apprehensive genius of the Indo-European race, the race which invented the Muses, and chivalry, and the Madonna, is to find its last word on this question in the institutions of a Semitic people, whose wisest king had seven hundred wives and three hundred con- cubines?   (p. 208, lines 27–35)

And an inverted anticlimax, if it can be called such – a climax subverted in advance – crowns this sentence: 'It is notorious that our middle-class Liberals have long looked forward to this consummation, when the working class shall join forces with them, aid them heartily to carry forward their great works, go in a body to their tea-meetings, and, in short, enable them to bring about their millennium' (p. 142, lines 25–30).

At least one anticlimax Arnold owed, as he did certain hints for the shaping of his fictive self, to his ever-appreciative reading of public men's recent utterances. This was the passage in which he speaks of having gone to Oxford 'in the bad old times, when we were stuffed with Greek and Aristotle, and thought nothing of preparing ourselves by the study of modern languages, – as after Mr Lowe's great speech at Edinburgh we shall do, – to fight the battle of life with the waiters in foreign hotels' (p. 126, lines 33–7). Arnold somewhat bent Lowe's intended point, but Lowe had unquestionably said that 'the advantage of knowing French would be that when [an Englishman] goes to Paris he would able to order his dinner at the café, and to squabble over his bill without making himself a laughingstock to every one present' (Super, p. 429).

Among all the absurdities – as he regarded them – that Victorian politics and popular culture laid ready to his hand, one source of anticlimax seemed almost providentially designed for his purpose: the much-derided Deceased Wife's Sister Bill, 'that annual blister' as it was to be called in *Iolanthe* (1882). Regularly introduced, debated at length, and defeated ever since 1835, this piece of legislation was meant to nullify the canonical prohibition against a man's marrying his deceased wife's sister. Arnold could scarcely have avoided using the current parliamentary session's consideration of the bill as a satirical illustration of 'the practical operations by which our Liberal friends work for the removal of definite evils' (p. 205, lines 17–19). The main concerns of middle-class Liberalism, he declares, have been 'the advocacy of free trade, of Parliamentary reform, of abolition of church-rates, of voluntaryism in religion and education, of non-interference of the State between employers and employed, and of marriage with one's deceased wife's sister' (p. 128, lines 23–7). Arnold liked the ring of this, so he used it again a paragraph later: 'An American friend of the English Liberals says, indeed, that their Dissidence of Dissent has been a mere instrument of the political Dissenters for making reason and the will of God prevail (and no doubt he would say the same of marriage with one's deceased wife's sister)' (p. 129, lines 3–7). The extended passage devoted to excoriating political Hebraism, with the bill as a prime example, may strike some as an uneasy combination of Arnoldian witticisms and Arnoldian eloquence, notably in the paragraph beginning 'But here, as elsewhere, what we seek . . .' (p. 207, line 8). At this point the risibility of the Deceased Wife's Sister issue does not comport well with Arnold's basic seriousness; he seems torn between exploiting its comic potential and serving his deeper purpose. In any case, he valued the fatuous controversy so highly that he used it to crown his peroration. The last paragraph of *Culture and Anarchy* begins: 'Docile echoes of the eternal voice, pliant organs of the infinite will' – cadences recalling 'The Scholar Gypsy'. The paragraph – and the book – ends: 'But now we go the way the human race is going, while they abolish the Irish Church by the power of the Nonconformists' antipathy to establishments, or they enable a man to marry his deceased wife's sister' (p. 229, lines 23–33).

The incongruity that is the soul of anticlimax manifests itself in still other ways. Ironic juxtaposition and specious elevation are the principal devices by which Arnold pays his measured respects to contemporary journals of opinion. *The Times* and the *Daily News* are 'our philosophical teacher[s]' (p. 157, lines 37–8), the latter being distinguished also by its 'subtle dialectics' (p. 158, line 22). He speaks of the 'imposing and colossal necessitarianism of the *Times*' (p. 213, lines 19–20), through whose 'mastery of style' the 'sad picture' of contemporary national education 'assumes the iron and inexorable solemnity of tragic Destiny' (p. 157, lines 34–6). Persons are subjected to the same treatment, as when the dashing Colonel Dickson, factitious hero of the Hyde Park disturbances, is linked with Julius Caesar and Mirabeau (p. 133, line 15). The 'symbolical Truss Manufactory' which occupied what was called 'the finest site in Europe', facing Trafalgar Square, served Arnold as an architectural anticlimax (p. 121, lines 36–8), as did the British College of Health, ennobled, as readers of 'The Function of Criticism at the Present Time' would have recalled, with a plaster statue of Hygeia, and mentioned in *Culture and Anarchy* just following Westminster Abbey, Notre Dame and Spurgeon's great Tabernacle (p. 198, lines 11–12).

On occasion, Arnold uses verbal deflation. As if to meet his adversaries' rebuke that his disputatious style is too elegant, he salts his 'urbane' language with an unexpected colloquialism on the order of 'outrunning the constable'. Having established the idea that true culture consists of discovering the promptings of man's best self, his right reason, he declares that 'to say that we shall learn virtue by performing any acts to which our natural taste for the bathos carries us,[7] that the fanatical Protestant comes at his best self by Papist-baiting, or Newman Weeks and Deborah Butler at right reason *by following their noses*, this certainly does appear over-sanguine' (p. 159, lines 31–5, my emphasis).[8]

The techniques Arnold uses to anatomise the several social classes have their comic elements, but they are matters of dialectic strategy rather than of style and, as such, demand a separate analysis for which there is no room here. Something must be said, however, about the way that current events, like the utterances of contemporary politicians and other public figures, obliged Arnold's penchant for mordant comedy. In a 'tabernacle' at Birmingham, an 'agent of the London Protestant Electoral Union' named William Murphy had undertaken a series of anti-Popery lectures which resulted in the police and hussars being mobilised to preserve order.[9] In the face of imminent disturbance Murphy insisted on his right to free speech. 'Mr Murphy', wrote Arnold three or four months later in what became the second chapter of *Culture and Anarchy*, 'lectures at Birmingham, and showers on the Catholic population of that town "words", says the Home Secretary, "only fit to be addressed to thieves or murderers". . . . But, above all, he [Murphy] is doing as he likes; or, in worthier language, asserting his personal liberty' (pp. 119, lines 37–120, line 7). In the fortuitously supplied name 'Murphy' Arnold, always fastidious in such matters, found an attractive way of intensifying his ridicule of the masses' alleged right to act and speak as they liked. In a day when Fenianism was reviving in all its stridency (and occasional dynamiting) and fanatical Irish Catholics were out-Hebraising the Hebraists in their propaganda, the name 'Murphy' epitomised all that was regarded as deplorable and dangerous in the Irish character and aroused all the considerable anti-Hibernianism of which the popular English temper was then capable. One might reasonably have expected a man named Murphy to be, if anything, a rabid anti-Protestant, and Arnold must have found extra ironic delight in the spectacle of a Murphy preaching anti-Catholicism – the ultimate expression of the 'dismal and illiberal' atmosphere of Dissent, and of Dissenting propaganda at its raucous, bigoted worst (p. 140, lines 16–17).

By an ambiguity in reporting, *The Times* ascribed to a Rev. William Cassel, a Methodist preacher who presided at the Birmingham meeting, Murphy's warning to Protestant husbands to *'Take care of your wives!'* (p. 131, lines 15–16, Arnold's emphasis. 'He suspects', Arnold had observed earlier, 'the Roman Catholic Church of designs upon Mrs Murphy': p. 120, lines 3–4). When *Culture and Anarchy* was serialised in the *Cornhill*, Arnold referred a dozen times to 'Cassel's' remarks. Only as the serialisation was drawing to an end did he learn that 'Cassel' was really 'Cattle'. He corrected the error throughout when the separate papers were collected as a book, and in so doing he was able to add another happy touch, the name 'the Rev. W. Cattle', epitomising all that was unlovely and reproachable in Dissent. In Arnold's bag of stylistic tricks, the bovine Rev. W. Cattle was dignified over the unfortunate Wragg of celebrated memory, not to say Higginbottom, Stiggins and Bugg ('our old Anglo-Saxon breed'), only by the margin of a truncated honorific and a similarly truncated Christian name. (Readers of subsequent editions are deprived of this not inconsiderable comic detail, Arnold having expunged Cattle, along with numerous other names, in order to reduce the 'personalities' of which critics complained, as well as to remove the misattribution of observations that were actually Murphy's.)

For the first edition of 1869 Arnold prepared a brief introduction, in which he added one more tongue-in-cheek mention of Bright as a 'fine speaker and famous Liberal' (p. 87, lines 1–2) and in another ironic vein identified himself as a Liberal like Bright, Harrison, the editor of the *Daily Telegraph*, 'and a large body of valued friends of mine' (p. 88, lines 33–5). The introduction was followed by a long preface, which, insofar as it concentrates on particular issues of the moment and expands some of the ideas expressed in the book proper, might better be regarded as an additional chapter, a coda rather than an overture. Laden as it is with arguments over narrow and ephemeral issues like church discipline, much of it, like most of ch. vi, has a pamphleteering air; certainly it is one of the least inviting entryways a famous book has ever acquired. Its rhetorical effect is lessened when it is placed at the beginning, because that effect depends on the reader's prior familiarity with the various themes and stylistic motifs established in the course of the six chapters: 'stock notions', 'fetishes', 'the one thing needful', the Philistines' 'natural taste for the bathos', and quoted phrases like 'walk staunchly by the best light we have' and 'make reason and the will of God prevail'.

Here, too, by a kind of *post-hoc* preparation as it were, Arnold assumed in advance the persona the reader would again meet in ch. ii. The mock self-depreciation ('we might gladly, if we could, try in our unsystematic way to take part in labours at once so philosophical and so popular': p. 237, lines 4–6); his ironically improbable association of himself with the Society for Promoting Christian Knowledge, mention of which gets the preface off to an artfully bathetic start (p. 231, lines 1–5); his smiling reference to 'our dear old friends the Hebraising Philistines, gathered in force in the Valley of Jehoshaphat previous to their final conversion' (p. 254, lines 36–8) – all supply foretastes of the fictive character to be developed after ch. 1. So also do the preliminary samples of Arnold's suspect praise: his allusions to Bright's 'noble oratory' (p. 241, line 33) and to the Rev. Edward White's 'temperate and well-reasoned pamphlet against Church Establishments' (p. 237, lines 20–1).

But on one occasion he again beclouds his intention. Immediately after speaking of John Bright as 'representing himself' as above all, 'a promoter of reason and of the simple natural truth of things, and his policy as a fostering of the growth of intelligence' (pp. 240, line 36–241, line 1), Arnold refers to Renan, 'another friend of reason and the simple natural truth of things' whose opinion of America 'seems to conflict violently with what Mr Bright says' (p. 241, lines 9–12). At first glance, Arnold's ironic dismissal of Bright would seem to carry over to Renan; so, at least, his familiar habit of ironically repeated phraseology would seem to suggest. He links them, further on, as 'these two friends of light' (p. 241, line 25). Only as we read on do we learn that in fact one is a false, the other a true, friend of light.

Murphy and the Rev. W. Cattle are absent from the preface, but Arnold doubtless found a similar pleasure in writing the name of Ezra Cornell, 'Ezra' being so suggestive of brick-and-mortar chapel Dissent as to qualify if not negate the praise of Cornell's university, 'a really noble monument of his munificence' (p. 244, lines 37–8). Two other touches in the preface are perhaps more subtle than any in the main text. In the second sentence of the following passage there are familiar devices – first, suspect praise and then a resounding anticlimax in the allusion to G. A. Sala, the prolific journalist and *bon vivant* whom Arnold uses to represent the antithesis of what an Academy should stand for:

> One can see the happy family in one's mind's eye as distinctly as if it were already constituted. Lord Stanhope, the Dean of St Paul's, the Bishop of Oxford, Mr Gladstone, the Dean of Westminster, Mr Froude, Mr Henry Reeve, – everything which is influential, accomplished, and distinguished; and then, some fine morning, a dissatisfaction of the public mind with this brilliant and select coterie, a flight of Corinthian leading articles, and an irruption of Mr G. A. Sala.   (pp. 234, line 30–235, line 1)

But the sly subversion lies in the first sentence. In the Victorian mind 'the happy family' referred to a popular type of street exhibition by that name, a large cage filled with a variety of small animals living in harmony, in the spirit of the American painter Edward Hicks's

famous picture of *The Peaceable Kingdom*. One such show had been
invited inside Buckingham Palace in 1842; a decade or so later,
Henry Mayhew had included a detailed description of the 'happy
family' trade in his *London Labour and the London Poor*; and in 1854
W. P. Frith had introduced a happy family into his celebrated painting
Life at the Seaside (Ramsgate Sands). There was even a parlour game
so called. The term had, therefore, acquired lasting jocose
connotations by Arnold's time. The reader encountering his
enumeration of the brilliant and select coterie, Lord Stanhope,
Gladstone and the rest, in all probability would have imaged them
in the form of a domestic menagerie, evoked all the more readily by
recollections of the many *Punch* cartoons by John Tenniel, who
specialised in portraying public figures with heads of animals and
birds.

In the preface to the 1869 edition, also, Arnold included a lengthy
paragraph on Oscar Browning which cut too close to the knuckle of
good taste and was therefore excised from subsequent editions. It
had its abundance of characteristic Arnoldian comic effects,
exemplified in the double-edged remark that 'it is impossible not to
read with pleasure [malicious pleasure?]' what Browning says in the
Quarterly Review (p. 530, lines 38–9). Much less obtrusive was the
sting implied in a preceding sentence which began, 'Mr Oscar
Browning gives us to understand that at Eton he and others, with
perfect satisfaction to themselves and the public, combine the
functions of teaching and of keeping a boarding-house.' The
allusion to teaching and boarding-houses helps clarify the
vulgarising implication of 'with perfect satisfaction', for the phrase
was specifically associated with routine letters of recommendation
that Victorian householders wrote on behalf of servants, including
governesses, who had left their employment, or of proprietors of
cheap schools to which they had sent their children.

The effect of thus examining the comedy of *Culture and Anarchy* is,
I think, to justify in the main the reaction of many of its first readers.
It is probably just as well that the comic touches are brief – usually a
matter of detached phrases and sentences – and no more frequent
than they are, and that they are largely concentrated in two or three
chapters (II, III and to some extent IV). Apart from the witty dialectic
of Arnold's description of the Barbarian character there is only one
protracted comic passage, that in ch. VI in which Arnold engages *The
Times* and Robert Buchanan on the topic of excess population and
has mordant fun with the unrealistic notion that children are 'sent'

into the world by a Divinity afflicted, like the British Philistine and the poorer class of Irish, with incurable philoprogenitiveness (p. 214, lines 33–5; cf. p. 217, lines 10–12). The fun is heavy-handed enough to preclude any wish that Arnold had indulged his taste for sustained irony elsewhere in the book. Even in short passages, his touch, as we have already noted, is not sure. He is successful, one feels, in such a passage as this:

> Another American defender of theirs [the Liberals] says just the same of their industrialism and free trade; indeed, this gentleman, taking the bull by the horns, proposes that we should for the future call industrialism culture, and the industrialists the men of culture, and then of course there can be no longer any misapprehension about their true character; and besides the pleasure of being wealthy and comfortable, they will have authentic recognition as vessels of sweetness and light.
> All this is undoubtedly specious. . . .   (p. 129, lines 9–18)

The wit of the last words lies in their very gratuitousness; the speciousness of the notion is so blatant that it requires no comment, and Arnold's pointing it out anyway is part of the joke. On the other hand, a humorous effect is hardly enhanced when the author feels obliged to explain it. Hepworth Dixon, says Arnold, 'may almost be called the Colenso of love and marriage': a fancy that might have been allowed to stand on its own merit. But Arnold hastens to write a ponderous gloss: 'such a revolution does he make in our ideas on these matters, just as Dr Colenso does in our ideas on religion' (p. 206, lines 11–13).

The criticism implied in the *Vanity Fair* and Beerbohm caricatures strikes to the heart of the matter: Arnold's flippantly intrusive self distracts from his seriousness; too often it is personality, in two senses, rather than ideas which claims the reader's attention. Arnold's persona – and in this respect it is identical with Arnold himself – is capable of comedy but not of true humour; his self-mockery fails to conceal self-righteousness; his temperament is neither tolerant nor generous. The humility is not only too patently a pose, but too much insisted upon. The irony is too formulaic. The comic themes, like the notorious catch-phrases, recur too often. What wears best, no doubt, is the kind of wit that, once it has hit the target, Arnold does not frugally retrieve for repeated use later on.

Too often we have the feeling that Arnold is not so much debating as indulging in a protracted exchange of genteel Billingsgate. The abundance of 'personalities' typifies the level on which Arnold (pressed by his adversaries, no doubt; but he showed no reluctance to meet them on their own ground) chose to wage his campaign. Of the high-mindedness of his aims as a social critic there can be no question, but the methods he uses are doubtful. Granted that any man must be held responsible for his inane and asinine opinions, not least when they are expressed with the sublime assurance of a Murphy or a Rev. W. Cattle, still it must be affirmed that combating them with hollow praise of a speaker's eloquence or the beauty or profundity of a newspaper's leading article evades the intellectual issue. As to the ethics of Arnold's rhetorical tactics, his observance of the Queensberry rules of verbal sparring, every reader must judge for himself. But it does seem too bad, even allowing for his ironic intent and with due admiration of his skill in turning his opponents' tactics to his own advantage, that he sought sympathy for himself as the blameless victim of his 'Liberal friends', stoically 'disregarding their impatience, taunts, and reproaches' (p. 222, lines 6–7), at the same time as he was expressing his own impatience with them and hurling at them his own full measure of taunts and reproaches. There is something ultimately unsatisfactory about the comedy in *Culture and Anarchy*. A wit, yes; but the elegant Jeremiah was not a first-rate comedian.

Notes

1. Matthew Arnold, *Culture and Anarchy with Friendship's Garland and Some Literary Essays*, ed. R. H. Super (Ann Arbor: University of Michigan Press, 1965) pp. 412, 414. Factual material in this essay is from the apparatus in this volume, hereafter cited as 'Super', and from Sidney Coulling, *Matthew Arnold and His Critics: A Study of Arnold's Controversies* (Athens, Ohio: Ohio University Press, 1974), hereafter cited as 'Coulling'. In addition to tracing Arnold's whole career as a controversialist, Coulling shows how each instalment of *Culture and Anarchy*, except the first, was affected by Arnold's desire to respond to criticism of the preceding instalments in other organs of opinion. He also gathers contemporary comments on Arnold's authorial manner and its relation to his private personality (pp. 3–5) and information on his attacks on public men (pp. 10–14).

2. *Culture and Anarchy* consists of one lecture ('Sweetness and Light') and five essays, collectively titled 'Anarchy and Authority' in the serialisation.

3. Textual references, by page and line, are to Super's edition, which reproduces that of 1883.

4. J. Dover Wilson, in his edition of *Culture and Anarchy* (Cambridge: Cambridge University Press, 1950) p. 224.

5. Still another is at p. 184, lines 22–35: 'But many things are not seen in their true nature and as they really are, unless they are seen as beautiful. Behaviour is not intelligible, does not account for itself to the mind and show the reason for its existing, unless it is beautiful. The same with discourse, the same with song, the same with worship, all of them modes in which man proves his activity and expresses himself. To think that when one produces in these what is mean, or vulgar, or hideous, one can be permitted to plead that one has that within which passes show . . . this it is abhorrent to the nature of Hellenism to concede.' This passage is of additional interest as an example of Arnold's sly use of submerged quotations. Hamlet's poignant confession to his mother, 'I have that within which passeth show' (i.ii.85), is hardly congruous with the tenor of the passage: there is no discernible affinity between Hamlet and the Hebraists of whom Arnold is speaking, least of all with Murphy, the anti-Papist Irishman mentioned in the ensuing lines. Earlier, the same Shakespearean words had been applied with equal incongruity to 'the great Liberal middle class', which, says Arnold, 'has by this time grown cunning enough to answer that it always meant more by these things [the various examples of "machinery"] than meets the eye' (p. 128, lines 28–31).

6. One also detects a Menckenian flavour here: 'Why, a man may hear a young Dives of the aristocratic class, when the whim takes him to sing the praises of wealth and material comfort, sing them with a cynicism from which the conscience of the veriest Philistine of our industrial middle class would recoil in affright. And when . . . an unvarnished young Englishman of our aristocratic class applauds the absolute rulers on the Continent, he in general manages completely to miss the grounds of reason and intelligence which alone give any colour of justification, any possibility of existence, to those rules, and applauds them on grounds which it would make their own hair stand on end to listen to' (pp. 125, line 27–126, line 3).

7. It is tempting to seek a connection between Arnold's use of anticlimax and his argument that one of the characteristics of the Philistine middle class is its natural 'taste of the bathos' (p. 147, lines 13–14). Although bathos and anticlimax are closely related rhetorical devices, Arnold here uses the former term in a wide sense unrecognised by the *Oxford English Dictionary*. Expanding the Scriblerian definition, he designates as bathos a whole cluster of Philistine traits: cherishing of false values, veneration of the wrong authorities, clinging to obstinate prejudice, smugness, receptivity to flattery and claptrap. Perhaps it might be said that Arnold's rhetorical anticlimaxes are illustrations of middle-class bathos. He manipulates true and false values for comic effect, making clear distinctions between them, as if to exemplify by contrast the confusion of values, the inability to make distinctions, that is a mark of the Philistine.

8. There is something humorous, too, in Arnold's coinages, which Carlyle might not have disdained. In denouncing the proposal of the Licensed Victuallers and the Commercial Travellers to found their own schools in which to teach a new generation the precepts of the commercial middle class, Arnold characterises their spirit as 'licensed victualism' and 'bagmanism' (p. 154, lines 36–7).
9. For a full understanding of the connotations that Murphy's name had in the mind of Arnold's first readers, see Walter L. Arnstein, 'The Murphy Riots: a Victorian Dilemma', *Victorian Studies*, 19 (Sep. 1975) 51–71. Along with the Hyde Park riots, the disturbances and controversy stirred up by Murphy's virulently anti-Catholic crusade were the prime examples of what Arnold meant by 'anarchy' in its social, as opposed to intellectual, manifestations.

6

The View from John Street: Richard Whiteing's Social Realism

JEROME HAMILTON BUCKLEY

In Arnold Bennett's first novel, *A Man from the North*, published in 1898, the sardonic Mr Aked tells the hero, Richard Larch, an aspiring young writer very like Bennett himself, that a novelist may find all the drama he needs in the life and character of any single London street. Twenty-five years later, in *Riceyman Steps*, Bennett fully realised the aesthetic potential of a dreary Clerkenwell square. But Mr Aked's advice was as much descriptive of a current mode as prescriptive of a future fiction, for the London street, usually of a dreary kind, was already well established in the 1890s as an appropriate setting for realistic narrative. Arthur Morrison had followed up his *Tales of Mean Streets* (1895) with *A Child of the Jago* (1896), a grim report on violence in an East End slum block. Somerset Maugham began his career as storyteller with *Liza of Lambeth* (1897), the action of which, except for one scene, transpires entirely on and in a rowdy Vere Street, 'leading out of Westminster Bridge Road'. Richard Whiteing's *No. 5 John Street*, which appeared a year after *A Man from the North*, has been virtually forgotten, apart from an occasional mention alongside the Morrison and the Maugham in histories of English realism.[1] Yet it still, I believe, deserves attention not only as one slum-street novel among others, but also as a late-Victorian social and political satire of broader import, remarkable for its own qualities of intelligence, originality and wit.

Richard Whiteing (1840–1928), who was Thomas Hardy's exact contemporary, had something of Hardy's great compassion for the oppressed, but, of course, very little of Hardy's dramatic imagination. Like Hardy he was largely self-educated, widely read but erratic in his learning, prepared to season his writings liberally

145

with erudite allusions to history, literature and the fine arts. As a young man he had attended art classes at the Working Men's College in London; there he met John Ruskin, who probably first taught him to combine a keen interest in painting with a zeal for political justice. Whiteing passed much of his middle life abroad – in France, Italy, Germany and Russia – as foreign correspondent for British newspapers. In Paris, where he gathered materials for a late study of French manners and morals, he came to know some of the Impressionist artists and other Bohemian intellectuals, including the great ethnologist and notorious anarchist Jean Jacques Elisée Reclus, who appears, unlovably, as Azrael in *No. 5 John Street*. Though he expended most of his best energies on ephemeral journalism, he found time to write several novels and, after his retirement from the *Daily News*, his *Life of Paris* and *My Harvest*, an anecdotal but rather unrevealing autobiography.[2]

Though a unit in itself, *No. 5 John Street* is best approached as the sequel to a quite different work, not a street fiction at all, *The Island*, which Whiteing first published in 1888 but revised and reissued at the time of the later book.[3] A sharp satire as well as an engaging utopia, *The Island* purports to be the true narrative of 'a person of quality'. Standing one summer afternoon on the steps of the Royal Exchange, Lord ———— experiences a numbing revelation (a decisive 'epiphany', if you will): his own life seems suddenly empty and 'out of focus'; the whole social order of England, dandies and drudges alike, seems driven by an intricately meshed inhuman 'machinery'; throngs of city clerks, beggars, policemen and thieves surge dizzily past him, and 'for background the nondescript thousands in black and brown and russet and every neutral hue, with the sun over all, and between the sun and the thousands the London mist' (p. 3). (The vision looks back to its prototypes in Carlyle's *Sartor Resartus* and *Past and Present* and forward to the faceless throngs of *The Waste Land*.) In his bewilderment Lord ———— seeks refuge in a Parisian salon, described as '*grand monde* tinctured with literature'. But there he is repelled by the vapid elegance and affectation of the aesthetic *avant garde*, the Symbolists, the Decadents, the Neitzscheans, the Mystics (presumably of the Golden Dawn), the Diabolists propounding the efficacy of the Black Mass and finally the new 'light of the age', who is to be the *pièce de résistance* of the evening, the great Italian immoralist (unnamed but almost certainly the flamboyant Gabriel D'Annunzio).[4]

Hastily escaping all this, abandoning 'civilisation' altogether,

Lord ———— travels to the South Pacific, where he is soon lost to his ship and stranded on lonely Pitcairn Island. Settled by mutineers from *The Bounty* and their Tahitian spouses, the island has only very infrequent contact with Britain but none the less remains loyal to the distant unknown Motherland. Indeed the Ancient, who has been elected Governor, has named his beautiful daughter Victoria. Unlike Victorian Englishmen, however, the islanders have achieved a serene and happy society of simple laws and barter in homegrown yams, an economy of communal ownership, without luxury or poverty, greed or competition. In their pure religion, without dogma or hierarchy, they resemble 'the true Primitives, the joyous band of Galilean vagabonds, exulting in that new conception of the brotherhood of man whose secret we have forever lost'. Despite their innocent bliss, however, they are eager to hear of the great civilisation beyond the seas. Victoria, with whom Lord ———— promptly falls in love, entreats him, 'Civilize us. Make us like England. Give us large things to live for. . . . There must be something wanting, but I cannot tell what it is' (pp. 81, 106–7). Lord ———— then describes the English class system, the sophisticated worldliness of the rival churches, the uses of a belligerent foreign policy to maintain imperial supremacy. Like Gulliver in Brobdingnag, he exposes what he is ostensibly defending, till he grows ashamed of the conventions he has once accepted as essential and unalterable. When eventually he must go back to the civilised corruption of London, he leaves the island with a heavy heart and a firm resolve to return, as soon as possible, to its edenic goodness.

The less romantic *No. 5 John Street* begins with a brief explanation that Lord ———— apparently unable to re-adjust to his old way of life, has died suddenly from 'moral' as much as physical causes, or, as a later jargon might have it, from 'culture shock'. His friend and executor, Sir Charles ———— a man-about-town in Mayfair circles, picks up the narrative. The Ancient, he tells us, had asked Lord ———— to represent Pitcairn Island at the Queen's Diamond Jubilee. Sir Charles not only agrees to act as substitute but also decides to prepare a report on the general condition of London as well as the special Jubilee celebrations. But truly to understand how the populace lives, he must, he perceives, abandon for a while his status as a gentleman of leisured affluence, join the ranks of the labouring poor, and learn to support himself on a very minimal wage. Accordingly he finds temporary work in a dismal factory and moves to a room at No. 5 John Street, 'a four-sided hovel, in the very heart of a slum which lies between two of the finest thoroughfares of the West End' (the first sentence of *No. 5 John Street*).

This setting becomes Whiteing's theme, the slum-street between the fine avenues, the ironic juxtaposition of poverty and wealth. The narrator now contrasts not a real London and a distant island utopia, but two present realities, one of which excites his pity, the other his contempt. His social report to Pitcairn thus veers in tone between sermon and satire. Though himself by vocation an idle clubman, Sir Charles castigates, as emphatically as Thorstein Veblen did (in the same year as the novel), the conspicuous expenditure and waste of an extravagant leisure class. His portraits of Sir Marmaduke Ridler, the capitalist tycoon, and Seton Ridler, the 'dandy-athlete', are shrill caricatures of the *nouveaux riches* who are rapidly buying their way into power. Seton seems already to have acquired the patent of nobility, or at least of a new aristocracy of money, the air of one who 'might have done nothing for seven hundred years, such the calm of his manner, the unhastingness, such his tranquil and unobtrusive satisfaction with himself' (p. 152). The Ridlers are mere stereotypes of the time; Seton, given a readier wit, might have appeared in a Wilde comedy, and his father, if made more articulate about his business schemes, could anticipate a Shavian plutocrat. Neither is a rounded or well-motivated character; each stands primarily as a foil to the victims of the system, the helpless residents of John Street, whose plight is the narrator's more intense concern.

Sir Charles's first view of slum blight and squalor is detached and curiously aesthetic; a street brawl becomes a painterly 'arrangement':

> As an accessory figure of this gruesome composition yet still well in the center of it, is a faded-looking woman. . . . A touch of imagination would convert [a second figure in the tableau] into some well-preserved fragment of a bas-relief exhibiting Antiope on the war-path. To complete this idea of the statuesque, the little ragged boy at her feet makes a triangular base for the composition.   (pp. 25, 27)

The tone here recalls the clinical dispassion with which Maugham surveys his Lambeth street or Arthur Morrison's objective appraisal of the violent Jago. But nowhere in *No. 5 John Street* is there such carefully researched documentation of working conditions as we find in George Moore's naturalistic fictions. On the other hand, there is no revulsion from the urban poor, as in George Gissing's excursions into the lower depths, and there is very little of the condescension towards amusing Cockneys that marks the once popular stories of W. Pett Ridge.

Whiteing's (or Sir Charles's) descriptions have the virtue of an honest graphic journalism. The nameless ragged urchin, for example, is caught in sharp focus:

> His claim against society, nature, God – call it what you will – seems stupendous. He lacks everything – clothing, flesh to hang it on, all the amenities, presumptively, down to the A B C. He wears a shirt torn at the shoulder, and a pair of trousers which are but a picturesque ruin – just these and no more. A ridiculous fag-end of the shirt, itself a shred, sticks tailwise out behind through one of the rents. He is shoeless, capless, uncombed, and, even in this light, manifestly very dirty. With the dirt on his face there is a tiny dried-up rivulet of blood.   (p. 29)

The neglected babies of John Street supply a more general impression, but one still animated by circumstantial detail:

> Some are locked in all day, 'to keep 'em quiet', while their owners go forth to work or to booze. The infant faces, lined with their own dirt, and distorted by the smeared impurities of the window-panes, seem like the faces of actors made up for effects of old age. The poor little hands finger the panes without ceasing, as they might finger prison bars. The captives crawl over one another like caged insects, and all their gestures show the irritation of contact.   (p. 43)

Sir Charles's sympathy, as suggested here by a brief emotional charge of language ('the poor little hands'), mingles with his observation. But his narrative, from first to last in the urgent present tense, as if the raw sensations must remain unmediated, seldom sinks into a false sentimentalism or falters in its steady vision. The slum setting, which he sketches rapidly in a few telling details, achieves the authenticity of Charles Booth's monumental *Life and Labour of the People in London*, a comprehensive work in seventeen volumes, already well in progress at the time of *No. 5 John Street*.[5]

But the tenor of Whiteing's radicalism is more literary than sociological, recalling as it does the ardour of the early Carlyle and the anger of the moral Ruskin.

In *The Island* Lord ———— tells the utopians of a man named Swart, a typical late-Victorian slum denizen, yet a representative, too, of the whole English lower class, living for centuries on the rough edge of poverty. A chapter entitled 'Pedigree of a Poor Stupid' traces Swart's lineage, in Carlylean fashion, all the way back to the Peasants' Revolt when one Swyrte was 'deputy tub-bearer to the "mad priest of Kent", John Ball'. The 'poor stupid' is the 'simple soul' of the realist fiction of the 1890s, the resilient but unheroic protagonist, such as Moore's Esther Waters, the common worker, much put-upon yet lacking in the tragic sense of life that distinguishes Hardy's Tess and Jude. (On a somewhat higher level, the 'simple soul' engages both H. G. Wells and Arnold Bennett, in novels written not long after Whiteing's: the exuberant *Kipps* is subtitled 'The Story of a Simple Soul', and *Anna of the Five Towns* marks the demise of the unfortunate Willie Price as 'End of a Simple Soul'.) The slum figures of *No. 5 John Street* run true to type, insofar as they see, or actively seek, no escape from their lot and station. Nance as a drudge in Sir Marmaduke's rubber factory must submit to poisonous naphtha fumes if she is to earn a bare subsistence, and even Low Covey, for all his Dickensian resourcefulness and practical commonsense, has no notion of turning his energies to social protest and reform.

'Tilda, the coster-girl who dominates the plot, resembles these other simple souls in her basic goodwill and her forthright honesty of vision, but she also relates to a more specific literary type of the time. In *The Island* Lord ———— notes that there is 'no gaudier thing in nature than the coster-girl in her holiday dress of mauve, with the cruel plume that seems to have been dyed in blood' (p. 182). 'Tilda, as far as her limited means will permit, delights in such garish plumage – her huge hat on its hook is the single wall-decoration in her room. She shares her taste in clothing and her Cockney vigour of speech with Lizerunt (contracted from 'Eliza Hunt'), the pickle-factory girl in Morrison's *Tales of Mean Streets*. And Lizerunt is clearly the original of 'Liza in the *London Types* of William Ernest Henley (who first published Morrison's *Tales*):

> 'Liza's *old man's* perhaps a little *shady*,
> 'Liza's *old woman's* prone to *booze* and cringe;

But 'Liza deems herself *a perfect lady*,
And proves it in her feathers and her fringe.[6]

Lizerunt also anticipates Maugham's Liza of Lambeth, another girl of eighteen, who, in 'brilliant violet', crowned with feathers, electrifies Vere Street with her saucy retorts, her laughter, swagger and rowdy country-reel. Like these, who all too soon pay the price of abundant vitality and humour, 'Tilda must come to an untimely end. Yet her Cockney high spirits remain to suggest – perhaps even, I should guess, to inspire – the creation of yet another 'Liza, this one a flower-girl like 'Tilda: the redoubtable Eliza Doolittle of George Bernard Shaw's *Pygmalion*.

Whether or not Shaw needed a fictional prototype for his Eliza, *No. 5 John Street* is the kind of Radical satire he could have read, at least when young, with approval, and Whiteing's 'Tilda is clearly the sort of assertive, sensible, right-hearted woman he frequently chose to place at centre-stage. 'Tilda at any rate has not only the expected Cockney range of vituperation and difficulty with aspirates; she has also the more specific sense of un-self-consciously defined identity that Henry Higgins vainly tries to purge from Eliza:

> But this hen of the walk of our slums is really herself in all her effects. Her bad English is straight from the turbid well. Her manner is no garment; it is her very skin. . . . Who can jaw a copper like 'Tilda, or carney a Covent Garden salesman out of a bargain, or take the size of a chaffing swell? She is not in the least aware of her perfections in this kind.   (p. 214)

Again like Eliza, 'Tilda has enough natural wit to be educable, and Sir Charles attempts 'to do something for the improvement of her mind'. Classical music makes her restive and uneasy, but at the National Gallery she readily applies her standard of literal verisimilitude and, somewhat more aesthetically, responds to the radiant colours, 'Oh, mother! don't the paint make you feel good!' (p. 217). Her desire for self-betterment, however, is checked by her resentment at the thought of being used as an experiment or exploited as a class joke:

> 'Oh, I'm no good for a lidy, I ain't! Oh, why didn't yer ketch me when I was a kid? . . . I wish I could sling my 'ook; I wish I could sling my 'ook. I can't speak proper. I can't be'ave proper. I ain't no good. I stands in the gutter, I do; I can't git out. . . .

'It makes yer larf, like, to 'ear us talkin', and to see our funny
w'ys. But some time you'll see us jest as we are. Then you'll git the
'ump, an' cuss the d'y you tried to mike a lidy out of a fightin'
flower-gal.' (pp. 275–7)

Eliza, who does become a 'lidy', never quite loses 'Tilda's fighting
spirit.

The Jubilee festivities, which provide the sanction for Sir
Charles's narrative, bring 'Tilda her one brief moment of public
attention. Dazzled by the imperial pomp and pageantry, she makes
her own generous contribution to the occasion, flowers to bedeck
the John Street charity dinner. When the Princess of Wales, visiting
the hall, lingers a moment to thank her, 'Tilda replies at some
length, with due respect but also with brave confidence that the
Princess need only be told of the plight of the hungry street-children
to institute quick remedial action. Sir Charles has no such naïve
illusions as he reflects on the extravagant display and the
supporting tribute coaxed or exacted from the far-flung Empire.
Indeed few indictments of Jubilee imperialism (in which even
Kipling descried 'foolish pride and frantic boast') can have been so
sardonic as his report.

Azrael the anarchist passes his own embittered judgement on the
banquet as a 'princely dinner to the slums, which is to exhibit the
virtuous poor by the hundred thousand struggling, amid all this riot
of opulence, for a cut of beef and a ha'penny orange as their highest
attainable good in life'. By this time himself a Radical, Sir Charles
may assent to Azrael's diagnosis of the social malady, but he can in
nowise endorse anarchism as an intelligent or likely cure. Azrael is
the thwarted revolutionist, self-deluded by arid theory: 'He is a well
of science; he knows everything but the human heart; and, for want
of that knowledge, all his thinking processes fade off into that
logic of Cloud Cuckoo Land' (pp. 299–300). Yet his commitment
constitutes an immediate danger, for he is 'a wretch in a hurry', a
self-appointed avenger hissing with anger and hate, goading a
ragged audience to acts of terrorism. The death of Nance is all the
pretext he requires for a mad foray against Sir Marmaduke, who as
Nance's exploitive employer has been responsible for her fatal
illness. When 'Tilda wrestles to deter him, both perish by the
accidental discharge of his home-made bomb. To the narrator
Azrael is thus as inimical to human life as Sir Marmaduke, for

' 'Tilda was to die with Nance – both victims, the one to the curse of the disease, the other to the curse of the remedy' (p. 302).

The anarchist had been a figure of public concern throughout the 1890s, especially since 1894, when a Martial Bourdin attempted to demolish Greenwich Observatory but was himself exploded while planting his bomb.[7] David Christie Murray worked a variation on the theme in his popular novel, *The Martyred Fool*, where the hero, a gullible young anarchist, finally recanting, deliberately destroys himself and his fellow-nihilists. Less melodramatically, Arthur Morrison alluded directly to the Greenwich bomber in the most amusing story in *Tales of Mean Streets*. 'The Red Cow Group' relates the come-uppance of an anarchist agitator named Sotcher at the hands of some simple labourers, who, weary of his windy rhetoric and aware of what happened to Bourdin, resist incitement and force Sotcher himself to assault the local gas works – actually the bomb they arm him with is only a firecracker, and the panic-struck cowardly Sotcher is arrested by the police not for dire sabotage but for drunken vagrancy. A far more impressively sinister character than these, Azrael anticipates the intellectual anarchists of Conrad's *Secret Agent* (1907), which was to be, though long after the event, the most brilliant reflection of the Greenwich episode. But where Conrad's depiction of the heavy-lidded Verloc and his sorry crew succeeds through a sustained ironic detachment, Whiteing's portrait of Azrael suffers the burden of polemic, the direct undramatised denunciation of a vicious political creed.

For *No. 5 John Street* is essentially a political novel, most effective when its bias is implicit, least so when it becomes overt and doctrinaire. By the end of the novel Sir Charles is most sympathetic with the Social Democrats whom Azrael despises, and he is prepared to declare that 'the true business of literature is the new forces which are shaping man to democracy'. Yet he has no Fabian interest in Socialist economics, nor any confidence in technocratic progress. His dream of the future is far more likely to be satisfied by William Morris's *News from Nowhere* than by Edward Bellamy's *Looking Backward*, which he dismisses as 'merely visions of a glorified Poughkeepsie with superior drains'.[8] Like Morris, he would recover, if he could, the spirit of the medieval 'socialism' of John Ball and William Langland of Malvern. In grief at the senseless destruction of 'Tilda he actually retreats to the Malvern Hills, where he muses on the parallels between Langland's London, in another 'year of jubilee', and his own and on the message of *Piers Plowman*, 'the exposure of the world's wisdom and the squalor of its pomp'.[9] With the sense of Langland majestically looking down on him, 'under the compulsion of his gaze', he then begins his report to the uncivilised, uncorrupted people of Pitcairn.

Like other social realists of the period, the H. G. Wells of *Love and Mr Lewisham*, for example, or Arnold Bennett in *Anna of the Five Towns*,[10] Whiteing, through his narrator, assails organised religion as sanctioning inequality and exploitation. Sir Charles finds the clergy reluctant to condemn the inhumane greed of industrialists like Sir Marmaduke, yet 'capable of dooming a whole social order [namely, the oppressed workers] with a text'. He speaks ironically of a current 'system of therapeutics in which texts from Scripture take the place of drugs', and he is convinced, as Marx was, that religion has long been invoked as a general opiate (see pp. 192, 308). None the less, like many late Victorians, disillusioned with the practice of the established churches and deprived of the old faith, he adapts religious emotion, language and imagery to the ends of a secular humanism.[11] He himself is deeply religious in impulse; he seeks a new religion based on 'the iron laws of brotherhood' and a new church which 'may have its modest beginnings in any two or three gathered together with the resolve that they will stand side by side, alike in weal as in woe, and that they will not covet their neighbor's bread'. (p. 310). He thus concludes his narrative, which has modulated from comedy to pathos to fierce satire, on a solemn hortatory note, carrying us back to the earlier Victorian prophetic urgency of Carlyle and Ruskin, with now an earnest echo of *In Memoriam* and perhaps even, unexpectedly, a hint of Oscar Wilde's defence of art as man's protest against nature:

> Democracy must get rid of the natural man of each for himself, and have a new birth of the spiritual man, the ideal of each for all. . . . The very reproach that the thing is not natural is a sign that it is right. Man's work in life is to turn himself from the raw product into a piece of fine art. The Nike of Samothrace in the natural state is but a lump of clay. . . .
>
> Ring out the old, ring in the new, the great moral renaissance, the new learning of the mind and the heart, the new type of man and woman developed by liberty working within the domain of love and law. (pp. 309, 311).

Such passages – and there are a number of others, somewhat shorter, scattered throughout *No. 5 John Street* – suggest that

Whiteing, like Samuel Butler in *The Way of All Flesh*, was as much the essayist as the novelist. In both of these otherwise dissimilar books digression, generalisation, satiric aside and moralising judgement may be excused, at least in part, as characteristic of an invented narrator who is eager to interpret what he has learned from the incidents he has described. And, if the opinions of Overton or Sir Charles often seem intrusive or abstract, each narrative, apart from the commentary, still has a strong enough fictional element to qualify as a 'novel'. Butler's chronicle retains its place as a memorable and influential *Bildungsroman*, and Whiteing's, though it crosses several genres, deserves comparison, as I have tried to show, with the best work of the London realists of the 1890s.

After the first street scene, however, the 'realism' of *No. 5 John Street* bears little resemblance to the disengaged impersonal method of Flaubert and Maupassant, which was reproduced with some success in Maugham's *Liza of Lambeth*. Though Whiteing, too, had studied the French masters, his street novel derives most in spirit from an English tradition that carried no injunction to exclude an author's sympathy with his suffering characters or a moral judgement of their plight.[12] As a distinctly English realist he thus looks back to Dickens and Trollope and forward, in the grimmer context of his time, to the Edwardian achievement of Bennett and Wells, who were able to combine a warm compassion and humour with a close regard for specific social detail. We have only scant record of Richard Whiteing's later life, but we do know that he met both of these gifted younger contemporaries. And it seems appropriate, as a brief footnote in literary history, that Bennett, having encountered him at one of Wells's dinner parties, ten years after *No. 5 John Street*, should report joyfully back to his confidential journal that the 'deafish' old man had expressed 'a sort of startled enthusiasm for *The Old Wives' Tale*.[13]

Notes

1. Whiteing is discussed briefly, with some inaccuracies, in William C. Frierson, *L'Influence du naturalisme français sur les romanciers anglais de 1885 à 1900* (Paris: Giard, 1925) pp. 218–27, and again (with errors uncorrected) in Frierson, *The English Novel in Transition, 1885–1940* (Norman, Okla.: University of Oklahoma Press, 1942) pp. 93–8. Holbrook Jackson mentions him in *The Eighteen Nineties* (1913: repr. London: Pelican Books, 1939) p. 36: 'Richard Whiteing, veteran journalist, but unknown to the public by name, suddenly became

something like famous by the publication of *No. 5 John Street*, in the last year of the decade.' I have found no recent references to Whiteing.

2. See sketch by F. Page in the *Dictionary of National Biography* Suppl. *1922–1930*, pp. 907–8.

3. Richard Whiteing, *The Island, or An Adventure of a Person of Quality* (London: Longman, 1888), reissued with new subtitle (*The Adventures of a Person of Quality*), two new chapters and some other changes 'to make it more truly of its time' (with American spellings) (New York: Century, 1899). Citations to *The Island* throughout this chapter are from the 1899 edition.

4. See pp. 28–34. The narrator has earlier (p. 2) been reading D'Annunzio; in 1888 edition, Daudet rather than D'Annunzio.

5. Booth, *Life and Labour* (London: Macmillan, 1892–1902); in earlier and much shorter form, 1889–1891.

6. W. E. Henley, ' 'Liza', *London Types* (London: Heinemann, 1898). The volume contains thirteen of Henley's 'quatorzains', each boldly illustrated in colour by William Nicholson.

7. For a succinct review of the Greenwich Observatory affair, see Eloise Knapp Hay, *The Political Novels of Joseph Conrad* (Chicago, Ill.: University of Chicago Press, 1963) pp. 220–5. The fictional anarchists of the 1890s scarcely resembled Henry James's sensitive Hyacinth Robinson in *The Princess Casamassima* (1886), nor the scholarly theorist Prince Kropotkin in real life of the time.

8. P. 310. Bellamy, of course, writes of Boston, not Poughkeepsie; Whiteing may think the latter merely a typically ludicrous American place name. At any rate, he believes, however important good drains may be, 'The underground system of the human being is the thing that we must first set right'.

9. P. 304. Also on Langland, whom he never actually names, 'He was Chaucer's teacher, and a greater than Chaucer, though he sang less sweet, by reason that passion marred the evenness of his note' (pp. 303–4).

10. Both of these were written in large part by 1899; *Mr Lewisham* was published in 1900; *Anna* in 1902.

11. Richard Ellmann comments on the 'thoroughly secular' tone of literature from the 1890s to 1910 and at the same time the increased literary use of religious imagery. See his 'Two Faces of Edward', *Golden Codgers* (New York: Oxford University Press, 1973) pp. 116–23.

12. Donald D. Stone distinguishes relevantly between French 'realism' and the English sort, where the novelist evinces more active sympathy with his protagonists. See his essay 'The Art of Arnold Bennett', Robert Kiely (ed.), *Modernism Reconsidered* (Cambridge, Mass: Harvard University Press, 1983) pp. 17–45.

13. Entry of 21 Dec. 1909, *The Journal of Arnold Bennett, 1896–1910* (New York: Book League of America, 1932) p. 352.